Praise for the hardback edition of
EDUCATIONAL FAILURE AND WORKING CLASS
WHITE CHILDREN IN BRITAIN

'I was educated by this' – **Dame Marilyn Strathern**, Professor of Social
Anthropology at the University of Cambridge

'A wonderfully enlightening and entertaining book. An anthropologist
delivers an insider's account of life in inner London, and makes sense
of the educational failure of working class white boys' – **Adam Kuper**,
Professor of Social Anthropology, Brunel University

'A brilliant and highly entertaining study of a neglected subject' – **Andrew
Gimson**, *Daily Telegraph*

'A compelling, often uncomfortable journey of self-discovery, as well as
a fascinating insight into class and education in Britain. *Educational
Failure* . . . stands out for its honesty, its bravery and its originality' –
Patrick Butler, Editor, *Society Guardian*

'This book should be read by teachers, parents, academics and policy
makers, and by Bermondsey people. If they do, this book can be a
catalyst for change' – **Michael Holland**, ex-Bermondsey, playwright
and film-maker

Educational Failure and Working Class White Children in Britain

Gillian Evans

First published in hardback 2006
First published in paperback 2007 by

PALGRAVE MACMILLAN
Houndmills, Basingstoke, Hampshire RG21 6XS and
175 Fifth Avenue, New York, N.Y. 10010
Companies and representatives throughout the world

PALGRAVE MACMILLAN is the global academic imprint of the Palgrave Macmillan division of St. Martin's Press, LLC and of Palgrave Macmillan Ltd. Macmillan® is a registered trademark in the United States, United Kingdom and other countries. Palgrave is a registered trademark in the European Union and other countries.

ISBN-13: 978-1-4039-9216-1   hardback
ISBN-10: 1-4039-9216-9   hardback
ISBN-13: 978-0-230-55303-3   paperback
ISBN-10: 0-230-55303-6   paperback

This book is printed on paper suitable for recycling and made from fully managed and sustained forest sources. Logging, pulping and manufacturing processes are expected to conform to the environmental regulations of the country of origin.

A catalogue record for this book is available from the British Library.

Library of Congress Cataloging-in-Publication Data

Evans, Gillian, 1966–
    Educational failure and working class white children in Britain / Gillian Evans.
        p. cm.
    Includes bibliographical references and index.
    ISBN 1-4039-9216-9 (cloth) 0-230-55303-6 (pbk)
        1. Children with social disabilities—Education—Great Britain.
    2. Education, Urban—Great Britain. 3. Working class whites—Education—Great Britain. I. Title.

LC4096.G7E83 2006
371.826'24—dc22   2006042273

10   9   8   7   6   5   4   3   2   1
16   15 14 13 12 11 10 09 08 07

Printed and bound in Great Britain by
Antony Rowe Ltd, Chippenham and Eastbourne

For my dad: common-as-muck and highly professional, a leader in his field.

And for Sharon, who passed away in 2006 leaving three daughters who miss their mother dearly.

'These kids don't know they're working class; they won't know that until they leave school and realise that the dreams they've nurtured through childhood can't come true.'

Christine: Year Five/Six teacher
Tenter Ground Primary School
Bermondsey, 2000

Contents

List of Figures

Acknowledgements

This book would have been impossible to write if it were not for the generosity and hospitality of the people of Bermondsey. Thanks are due to all those families and individuals who invited me into their homes and patiently tolerated my ignorance of their ways. For unprecedented guidance and friendship, I am grateful to Michael Holland and Tracey O'Connor who gave me a way-in and had no qualms about securing the necessary introductions for a posh-cow, like me.

To all the staff, parents and pupils of Tenter Ground Primary School in 1999 and 2000: thank you for all your help and support and for putting up with me being in school for so long. I am especially indebted to those families whose lives have become the subject of the case studies of this book: special thanks to Sharon and Emma, Anne and Tom and to Gary; I hope you read it one day.

The research for this book was made possible by the kind support of the Laura Ashley Charitable Foundation and the Centre for Child-Focused Anthropological Research (CFAR) in the School of Social Sciences and Law at Brunel University. I am indebted to the British Academy for a post-doctoral fellowship which has allowed me time for further research and revision of the manuscript. For unwavering intellectual support I am grateful to Professor Christina Toren, and for moral support special thanks are due to family and friends who have waited too long for this book to be finished.

Preface to the Paperback Edition

'We're all middle class now', Tony Blair announced triumphantly in 1998. Not everyone rejoiced. Many of those increasing numbers of people who were economically defined as middle class refused to identify themselves as such. There followed an out pouring of working class pride and a prevailing attitude of inverse snobbery was revealed towards the middle classes.

Like the people who were defined economically as middle class but who identified themselves as working class my position was anomalous too, but for different reasons. As a middle class woman, living and raising my children on a council estate in Bermondsey, South-east London, I was defined economically as working class, but I was struggling to understand what working class pride was about. From a naive middle class point of view working class people are relatively poor because they are relatively uneducated and they lead relatively limited lives because of it. This limitation relates to income and employment, health, housing, education and even life expectancy.

Not wanting to lead lives defined by this limitation and not wanting this restriction of opportunity and standard of living for their children, middle class people tend to segregate themselves from the need to know anything more about working class life; they work hard to preserve their advantages, to get ahead and away; they are glad to be middle class.

Having fallen in love and had children with a struggling musician from the East End of London, I had failed to translate my university education into a well-paid career and so, finding myself living on a council estate and experiencing some of those limitations associated with working class life, I was in a perfect position to confront the segregation which middle class naivety depends upon. As far as I could see the people that I thought of as working class were alive and well but the New Labour pronouncement made me think: What did it mean to be working class in Britain at the turn of the twenty-first century? This book provides the beginnings of my answer to that question.

Rather than starting with economic, political or sociological classifications of social class I was concerned, as a social anthropologist, to explain how those people who are defined as working class understand their own lives. Of all the things I learned in Bermondsey what surprised me most was to discover that relatively poor people are not united by a shared preoccupation with their difficult economic position; on the contrary,

I found white working class people divided amongst themselves, lamenting the death of their community and struggling desperately to defend their way of life against the increasing influence of immigrants from Africa, Asia and the Caribbean. Here, despite the success of multiculturalism, which was being celebrated nationally as a resistance movement against racial and cultural prejudice in Britain, were white working class people crying out in defiance of this victory: 'What about us?' 'Why are we feeling under threat in our own neighbourhoods?' 'What about our way of life?' 'What about our culture?'

Following publication of the first hardback edition of this book I was commissioned by the editor of *Guardian Society* to write two consecutive articles which featured on 4 and 11 October 2006. Publication of them provoked a controversy. Why? Some right-of-centre Conservative commentators were angered because they like to believe that opportunity is equally available to all, that there is no such thing as the working class in Britain anymore and that overcoming the limitations of poverty is all about taking 'individual responsibility'. The problems with this point of view are threefold: firstly it is assumed that the institutions which deliver opportunity to the people of Britain function equally well at all times and in all places, an idea which this study of educational failure completely undermines. Secondly it is assumed that all people have the necessary educational, financial and emotional resources to stand alone as individuals (who have no need of society). This book explains why not everyone in Britain is in a position to take personal responsibility in the same way, which brings the politics of social responsibility into focus and indicates why individualism is more likely to be the prerogative of the middle classes. Finally, this 'individual responsibility' perspective ignores children completely. An analysis of social class is meaningless without an in-depth account of what childhood is like because if opportunity were equally available to all, children would no longer be constrained by the social and economic position of their parents. Only in this sense could the working class be said to be nonexistent. The problem in Britain at the moment is that children still are likely to reproduce the social class position of their parents. At what age, then, can children who are being failed at school, facing difficulties at home and learning how to survive on 'mean streets' be said to be responsible for themselves?

To others it seemed outrageous that the white working classes should be treated like a 'culture' and be analysed by a social anthropologist and a middle class one at that, when it is obvious that the working class is a politically and economically disadvantaged group of people who have had, historically, to work together collectively in order to fight against their employers for political rights, better conditions of employment and improvements in living standards. This is why a remark like, 'We're all middle class now' and from a Labour government too, caused a lot of anger. It implied that there was no longer any need (in a post-industrial, knowledge-based economy) for this government to think about or to represent the political and economic interests of its traditional supporters – the working or labouring classes. New Labour's task, it seemed, was to hold the centre ground; to maintain and increase the size of the middle class vote; to raise the aspirations and living standards of the poor (by, for example, increasing the minimum wage) and to undermine the privileges of the upper classes.

The anger about my having taken Bermondsey people's lead and analysed the white working class way of life as a 'culture' and, by implication, having been misinterpreted as implying that the difference between the classes is simply a cultural one, brought to the fore what was obscured when I was doing my research: whilst Bermondsey people were lamenting the death of their idea of community and preoccupied with trying to defend their way of life – learning 'how to have a cultural identity' in order to compete in a multicultural social climate – the political and economic struggles which have historically defined what it means to be working class in Britain were forced into the background and concealed. This highlighted the present danger which is that even as we celebrate multiculturalism, there is no institution – political or economic – through which relatively poor people – black, white and Asian – can come together to know themselves collectively as working class. What becomes interesting in this context and which the controversy brought to light, is the question of how, as a result of a particular complex combination of forces, the political and economic as opposed to cultural implications of what it means to be working class have become obscured.

Take the naive middle class assumption we began with as an example: working class people are relatively poor because they are relatively uneducated. This assumption leads those middle class people who are concerned to do something about the limitations associated with working class life to ask: 'Why are working class people relatively uneducated?' and to support as their remedy to this deficiency a policy commitment to, 'education, education, education'. This focus on education as a cure-all solution to the problems of poverty obscures, however, the other half of the social class equation and prevents the question from being asked with a different emphasis: 'Why are working class people relatively poor?' Once education is put in brackets for a moment the focus shifts onto the question of employment and onto the history of what working class people in Britain have had to endure in order to make even a meagre living out of the most badly paid routine or physically demanding kinds of jobs. This forces us to begin to have to think not just about what is going on culturally in contemporary white working class communities but also about what has happened in them historically.

The battle for improvement in the appalling living and working conditions of the poor since the Industrial Revolution has been fought largely through collective action, the two main ones of which have been the development of the Labour Party and the trade union movement. It is this collective struggle to fight against poverty and its associated limitations which, together with the intense loyalty felt towards closely knit and territorially defined communities have traditionally been the reasons for working class pride. This pride is about resilience in the face of adversity; it is about survival when all the economic odds are stacked against the poor and it is about the struggle for dignity in a country where, relative to dominant political, economic and social values, the working classes are at the bottom of the heap. This is why people who have done well for themselves don't want to be identified as middle class: being middle class means looking down on working class people and working class people (supposedly) don't look down on their own.

This understanding of history allows for a subtle but significant shift away from the cultural strategies of the white working classes, away from the naive middle class point of view and towards a renewed political perspective. It becomes clear that being relatively poor makes work, not education, the focus of life's struggle. The problem, however, is that in the past thirty years the influence of all those integrating collective movements, which were the source of working class strength, have been gradually undermined. To be valued in Britain at the beginning of the twenty-first century a person has to be either middle class or ethnic and with no viable way to participate publicly as themselves, this leaves white working class people feeling that rather than being valued as the primary movers against unfair hierarchies, they have become, ironically, a block to equality. Meanwhile, when made synonymous with the so-called underclass or non-working class (those people for whom the collapse of the community and disappearance of conventional sources of manufacturing employment has had the most devastating consequences), the white working class way of life, which some right-wing Conservative commentators feel would best be left to die out, is increasingly portrayed as a cultural disgrace.

Gillian Evans
December 2006

1
Introduction: Social Class and Education

While I was shopping in a supermarket on the Old Kent Road and during the time that I was conducting fieldwork research in Bermondsey, southeast London, I overheard the following conversation between two young men:

> *Young white guy* (about 16–18 years old, fed up, stacking shelves): 'I'm sick of this job [stacking shelves in the supermarket]: I wan' a propa job: ya know, where ya 'ave to wear a suit and all tha'[t] and ya get to tell uv[th]er people what to do.'
>
> *Young black guy* (similar age, laughing, stacking shelves): 'Yeah, bu[t] wha' d' yer mum and dad do for a livin'?'
>
> *Young white guy* (stops stacking shelves for a moment): 'Me dad drives a van and me mum works in a caf'[é].'
>
> *Young black guy* (laughing): 'So, what d' ya expect then?'
>
> *Young white guy* (silent, continues stacking shelves, fed up).
>
> (Tesco, Old Kent Road, in the year 2000)[1]

I was struck by what the young men said because their concerns resonated with my own: my research focuses on the relationship between social class and education, and like other researchers before me,[2] I was trying to work out why, in Britain, at the beginning of the twenty-first century, despite a history of over fifty years of free access to compulsory education,[3] many working class children still end up in the same kind of low-status occupations as their parents. I continued shopping, asking myself the question which this book addresses: why hasn't education made any difference to young people like these two working in Tesco?

Listening to the young shelf-stackers, I had been particularly interested in the discrepancy between the young white guy's ambitions and the

1

reality of his working life; he wanted to do better for himself, imagined enjoying greater responsibility and was clearly disappointed and frustrated with the routine nature of his occupation. The young black guy, in contrast, appeared to be more accepting; he was light-hearted and cheerful, perhaps because he felt that he understood his colleague's (and by implication his own) situation. His analysis was certainly incisive; he struck the nail on the head: young people's expectations, employment opportunities and chances of self-fulfilment continue to be largely governed by their parents' achievements. This is a problem because, in this day and age, young people's futures are no longer supposed to be determined by the social class they are born into. Education is assumed to be the key to opportunity, merit and social mobility in later life, but if the education system is failing many working class children the only doors open to them will be those that their parents have already unlocked.

Social, educational and economic inequality

At a press conference in February 2005, David Bell, Her Majesty's Chief Inspector of Schools in Britain, introduced his annual report.[4] He outlined recent achievements and emphasised two major concerns:

> One is the variability in the performance of otherwise similar schools [for example, those schools with similar levels of free school meals] and colleges and the extent to which social class still appears to play a role in defining the success of our young people.

He went on to stress:

> There are no simple solutions to deep-seated problems of social, educational and economic inequality. But in these early years of the twenty-first century, we cannot accept the fact that too many young people fail to achieve their potential. The consequences are not just educational: they impact much more widely and for that reason alone, we should continue to be concerned about too much variation in our education system.

David Bell's comments refocus our attention on the enduring relationship between social class and children and young people's chances of success at school and fulfilment in later life. He recognises that it is not a level playing field; the children of working class parents are often, for various reasons, at a disadvantage before they even get to school. Recent research,[5] for example, suggests that children's early educational achievement is heavily influenced by factors outside school and especially the educational and economic status of parents. The research shows how it is possible to combine socio-economic classification of the household with the child's overall developmental score at age 22 months to accurately predict educational qualifications at the age of 26 years. This is astonishing because it indicates that during those intervening years education makes no impact on pre-school developmental trends and it certainly doesn't do what education is supposed to do for working class children, which is to reverse them. Family background is, therefore, critical for children's educational future.

The significance of mothers/principal carers

The statistical analysis also reveals how far, by the age of 22 months, children's developmental score is already stratified by social class (measured by parents' occupational status and level of education) and how this stratification has increased significantly by the age of 10 years. The research also demonstrates that children of wealthy or educated parents, who scored poorly on the developmental index in their early years, were still likely to catch up in later years whereas the children of poorer parents were extremely unlikely to do so. Equally, those children from poorer families who scored highly in their early years are still much more likely to fall behind their wealthier peers who got low scores at 22 months. The most significant factor associated with whether or not a child scores highly on the developmental index is the educational level of the mother or principal carer. The father's educational background doesn't become statistically significant until the child is 5 years old and the father's socio-economic status isn't significant until the child is 10.

My own experience suggests that middle class mothers, who are usually educated to degree level, take it for granted that formal-learning-type skills, such as those associated with literacy (speaking, listening, reading and writing), numeracy (counting, calculating and problem-solving with numbers), arts and crafts (colour and shape recognition, hand-to-eye co-ordination, fine motor skills such as those necessary for drawing, painting and cutting) and science (developed sense of curiosity about the world and some understanding of the forces that are at work in it) as well as sport (physical co-ordination and physical competence in particular activities such as swimming) should be incorporated, in an informal, playful way, into the caring relationship with the child at home. In this way middle class children often come, early on in their lives, to love formal learning because formal-learning-type tasks are what the loving relationship with the mother largely consists of. It is no surprise, then, that even by the age of 2 children whose mothers are well educated are likely to be doing better in pre-school learning tasks than their peers whose mothers are relatively uneducated.[6]

Situated learning

Because the average differences in educational attainment between the social classes manifest themselves very early on in children's lives and because the gap in attainment has persisted over time and despite many government strategies to reduce it, a minority of researchers have pursued the argument that, on average, working class children have naturally differing and lower levels of intelligence than their middle class peers.[7] This kind of research distracts, however, from the success of those working class children who do exceptionally well at school and it also fails to account for those working class people who, even after having failed at school, successfully take on the intellectual challenge of self-education in later life.[8] It is important to remember that the statistics about educational attainment are based on average figures and we rarely, therefore, get any sense of the individual achievements of working class children who are doing very well at school, neither do we learn about the individual failures of middle class drop-outs.

Anyhow, if we were to accept the genetic explanation for the difference between the social classes we could stop treating the distinction as a social one. It would then become pointless to continue investing in the endeavour to educate working class children to the same level as middle class children and we could turn our backs on the ideal, which is to make the opportunities that education affords more equally available to all. It is not difficult to see how potentially insidious are the implications of the genetic explanation, the least of which would be the development of less challenging forms of education for the working classes.

In this book I assume from the beginning that the range of what individual middle or working class children are intellectually capable of is the same, and I focus on research which suggests that the reason for the lower average level of educational attainment among working class children is to do with a complex combination of institutional bias against them, a lack of social preparedness, in the family, for the school environment and, in some cases, institutional failure and/or familial breakdown. Intelligence, which is often used as a measure of children's ability to do well at school, is better understood, in this kind of analysis, as a social process. This means that intelligence can be thought of, yes, as an innate capacity and heritable attribute, which varies from one individual to another, but not as a trait which develops separately from social interaction in the infant and child's immediate surroundings: family, neighbourhood and school.

The social structure of intelligence

It is important to emphasise, therefore, that children are, all the time, learning, but what they learn depends largely on the kinds of activities to which the significant adults in their lives expect them to apply their intelligence. For example, a child who has grown up around and been inseparable from a father who is an expert carpenter, and been allowed, expected and encouraged to try his hand at woodwork will, in time and given the necessary patience and inclination, learn the skills and finely differentiated sense of appreciation that becoming a craftsman requires. This process may take as long as fifteen years, if not longer. In this case, woodwork is the use to which this child's intelligence is put. The boy's social relationship with the father involves a particular form of practical learning: they do carpentry together. Learning a particular skill and learning how to relate to others socially are, therefore, inseparable processes and learning is always socially situated.[9]

As the child learns to make structures from wood he is, then, also learning about another kind of structure – a social one – which is the relationship with his father. This social structure, which seems to be less tangible than the wood, but which is, nevertheless, constantly in the process of being crafted, has, just like the piece of woodwork, a specific form. The father crafts wood and the boy learns through crafting wood himself about his own social position relative to his father. Comparing his own experience with that of other boys the child learns about what form is taken among his people by the father/son relation in general. Probably the relationship is one of respect in which the father exerts his power and authority over the boy as he teaches him what he needs to know, and the boy who is the attentive, but never passive novice with everything to learn, submits to that authority and gains respect from his father as his skill in the craft increases.

The more the child learns about the practical skill of making things with wood, the more he learns about the social skill of building a relationship with his father. Via these particular practical and social skills the boy is, then, also simultaneously bringing his understanding of himself into being: the question of who he can be is inseparable from the question of who he is expected, by significant others, to become. Learning how to do what others think is appropriate, the boy must strike a balance between his readiness to acquiesce in adult expectations and his desire to resist them. His success in this balancing act depends on his emotional reasoning about the value – the goodness or rightness – of what participation and increasing incorporation into the family/community feels like and is worth. A degree of emotional tension is, therefore, always going to be a dynamic feature of the boy's emerging relations with those people who are significant in his life. In time, as he learns more about what adults think it is right for a boy to do, he comes to understand what counts among his people as an ethical disposition. This disposition, which the boy learns, in time, to adopt for himself, is a continuously emerging and embodied understanding about what is good and, by implication, bad for boys to do, and through doing, to become. In learning about what is considered to be appropriate, the boy begins to take a particular stance towards the world and other people in it, but it is only with time that the specific social, educational and economic consequences of that stance – that socially structured way of being in the world – will become clear to him.

Learning as participation

In order to be precise and also to emphasise its active quality, let's call the particular form of learning that is required of children by adults, participation. The questions we then have to ask ourselves, in all cases, if we are interested in children's (and indeed adults') learning, are as follows: what form does participation take and how, via involvement in particular forms of participation, are social relations between people structured? If we want to compare different social situations as learning environments, for example, in order to understand the difference between what this boy, who likes doing woodwork with his father, learns when he is with his mother, we simply need to ask ourselves what kind of participation the mother requires of the child. Perhaps the boy learns very different skills with her, like gardening or cooking, reading or writing or perhaps they spend a lot of time watching television together. Maybe the mother expects the child to leave her alone while she gets on with her work around the home, and for this the boy would have to develop an advanced sense of self-reliance and learn how to learn through playing on his own or with siblings and friends. Each of these skills, even if it is a quiet and still activity, like sitting on the mother's lap to listen to her read, requires from the child a growing appreciation of a different form of practical participation. The point to emphasise is that in different social situations our intelligence is put to different uses and learning takes, therefore, various forms.

For the boy, this means that he must continuously accommodate what he learns in one situation to what he learns in another.

Education as a particular form of learning

From this point of view it becomes important to distinguish learning in general from education in particular. Education requires of children a particular form of participation involving explicit and formalised task-oriented instruction in a highly specific and institutionalised social environment, which is usually a school. The school, understood as a distinctive social situation, is likely to be, in many ways, a very different learning environment to the one the child is used to at home. To understand the problem of the relatively low average educational attainment of working class children, it makes sense, then, firstly to investigate and describe the precise form of participation that education requires of children, and secondly to compare and contrast school-based learning with the specific forms of participation that are required of working class children outside school.

The suggestion is that problems are more likely to arise, at school, for working class children not only because the schools they go to are more likely to be failing and their parents are less likely to be either well-off financially or well educated themselves, but also because the form of participation that is required of them at school doesn't closely match the one that is required of them at home and in their immediate surroundings. Educated middle class parents, in contrast, tend to be better-off, better educated and require of their children at home a form of participation that matches more closely what is expected of children at school. This means that compared to their middle class peers, working class children tend to be at a disadvantage when they get to school where they first have to learn all about a new form of learning, which is called education.

This argument does not, however, necessarily lead to a social deprivation model, which implies that working class children tend not to do well at school because the social relations in their immediate families and wider neighbourhoods are somehow deficient. If we were to go with a social deprivation model the resolution of the problem would be simple: all we would have to do would be to provide increased opportunities for working class people to learn the forms of participation that middle class people take for granted and which educational institutions require of children. Exactly this kind of logic lies behind the government drive to get working class children away from their parents as early as possible, and for as long as possible, into nurseries and centres of early learning which will familiarise them with the form of participation that education requires. The problem with this strategy is that it makes it seem as if working class parents are a bad influence on their children. A social variation model, in contrast, allows for investigation of the differences and discrepancies between school and outside-school learning environments and seeks to understand how different forms of participation come, as a result of education, to be unequally valued.

How to be 'clever'

Research[10] on middle class parents shows, for example, how far middle class parents, and mothers in particular, are prepared to invest considerable time, energies and resources in making sure that their children have the necessary skills to be thought of as 'clever' in a way that will be valued at school. This kind of parenting has been described as 'intensive' and it often results in the precocious development in children of proficiencies in formal-learning-type skills that are worth a great deal to the child when it enters the school environment where basic abilities are transformed into merit and rewarded. According to this argument even middle class children of average and lower intellectual capacity are likely to reach their potential at school precisely because they benefit from this kind of intensive parenting.

Having invested so much energy at home in making their child clever, middle class parents tend to be far more discriminating and strategic about which school to send their child to. They are keen that the school should continue the work they feel they have started at home, work which is all about fostering their child's intellectual development in a particular direction and they want to make sure that their child will meet, at school, like-minded peers and families. This degree of strategic thinking among middle class parents tends to lead, in time, to the segregation of middle- and working class school children, with the middle class ones being more likely to attend good schools.[11] These schools often achieve higher results precisely because their pupil intake includes a majority of children who are strongly supported in their school work at home and who are likely to have been competent in formal-learning-type tasks before they ever started school.

In addition, the parent body, in schools like this, largely consists of educated people who are constantly vigilant about the standard of education which the school is providing. When a problem arises they have no qualms about exercising their right to complain because their confidence in their own education gives middle class parents the self-assurance they need to make teachers accountable to them rather than the other way round. The important point to emphasise is that for middle class families formal learning and caring are synonymous: education is central to middle class values. This does not mean that working class parents don't value education. A focus on the social processes that underlie our notions of intelligence and merit can help us to appreciate that for working class parents formal learning and caring tend not to be synonymous and often the expectation among them is that formal learning is what happens at school. This doesn't mean that working class parents don't care properly or that working class children don't want to learn at school. Of course working class parents care for their children, but usually in a different way to middle class parents, one that focuses on other kinds of core values and which tends not to hinge on the development at home of success in formal-learning-type tasks.

The working class child is, therefore, less prepared for and at a disadvantage in an education system which rewards success in and expects children to be prepared at home for formal learning at school: schools embody middle class values. This doesn't mean that working class children can't do well at school. The vast majority of working class parents appreciate the value of education and encourage their children to do well in it and many working class children have no problem with the form of participation that doing well at school requires of them. Even if it is different to what they are used to at home, they enjoy the different form that learning takes at school; they thrive on it and do well. Others do not, and it is these children, and especially, but not exclusively boys, that I focus on in this book.

How do people come to be unequally valued in Britain?

Not surprisingly, since middle class people value education above all else, the comparatively low level of average educational attainment amongst the working classes is a source of middle class prejudice against working class people. To a certain extent the same prejudice also exists among working class people against themselves, which is not astonishing either since the education system works to legitimate success at school as a dominant form of merit and therefore self-worth. The logic of that prejudice works as follows: working class people have low status in society because they haven't got 'good' jobs; they haven't got 'good' jobs because they didn't do well at school; and they didn't do well at school because they weren't 'clever' enough. The central premise of this logic rests on the assumption that people are either naturally clever or they are not and it follows from this that those people who are clever should naturally occupy the best positions in society and feel fortunate.

If we undermine this premise and suggest instead that clever is something children become as the outcome of specific kinds of social participation at home and in school, and we understand that this kind of participation centres around increasing familiarity with and skill in formal-learning-type tasks, then we can begin to appreciate just how far education is a social achievement. At school a particular kind of participation is enforced and made legitimate. By implication, other kinds of learning, those which foster different kinds of skills, are rendered illegitimate and therefore of less worth. For the child who cannot or refuses to overcome the discrepancy between the various forms of participation that are required of him/her in and outside of school, the conditions for school failure are thus established. As the particular form of merit is structured and made legitimate at school so is created the basis for the unequal form of relations between people of merit and those of less worth.

Once the unequal form of relations between young people at school becomes substantiated and objectified in educational qualifications, the trajectory of education, as a specific kind of structuring force, is established. For young people, the end result is a relatively higher or lower position in a social structure which is based on the various kinds of employment that different educational qualifications can secure. This is how social class in Britain works; it is about an ongoing relationship between people grouped according to occupational status, in which the relative value of each group is worked out on the basis of a continuous differentiation of value and consequent reward. The basis for this differentiation is established at school, consolidated in the workplace and finally symbolised by relative wealth.

Resisting education and middle class values

Tension is created within this social class structure, however, because the system for establishing value through formal educational qualification, which, by force of law, is the legitimate one, conflicts with other means for gaining status that depend on completely different kinds of social participation about which working class people might be fiercely proud. There is, therefore, amongst working class people, likely to be a considerable degree of resistance to the forces of legitimation that education represents. This is probable even when those forces emanate from the good will of the (usually middle class) powers that be whose intention it is to offer education to all as the means for self-improvement.

And, in effect, isn't this what schools require of children and young people: that they learn how to be middle class? Certainly the policy assumption seems to be that if only everyone could be middle class then everything in Britain would be all right, but what if, for the majority of working class people, the last thing on earth they want is to be just like middle class people? What if they want to continue to be just like the working class people they know and love, but they also want to be wealthy? Is that possible? After all, what is distinctive about contemporary capitalism is the way that we are united by our desire for the good things in life and differentiated on the basis of our ability to afford them. And what of those working class people who are ambitious for advanced levels of education and jobs which have professional status and high levels of income; can they aspire to such ambitions without having to become just like middle class people?

What is at stake here is the question, not just of who gets the best jobs and makes the most money, but of what it means, in Britain, to become a viable person. If the working and middle classes have significantly different ideas about what it means to be a person – different ideas about the appropriate way to be in the world – different stances, if you like, and it turns out that education, which is supposed to broker that difference, is heavily biased in favour of the middle classes, then the inevitable result is that, at school, the working class idea of the person is eclipsed and forced into the background of educated life. The problem with this is that we are then none the wiser about working class life and values and it becomes impossible for us to understand why young working class people would want to resist what it means to become middle class and well educated at school.

If, for example, young working class men, like those shelf-stackers in Tesco, prefer the working class way of being a person, which is what might have led them, in the first place, to resist and, therefore, to fail in their schooling, why are they, then, so dissatisfied with routine working class jobs? Perhaps their disgruntlement arises because they don't fully realise, until they actually leave school and have to make their own money, that their taken-for-granted way of being a certain kind of person becomes translated, in the labour market, into a negative socio-economic consequence, which is a relatively low occupational status. If young men, like this, have, all along, been filled with pride about who they are, it is inevitably going to be hard for them to come to terms with the actual lowliness of their status. Only then might they begin to realise, relative to their middle class peers, the limitations which their social position places on the range of opportunities available to them in the world of work.

If young men, like these, are so determined to become working class and they resolutely reject the educated way of being a person, then the problem really is one of why they aren't being adequately prepared, at school, for the occupational implications of working class life. We then have to ask ourselves why the young shelf-stackers haven't gained, during eleven years of compulsory schooling, the kinds of skills they need to create the kind of working class life that they imagine for themselves. They might not be content with routine occupations but they are aware that they are inadequately qualified for a whole range of other kinds of working class jobs that they might have been better suited for.

Acknowledging the different values associated with a working class way of life, we need to make it clear to ourselves, and to young people, that it is perfectly possible to lead a decent, prosperous and fulfilling life without being middle class and without necessarily having done well and become highly qualified at school. Being highly educated and middle class is not the be all and end all of life in Britain. This realisation leads us to ask the following questions: what is a working class way of being a person in Britain? What does it mean for a child to learn how to be working class? How is it different for boys and girls? How is it different for black, white and Asian working class children in Britain? And how does this kind of learning make working class children so much more likely than their middle class peers to fail at or to reject what it means to do well at school? On the one hand, we need to understand the attractions of what people take for granted as the working class way of being a person and yet, on the other, we also need to be able to explain why some working class young people, for example those who have gone on to do well at school, gone to university and made professional careers for themselves, talk as if working class life was something that they had survived and escaped from.

I raise these issues here, not because I claim to have encompassed the complexity of them in this book, but because I want to provoke researchers and give middle class people some sense of the education that they require, which is to gain an appreciation of the diversity of working class life in Britain and to understand something about working class values. My focus is on those working class children and young people who are failing or have failed at school, but I do not want to give the impression that the picture of working class life that I portray is representative, because it is not. My intention is to generate hypotheses and in so doing, I touch only the tip of the iceberg. For now, the point I want to emphasise is that given the reality of working class pride there is bound to be a degree of conflict within a system of meritocracy which is heavily biased towards middle class values.

Failing schools

Education, then, is not simply a question of finding out who amongst us is more intelligent, it is about finding out which of us are most prepared to meet the particular form of participation that formal learning requires. Education is, as I have already stressed, a social achievement for which some of us are more prepared than others. Working class children, for example, are less likely to benefit from the same degree of strategic parental support as their middle class peers; working class parents may themselves have had negative experiences of school and had problems with formal learning that were never resolved. As a consequence, they are less likely than educated middle class parents to know what to do about any difficulties their children might be having at school. This leaves the family at the mercy of what the teacher understands about the situation, and the comparatively low level of economic resources in working class families compared to middle class ones means that they usually have to rely, for resolution of the problem, on the resources which the teacher has at her disposal within school. In a good school this might not be a problem; in a failing school it is disastrous.

It is just such a scenario that David Bell, Her Majesty's Chief Inspector of Schools, is concerned about and which I address in my research. Apart from the existence of an intrinsic middle class bias in the education system and the fact that outside-school factors clearly influence children's chances of educational success, working class children also face another disadvantage. David Bell refers in his report to what he finds especially unacceptable in the contemporary situation, which is inequalities in educational provision. It has become clear that working class children, even when they go to schools which have a similar pupil intake, for example in terms of levels of free school meals, don't have an equal chance of going to a good school: too many schools in working class neighbourhoods are failing. Working class children are less likely, therefore, to benefit from the opportunity that access to good schooling is supposed to provide. The important questions, which David Bell reminds us of, are as follows: why are working class children more likely to fail at school and how, exactly, are they being failed?

In my research I approach these questions about educational failure via ethnographic case studies of working class children and their families and I begin to ask myself the following kinds of questions: What forms of participation are required of working class children outside school? What is the discrepancy between these forms of participation and what is expected of children at school? What is distinctive about the social situation of the working classes in Britain? Take one case study location, for example, Bermondsey, in southeast London. What kinds of working class people are to be found there? I focus on the white working classes in Bermondsey, endeavouring to explain their preoccupations from the point of view of their pride in who they are and I show how, in trying to work out their values, I am inevitably thrown self-consciously back against my own middle class ideals.

Part I
Common Knowledge

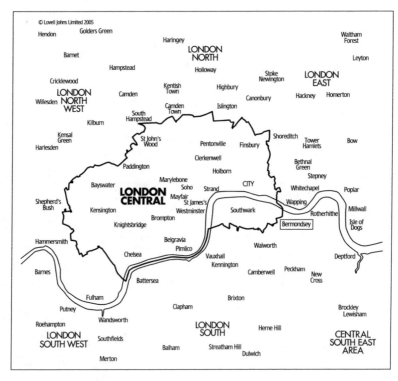

Figure 1   Map of central London showing Bermondsey

2
Sharon: Common-as-Shit

'Ask them what I am: I'm common-as-shit; I wasn't brought up – I was dragged up – on the Old Kent Road; I wasn't taught to mind my Ps 'n Qs and my favourite word is cunt.'

Sharon, Bermondsey, 2000

Describing herself and seeking confirmation from her teenage daughters about what kind of woman she is, Sharon sits with me on the sofa in the living room of her small three-bedroom council flat, where we are drinking tea and chatting about what it means to be a Bermondsey person. By this stage, having already done a year's research and being a Bermondsey resident myself, I know that residency isn't a sufficient criterion for belonging. I notice, however, that Sharon purposefully defines herself in contrast to everything that she imagines Bermondsey people to be and I am aware that her self-description opposes both me, as what she calls a posh woman,[1] and the kind of woman her mother was proud to be, which is Bermondsey, born and bred.

Sharon and her five sisters grew up on the Hops Road Estate[2] adjacent to the Old Kent Road and Sharon, youngest amongst them, now lives and is bringing up her own daughters on the periphery of Bermondsey not far from the Chaucer Estate where I have lived for thirteen years. Hops Road is on the wrong side of Bermondsey, too close to the Old Kent Road, which forms the southern boundary with Peckham. People from Peckham in the southwest and Walworth, which is beyond the Walworth Road in the west, are known as 'Roaders', who are traditionally the arch enemies of Bermondsey people. Speaking proudly about being dragged up on the Old Kent Road is not something a 'real' Bermondsey person would do. So-called real Bermondsey people are keenly aware of the clearly defined boundaries of the territory – their manor[3] – and they are able to make the necessary distinctions about the kind of people who live inside and outside of those boundaries. The Old Kent and Walworth Roads stand for everything that Bermondsey people are not.

Although Sharon meets the formal criteria of belonging because she can claim residence herself and attest to the residence of the previous generation of her family on her mother's side as well as numerous other familial connections and could, if she chose, assume the status of 'being Bermondsey', she shuns the pretension that she presumes pride to be and makes herself simply a resident, albeit a different one to me. Compared to Sharon I am a newcomer in Bermondsey; I have lived and raised my own daughters close to the northern boundary for thirteen years, but the length of my residence barely approaches a respectable presence. Nevertheless it does make a difference to Bermondsey people when they are trying to assess what kind of person I am and whether my interest in the place they proudly call their own is legitimate; I am a relative new-comer but not a complete outsider. The anomaly of my status as a resident is, however, pronounced: firstly because I am, as Sharon continuously reminds me, posh and not common like her, and secondly, because my partner and the father of my children is black and specifically of African origin. The problem is that posh people don't live on council estates – they live in nice apartments and big houses – and Bermondsey people don't marry 'blacks' and especially not Nigerians.

Being posh and finding myself living and raising my children on a council estate because I have none of the money that equates with the manners (and education) that distinguish posh from common people, I have been forced, over the years, to come to terms with what it means to go down in Britain's social hierarchy. I have confronted the segrega-tion that separates the classes and endeavoured to understand what it means to become working or lower class or what Sharon calls common. Writing this book is part of that process; I compare what I have learnt as an outsider in Bermondsey with what working class children and young people learn when they grow up there and make sense, over time, of adult ideas about the kinds of persons they are expected to become.

The manor

Having lived close to the northern border with the borough and close to Borough High Street for ten years prior to beginning my research in 1999, I didn't, at that time, think of myself as a Bermondsey resident. I knew nothing about the place or its people because my mind was elsewhere. I sought the green spaces of Battersea and Greenwich and the fashionable shops and artistic attractions of Chelsea, the South Bank and the West End. Distance was no object if I could escape what I thought of then as the grim council estates, which sprawled for miles to the south and southeast, and get to places where I thought there would be like-minded, middle class people like me. Like most outsiders, my only orientation to Bermondsey was the knowledge that every Friday morning there was a famous antiques market in the square where the end of Bermondsey Street meets the junction with Tower Bridge Road and Long Lane.

The first time I began to think differently about Bermondsey was in the playground of my daughters' (who were, at that time, aged 9 and 6) primary school in Blackfriars when I overheard conversations between two mothers, one of whom – Anita – had just recently moved into Bermondsey on a council housing transfer from Waterloo and the other – Jean – who had moved here fourteen years ago from Kennington to a housing association house not far from the antiques market. Sharing stories about what Bermondsey is like for newcomers, the women made jokes about a people who never come out of their territory unless they have to; they described a people to whom the rest of the world, which begins just beyond Bermondsey's boundaries, is strange and suspicious. They commented on the distinctive appearance of the people, saying, 'You can tell a Bermondsey bird [woman] a mile off.' Later I asked Jean and Anita to explain how they could tell a person was from Bermondsey just by looking at them, but in response they emphasised that they just knew one when they saw one. When I pressed them to think about it more they tried to describe what is distinctive about the way that Bermondsey men walk, how they wear their clothes and cut their hair, and they tried to explain the subtle markers of difference such as the distinct way in which Bermondsey women wear their gold jewellery. Acknowledging the impossibility of them ever truly belonging in Bermondsey because they don't have the right look or familial connections, the women laughed and explained, 'Bermondsey's like Alabama – everyone is related to everyone else.'[4]

Of most interest to me in the beginning was the fact that Anita and Jean – the outsiders – were, to my mind, white and working class just like the Bermondsey people they spoke of and yet they described Bermondsey, which is a place less than half a mile away from Blackfriars, as if it were a foreign country whose people are strange, having customs which are impossible to understand. My assumption about white working class homogeneity quickly dissolved and I learned in time what anyone moving through working class London ought to know: the city is historically divided into manors, which were, and sometimes continue to be, closely defined territories about which people are often fiercely proud and protective. In appreciating the close tie between spatial and social distinctions I was beginning to learn something about the significance of working class life in Bermondsey specifically and in south London more generally.

I was intrigued by the possibility that in all those years that I had lived in Bermondsey I had missed something important because, blinkered by middle class snobbery, I had been looking the other way. Here, on my doorstep in the centre of modern metropolitan London, at the end of the twentieth century, were a people who seemed to be just like what anthropologists would once have called a 'tribe'. Here was a place in which people couldn't be less like the city dwellers we imagine in the modern characterisation: these were not isolated individuals cut off from family connections outside the city, who socialised via networks of friendship and work-related associations that spanned the city. Bermondsey was more akin to a typical English village occupied by a group of people closely tied to a particular location through a specific economic history and in-marrying links of kinship and residence.[5] As newcomers to Bermondsey, Anita and Jean obviously felt, even though they were bona fide residents, that they didn't belong. Determined to investigate what the criteria of belonging were and how Bermondsey was imagined from the inside, I resolved to try and overcome my previous efforts to distance myself from the people among whom I found myself living.

Bermondsey

Bermondsey now forms part of the London Borough of Southwark, but until 1965 it was a borough unto itself; it lies southeast of the central zone of London, occupying roughly a square mile, which has the River Thames between London Bridge and Tower Bridge as its northern boundary, Rotherhithe to the east and the Old Kent Road and Walworth Road in the south and west respectively. During the Industrial Revolution Bermondsey was known as the Larder of London because of an industry focused around dockside warehouses and factories processing foodstuffs imported via the docks from countries the world over. There were other industries too, including those focusing on hops, leather, wool and printing, but many Bermondsey men, their sons and close male relatives worked as casual labourers on the dockside in a tough and closely protected industry where much-needed, but insecure jobs were first allocated according to religious and kin affiliations; the Catholics controlled the docks and sons followed their fathers into the same kinds of employment. Women and daughters, meanwhile, worked in any one of the numerous nearby food processing factories, like Peak Freans' Biscuits, Sarson's Vinegar, Hartley's Jam or Courage Breweries.

Bermondsey's thriving industry centred, then, about a relatively small geographical area in which, before the war and prior to the construction of council housing, private landlords let accommodation on the basis of tenants' familial connections. Protectionism over jobs and places to live led, in time, to the development of a closely-knit, largely white, working class community. Despite the prosperity of the docks, however, Bermondsey people didn't reap the benefits of the wealth they worked to generate. Like most working class people of that time, they experienced real social and economic insecurity and suffered the worst effects of impoverishment. Illness claimed the lives of hundreds of Bermondsey children every year mainly because, as a result of poverty, people's diets were inadequate, housing was badly overcrowded and, by today's modern standards, shockingly unsanitary. Not surprisingly, the stories that older people and their descendants tell of that era are narratives about struggling to survive at a time when the powers that be were indifferent to the conditions of ordinary people's lives.

Despite increases in living standards in the last fifty years and, more recently, development resulting from private and public schemes for urban renovation in the area, parts of Bermondsey are still classified as amongst the most deprived areas of London and England. Mirroring the situation in the nation as a whole, there is, in Bermondsey, relative to a politically active past, also a marked decline in people's participation in the political process; only just over 50 per cent of eligible voters turned out for the most recent general election which was 10 per cent less than in 1997. In contemporary times the political struggle has been led by Simon Hughes, Liberal Democrat Member of Parliament for North Southwark and Bermondsey, who lives locally and has held the seat for more than twenty years. Historically, however, Bermondsey politics was dominated by the Labour Party; their most famous Member of Parliament (MP) was the socialist politician Dr Alfred Salter who was elected in 1922. Along with his wife, Ada, Dr Salter sacrificed personal prosperity and comfort in order to fight against the appalling conditions in which Bermondsey's poor lived and laboured. The couple's determination to live amongst the poor and, thereby, to try to understand and improve the squalid conditions in which they were living, led to the tragic death of the Salters' only child, Joyce; she died of scarlet fever. Realising that politics and not medicine was the only way to effect real change in Bermondsey, the Salters fought, as politicians, for Bermondsey's improvement; they championed many successful causes including innovative schemes for health and housing.

Nowadays, despite demographic disruption during and following World War Two (Bermondsey was one of the most bombed areas of the country), slum clearances, profound economic transformations arising from the closure of the docks in the 1970s and recent processes of gentrification, those remaining ex-dockers and factory workers, their families and descendants, continue to imagine the community in terms of closely-knit ties of both residence and kinship criteria or what people refer to as being born-and-bred Bermondsey. The historical precedence of fierce territorial rivalry between Bermondsey people and 'Roaders' who are white working class people living on the wrong side of the Old Kent and Walworth Roads, undermines any idea of a homogeneous white working class in London, and reveals the overarching significance of Bermondsey people's sense of place, highlighting their continuing allegiance to their manor. However, apart from these territorial distinctions there are several other relevant social distinctions within Bermondsey itself. In Sharon's home I discover that class distinctions are best understood ethnographically in terms of the difference between kinds of persons in England – common and posh – and, in time, I begin to understand the significance of the further distinctions which are drawn between kinds of common people in Bermondsey as well as kinds of outsiders.

Bermondsey girls

Denying that there is anything special about Bermondsey people, Sharon emphasises that 'Everyone, on *both* sides of the Old Kent Road, grew up the same.' She reduces everybody on either side of Bermondsey's boundaries to a common economic denominator. For Sharon all that matters is that the people live in similar flats on the same kinds of council estates because they do similar kinds of jobs for a similar wage. She adds, 'I see young guys bowlin'[6] around thinkin' they's real Bermondsey bods[7] and they ain't; they just think they are. There ain't nothin' special about Bermondsey; I think you might be wastin' your time.' With that Sharon lets out a raucous laugh, teasing me because she knows that I would like to think that my research about Bermondsey people is worthwhile and interesting. Tracey (age 16), one of Sharon's teenage daughters, interjects to reinforce her mother's point, which is that Bermondsey people certainly think that they are something special. She explains, 'I was coming 'ome the other day and these two girls was standing on the pavement and I couldn't get f[th]rough and they didn't move. I wasn't gonna step in the road so I says, "Excuse me!" and they still didn't move so I barged f[th]rough.' Tracey's elder sister, Sophie (age 18), adds for emphasis, 'Bermondsey girls're bitches, f[th]inkin' they own the pavement, just 'cos they're Bermondsey.'

In relation to their mother's perception of her own upbringing, not having been brought up, but 'dragged up on the Old Kent Road', Tracey and Sophie are learning about the value of distancing themselves from Bermondsey people's pride and in particular pride deriving from possession of the place itself. It is clear that even though they are not landowners, Bermondsey people claim the estates as theirs and even the pavements too. Sharon insists that in reality there's nothing special or different about Bermondsey people; she stresses that no matter what they think of themselves, Bermondsey people are just like everyone else in the wider area that spans Bermondsey, Peckham and Walworth. As my research progresses, however, I come to realise that shared economic position is a denial of everything that preoccupies so-called real Bermondsey people. Real Bermondsey people are fiercely proud about being from Bermondsey and nowhere else, except also being from England and sometimes, but only in specific contexts, Britain too. For them, their way of life and particular history is alive and in need of protection from outside influences; determined not to let it become a thing of the past, they struggle to sustain their pride as a hope for the future of the next generation. The place called Bermondsey, the actual space, being born and bred there and, therefore, being inseparable from a history and experience that is shared and lived in common, is what makes all the difference. It is a pride that makes a social value out of territoriality; it overrides and forces into the background the solidarity that shared class position across the Old Kent and Walworth Roads would seem to make logical.

Common-as-shit

Unlike the example set by her proud Bermondsey mother, Sharon takes pride in being common-as-shit and she uses this as the baseline against which to judge others. She constantly makes evaluations of people, including her own children, on the basis of how common they are in relation to her. When I ask Sharon what being common means, she tells me: 'Bein' common is about bein' down to earth, not f[th]inkin' you're upper [better than other people]; it means tellin' it like it is [talking straight – telling the truth in plain language], and it means ya don't mind yer Ps n' Qs: ya don't try to talk proper.' In Sharon's home being common means that swearing (foul language) – shit, fuck, bastard, fucking, fucking-hell and cunt – is a familiar part of everyday speech. When I ask other people what being common means they tell me that it is about, 'Knowin' what it is like to be skint – down to your last two quid [£] – there's no more money until next week and there's kids to feed.' Being common clearly has something to do, then, with economic position and in particular the experience of what it is like to be constrained by the limited availability of money because disposable income is in short supply, but being common is about much more than that too. Sharon goes on to explain that being common also means, 'Knowin' [h]ow to 'ave a good laugh 'cos you're not stuck up.' Having none of the obsessive modesty of prudish politeness, Sharon revels in the permanent joke of the body's sexual and excretory functions and she makes no attempt to conceal them for the sake of civility. Without a doubt, being common is, for Sharon, about a particular relationship to the question of what counts in polite society as good manners and it is a relationship of opposition. With her radically common stance, she opposes all those who think they are 'upper' and she makes it clear that she can't stand pretension. She thinks that the pride of Bermondsey people is pretension and she thinks that I am pretentious because I am, as she constantly reminds me, posh.

Posh cow

To some extent Sharon plays to the gallery, relishing her favourite word – cunt – hoping to offend me. Being labelled as posh, having the manners and demeanour that distinguish me as such, and yet living in a council flat in Bermondsey, makes me an anomaly and an object of curiosity to Sharon. Living on a council estate means, as Sharon emphasises, that people there share more or less the same economic fate, but because my manner differentiates me and stands for my upbringing, it leads Sharon to speculate about my past and have different expectations for my future. She knows that posh people don't live on council estates so I can't be that posh and yet I'm obviously not common either. From my point of view, trying to make sense of what kind of person I am becoming in Bermondsey, I begin to understand that social class position is the outcome of an inextricable relationship between money and manners. Ways of getting money and ways of being in the world are inseparable and it is this complex and specific conjunction that defines what it means to be a particular kind of English and British person.

Subtle markers of speech, clothing, ways of walking, wearing jewellery, hairstyle, physical bearing, posture and demeanour come, in time, to signify a particular stance, which symbolises the social and economic relationships a person was born into and points towards the future she or he is likely to arrive at. Sharon never lets me escape from the apparently determining effect of my manner and she assumes that because I am posh, I must, by definition, think that I'm upper, that is to say, a better person than she is and she's right, I do. She refuses, however, to acknowledge that being upper is something anyone can ever actually be, and asserts in her own manner of being, the idea that superiority can only ever be a function of pretension. Sharon cannot conceive of the idea that my posh manners are just as much a taken-for-granted aspect of my way of being as her common manners are. She presumes that I am constantly and self-consciously trying to be posh and trying to talk proper because, according to her way of thinking, everyone is common inside no matter what front is put up on the outside. From Sharon's point of view, inside every posh person there is a common person just waiting to get out. Being posh is, therefore, in her eyes, not something anyone can actually be – it is all pretension – a put on. From my point of view, however, the truth is that I didn't explicitly know what it meant to be posh until I encountered myself at the interface with people who think of themselves as common. I begin to appreciate how relative any person's social class position is; one kind of person is constantly being defined as distinctive through a hierarchically valued relationship of opposition to another kind of person's difference. When I discuss this with Anita – one of the Bermondsey outsiders – she summarises the situation for me, 'There is a cultural divide in this country that is never going to be overcome.'

With Sharon I am doomed from the beginning. Even as I begin to learn what it means to be common by trying harder to have empathy and 'fit in' and my demeanour begins to change, this is evidence to Sharon that I had been common all along and was, in the first place, just putting on 'airs and graces'. Having left a message on her mobile phone one morning, I see her later in the afternoon and Sharon tells me that when she listened to it, she had said to herself, 'I can't believe I've got this posh cow leavin' messages on my phone.' As I spend more and more time with Sharon, observing what being common-as-shit entails for a woman, I recognise that it is a lot to do with learning to enjoy the fun of bawdy talk. I watch her draw out the lewd suggestion in each new scenario: the barbecue tongs that are just like a woman's legs opening and closing; the corkscrew that screws, and so on ad infinitum and I quickly learn how to rouse her licentious laughter. This isn't difficult since my father was always crude in private, but I was taught constraint in this by my mother who despaired of my father's manners and insisted on the importance of politeness and restraint, especially in public.

Coming out of myself

Taking me under her wing, Anita invites me to accompany her to my first Ann Summers party in the home of one of the mums from our daughters' school. Accepting gladly, I enjoy the hospitality of the host who provides food and drink for all of the ladies gathered in her front room where we are to be entertained by the Ann Summers sales representative. The rep creates a riotous mood, getting everyone to join in lewd games and compete for obscene prizes (I win a pack of playing cards featuring nude men proudly bearing massive erections that make us scream in mock horror). After this, the serious business of selling begins; the Ann Summers rep introduces items from the latest catalogue containing sexy underwear and sex toys and women then have time to browse through, deciding what to buy. They are eager to spend because everyone knows that a share of the evening's sales goes to the host who has taken the trouble to organise the party. During this time the guests entertain one another, joking about their choice of items and teasing each other about what the implications are for their sex lives. Entering into the spirit of the evening and having a good laugh, I buy a lacy g-string for myself and three bright purple vibrators as gifts to outrage my friends with, but I'm self-consciously aware that I can't imagine ever getting turned on by one. As soon as I get home, because I don't want my daughters or my partner to see them, I hide my pack of cards and the vibrators because I don't want them to think that the things that I am learning to enjoy among these women are appropriate things for a woman like me to celebrate. Even though I enjoyed the party, I feel slightly ashamed of myself and am aware, at the same time, how prudish to these common women my romantic reservations would seem.

The next week at school when Anita and I see the host of the party in the school playground I make a crude joke about something or other and the woman says, as if she is critical of my attempts to fit in with them, 'I didn't think you were crude Gillian, what 'appened to you?' Before I can respond Anita jumps to my defence, 'Leave her, she's all right, she's just comin' out of 'erself.' And Anita is right: I am coming out of myself; I'm becoming someone whom I don't even recognise in myself; a woman whom my partner is beginning to be revolted by. The more common I become the less he desires me. Women who are common-as-muck are part of what he has endeavoured to escape from in the East End of London; bawdy women who come home from a night out 'pissed' (drunk), smelling of booze (alcohol) and fags (cigarettes). Painfully then, I begin to realise that social class is to do with a lot more than the differentiation of occupations, income, education and manner of speaking; it is also about the more intimate and bodily questions of how sensuality comes to be structured as desire, the corollary of which is the creation of parallel configurations of disgust and shame.

Meanwhile, in Sharon's home, Emma, Sharon's youngest daughter who is ten years old, watches in horror as the respectable 'teacher' who she is so proud to have brought home from school (where I began my research), descends into her mother's world. As my vigilance about appropriate behaviour relaxes I break the taboo that posh people have of not swearing in front of children. Chatting to Sharon in the living room and forgetting for a moment that Emma is there, I swear and call someone that we are talking about a bastard. Emma pulls away from the affectionate proximity she was enjoying while sitting with me on the sofa, 'Oh Gillian, why did you swear? I didn't f[th]ink you swore.' In response, Sharon roars with laughter. Delighted that I have gone down in Emma's estimation, she explains to Emma, 'She swears, of course she swears. What did you f[th]ink she was – a bloody saint?' Growing up in a household full of tough and brash women, who 'tell it like it is', Emma lives in a common home where there is little tolerance for the so-called precious innocence of childhood that is cultivated in posh homes like mine. I acknowledge that she must grow up fast and fit in quickly with the adult world that proceeds uncensored around her.

Being upper: talking proper

Before long, at Tracey's sixteenth birthday party, Sharon introduces me to some of her friends. Pleased that I am doing well because I have made everyone laugh with a crude suggestion, she explains to them, 'I used to f[th]ink she was posh but she's not ya see.' As all the taboos of my 'proper' upbringing are challenged, I begin first to be self-conscious about and then gradually to become aware of how the way that I speak and the content of my conversation is changing as I slowly learn how common women talk. Even though we all apparently speak English, it takes me a long time before I can confidently strike up a conversation, know how to greet people properly, what to talk about and how to make a joke and have a laugh in a new and different way. Unlearning what it means to be posh is a slow and excruciating process because it means undoing the value judgement that talking proper implies in relation to common speech. I realise that the educated and expensive talk of the middle classes is useless to me with Sharon; I no longer need to demonstrate how knowledgeable I am about the world, how broad and diverse my experience of it is and how ambitious I am to get on in life and improve myself. When I resort to such talk I am teased mercilessly about being posh and I quickly learn to keep the diversity and breadth of my education and experience firmly in the background of everyday interactions. I need only to focus on the essential business of everyday life: my family's welfare, our health (conversations about the vagaries of the unruly body predominate), work and ways to get money, housework, the drama of relationships, shopping, sex and gossip about my own or other people's troubles.[8] As long as I can talk about what seem to be the fundamental things in life and demonstrate that I can share stories about often-insurmountable difficulties, which I can also laugh about, then that is all that matters to Sharon.

As time goes on I begin to lose the polish of my posh accent, dropping consonants, blending and shortening words; my speaking tone gets coarse and louder in raucous moments. I become aware of the charisma of a new language in practice and I realise that as the way that I speak changes and I stop talking 'proper' I am becoming a person of less worth in my own eyes and that paradoxically that is a good thing. As I set out to get to know Bermondsey people and find out what makes them unique, I realise that I am also, via an examination of my own transforming feelings, exploring how the relationship between the social classes in England hinges on a segregation that is emotionally structured through mutual disdain; in other words I am becoming conscious that the differences between people of distinct classes are deeply felt and not just occupationally defined. Overcoming them is not, therefore, going to be a simple intellectual decision or even the inevitable outcome of the change in my economic fortunes or political will, it is going to be a question of how far I can overcome the embodied and largely unconscious history of how I have come, vis-à-vis others, to value myself as a particular kind of British and specifically English person.

One day, in conversation with a professor at university, I notice that without being able to stop myself I use the word 'gonna' instead of 'going to' and I am completely shocked. Despite myself I am taken aback by the changes in me which are being forged during the process of my fieldwork research. Anita, the woman whose move to Bermondsey and learning about what it means to belong here happens in parallel with my own, watches me go through all these changes as my research progresses and often has a good laugh at my expense. At least she is, as she describes herself, common to start with and all she has to learn about is the specific subtleties of what being a common woman in Bermondsey means. One day, having just completed a fantastic interview with a market stall holder 'down The Blue,'[9] I phone Anita to tell her about it and I shout excitedly into the phone, 'Anita, it was blindin [brilliant]!' Too polite to burst out laughing on the spot she phones me the next day, asks me about the interview again and mimicking my posh voice she teases, 'So it was excellent, then, was it?' In the school playground, subjecting me to further friendly ridicule, Anita tells me that she couldn't believe it, hearing me talking like that on the phone and that she had thought to herself, 'How the mighty they have fallen!' 'Never mind,' she says. 'You're on the dark side now – you'll have a better time.'

Interesting about Anita's reassurance is the way that it reveals how becoming common means moving out of the light, into the dark, towards the wrong side of righteous, no longer high and mighty. The metaphors mix height (being above/upper) and virtue (being good) implying that I have now fallen from grace, from the sacred pedestal of posh. On a more serious note, and in private, Anita tells me that she is worried that I am going to lose myself, stop being me in the way that I am, go too far with my research. She delights in seeing me cured of my snobbery but doesn't want to see me corrupted by the changes I am embracing. She intimates that there are different degrees of commonness and advises me that I shouldn't go too far. 'You wouldn't wanna be common-as-muck,' she explains. This is the first intimation I have that within one relatively small area of London, and within one community like Bermondsey, there are different kinds of working class people. Apart from the gendered differences between men and women I soon realise that women are very careful of, and attentive to, the distinctions between kinds of common people. Anita gives me a pointer to lead me away from a descent into being the kind of common person that she feels it wouldn't suit me to become and indicates that there are other kinds of common women that I can be more like. These are the kinds of women she is meeting in Bermondsey and with respect to whom she is transforming, in relation to her own rather disreputable past in Waterloo, her aspirations about her life and her children's future.

Making good

Anita also emphasises how Sharon's philosophy – of reducing all common people to the same level – represents a disavowal of the achievements of working class people who are proud to have worked hard and 'made good', which means to have done well enough in life to own their own homes, have a decent education, respectable white-collar jobs, take holidays abroad and enjoy high levels of disposable income. She explains that there are plenty of Bermondsey people like this, some of whom have stayed in Bermondsey, but many of whom have moved out, to Bromley and further afield to Kent. These people are then judged on the basis of their attitude to the friends and relatives that they have left behind on the estates; there is nothing wrong with making good but if a person makes good and then starts to look down on close friends and relatives, she/he will be despised for it.

To illustrate her point Anita tells me about her sister who lives in Kent. Anita explains that her ex-husband used to call her sister 'the Duchess' because her sister thought she was so posh. Anita says that she thinks it is sad that people who live in areas like Bromley work so hard to distance themselves from people, even members of their own family, who are considered now to be too common to associate with. She remembers when she used to visit her, how her sister would say things like, 'Oh, I didn't know you vacuumed everyday like me.' Or, 'Of course, you probably only eat frozen vegetables not fresh ones like me.' Anita, laughing, tells me how her sister's pride about her new home preceded a fall-out with her posh neighbour in Kent. The neighbour had an apple tree in her garden with branches that leaned over Anita's sister's garden. In autumn, the apples would fall on both sides of the garden fence and when Anita's sister complained to her neighbour the posh woman said disdainfully, 'I would have thought that people like you would be glad of a few free apples.' In response, Anita's sister had lost her temper, replying vehemently, 'You f[th]ink I'm common? I'll show you who's fuckin' common.' She then came back with a chain saw, cut through the fence and without a second thought, cut the apple tree down. Years later, Anita says, the two women are still not speaking to each other.

Anita emphasises that there are also people who have 'made good' who choose to stay on the estates. One woman that I interview, for example, lives in and owns her own council flat but also has a country cottage in Normandy in France. Trying to explain her position she insists that there is a need for a new name for a new class of people: these are people, like herself, who have achieved the same standard of living as middle class people but who would never want to be thought of as being middle class because they are proud of their own working class roots and disdainful of the middle classes. She says that she describes people, like herself, as 'new [or upper] working class' and instances herself and her parents, who have just bought property in Portugal, as members.

The secret of being working class

In contrast to this new-found pride among the working classes about rising living standards and higher levels of disposable income, Sharon, who is clearly not a member of the 'new working class', revels in being 'common-as-shit', and emphasises, therefore, equality between people as an affirmation of the value of the lowest common denominator. Sharon constantly denies the possibility of differential human value and it becomes clear to me that there is, therefore, a degree of tension among working class women about the different kinds of persons that they are proud to be. Common women stand in relation to common-as-muck women as posh women stand to common women in general. In Sharon's eyes these posh women think that they are upper, that is to say, better than her and she despises them for it. Anita, meanwhile, saves me from becoming common-as-shit in Sharon's house and explains, 'The secret of bein' working class is bein' 'appy with yer position, knowin' that you've done better than yer parents and makin' sure that yer kids will do better than you and that is enough. Un'appiness,' she spells out for me, 'is the result of desirin' a life you know you are never going to 'ave.'

The problem with this philosophy, however, is that it is obvious to me, and to Anita, that I haven't done better than my parents otherwise I'd be living in a posh house like the one that my parents actually live in. It is difficult, therefore, for me not to desire the life I have already known and become accustomed to. I have the upbringing and manners[10] that distinguish me as a posh person but none of the money that completes the equation.[11] Even during my research I didn't have what could be classified as a 'proper job' because I was at university studying social anthropology and nobody in Bermondsey really knew what on earth that meant, so it was difficult for people to classify what I was doing as legitimate work. Living on what Anita calls 'a sad council estate' makes me, by definition, working class but what kind of common woman could I become?

Eventually, I begin to understand that being of less worth in posh people's eyes is part of what the pride of working class people is all about. It flies in the face of the dominant (posh) value system that attempts to define and demean common people. 'It's them and us, that's 'ow it's always been, that's 'ow it'll always be,' Anita laments. 'We are the backbone of the nation and no one gives a fuck about us.' Reacting against dominance, then, working class pride creates the means for dignity; common people fight back defensively with their own values and being common entails, therefore, an inverse snobbery.[12] Posh people are pitied because 'They 'aven't got a clue [about "real" life]'. 'Even with all that education they've got no common sense [no practical skills or understanding about how to deal with common people].' 'They dunno what it means to get by [to know poverty, to struggle against it and survive]' and 'They dunno 'ow to 'ave a good laugh, 'cos of that stiff upper lip.' On the other hand, however, depending on the situation, certain kinds of posh people, like doctors, lawyers and teachers, are respected for their professional expertise. It all depends on the situation whether hatred, pity, resentment, envy or admiration for posh people is evinced. Anita is right, then, about the cultural divide in Britain: each social class is to the other as a people from a distant land with much mutual misunderstanding between the two.

The importance of this understanding from the point of view of education is as follows: if it is true, as I suggest it is, that the school, as a formal institution of the state, has come, over time, to represent and embody posh people's values, and make legitimate posh people's way of being in the world, then it is also true to say that common children, like Emma, Sharon's daughter, will encounter the formal, 'proper', 'posh' atmosphere of the school as if it were a foreign country. The strangeness of this encounter is probably no different in magnitude from what I felt on entering into Emma's home, which is only just down the road from my own flat, but which may as well have been in Outer Mongolia. The crucial difference between the two kinds of encounters, however, is that at school, and in life, middle class people behave as if they are doing working class people a favour, educating them, teaching them about how to live a 'proper' life and then wondering why it doesn't work; what they are not prepared for, however, is working class people's resistance to this process, a resistance which is born of a defiant pride about the value of common life and values. In the next chapter I consider working class pride in more depth. I begin by explaining how, even in one family, each person's relationship to what it means to be common is different and I end by exploring what the implications of this difference are for a common girl's chances of doing well at school.

3
Common Women: Working Class Values

Sharon has five sisters, about one of whom – Karen – Sharon tells me, 'She f[th]inks she's posh.' Sharon insists that Karen can't be posh because they all grew up the same and all her sisters still live on council estates in Bermondsey. I ask Sharon what Karen does for a living and she laughs, explaining, 'She's only an estate caretaker.' I ask Sharon to clarify for me what it is that makes Karen think she's posh and Sharon says, 'It's 'cos she's got nice f[th]ings and she f[th]inks she's upper: she's '[h]ouse-proud, obsessed about cleanin'.' Sharon explains that she can't stand women who are house-proud; she hates the way that women like that 'carry on' – as if they're upper – just because their homes are always clean and tidy and furnished with nice things.

It is not surprising to me, however, that dirt assumes a heightened importance among common women; the metaphors which describe what it means to be common liken common people to muck and shit, filth, dirt and waste products. Knowing what it's like to be dirty, either literally or sexually, is the constant background against which the battle for 'decency', cleanliness and 'respectability' is fought by women, like Anita and her new friends in Bermondsey, who want and need, unlike Sharon, to be able to differentiate between different kinds of common people. In time I come to appreciate that some of the most house-proud common women are those who spend their working hours cleaning up other people's dirt; cleaning is their expertise. Anita, for example, makes a living from cleaning posh people's homes. She emphasises how often she is disgusted by the state of posh people's houses and explains, 'I may be common but at least I'm not dirty.'

As for myself, during eighteen months' fieldwork I first resist, and then begin to appreciate the value of housework. I am used to middle class women joking about what a waste of time housework is and, like them, my assumption has always been that a woman who cleans too much in her own house is a woman who hasn't got anything better to do. Where once I had resented, neglected or paid another woman to do the work of cleaning my flat while I was trying to study and raise children, I begin to realise that to be valued by these common women in Bermondsey I will have to learn to appreciate the value of being a woman who can keep a tidy home. No matter if it is a council flat; if it is clean and nicely kept, a home on a council estate is something to be proud of. I feel ashamed when I go to the flats of women who work harder than I do but still manage, even with children to bring up, to keep their homes immaculately decorated, furnished and clean on a minimal budget.

Because I hadn't been proud of it, I hadn't appreciated what I had in my small two-bedroom council flat. Slowly, I learn how to take pride in and to take care of it myself. Daunted by the number of hours that could be devoted every day to cleaning, but making a start, nevertheless, on learning how to 'keep a tidy house', I am then able to participate, at least minimally, in the routine conversations about housework through which the pride of certain kinds of common women is established. Never ceasing to be amazed by conversations about, for example, net curtains, I learn that a woman's home can be judged from the outside on the basis of how white 'her nets' are, but I don't even have nets – I am the only woman in my block to have Venetian blinds – and not very clean ones at that. I notice, too, that women's talk about their ironing differentiates the degree of their dedication to cleanliness and tidiness: sheets, towels, children's clothes and even underwear get ironed, whereas I rarely find time to pick up an iron except very occasionally for a nice shirt.

Having nice things and being upper

Eventually I begin to understand that the same sense of pride about order and cleanliness in the home also extends to personal appearance. House-proud women and especially their children are turned out cleanly and smartly on a daily basis and not just for special occasions. Having nice clothes is just one way in which common women compete to differentiate themselves and their children from their less proud and less well-off friends and neighbours. Referring to this kind of competitiveness, Sharon explains that wanting to have nice things is the main source of problems between common people because friends and family members are always trying to outdo one another. By way of example she tells me about when she bought a new rug recently: her friend, who had come round to visit, noticed and admired the rug and then felt she had to go out and buy exactly the same one so as not to be outdone. In this way, consumption of desirable goods becomes the basis of a competition for equality among common women.

Sharon then tells me more about how she has become estranged from her 'posh' sister, Karen. Sharon and her daughters had been invited to Karen's wedding; they didn't go to the church service because Sharon hates churches, but they were expected at the reception dinner party. When Sharon and her girls arrived, however, no places had been allocated to them and they then had to suffer the humiliation of being tucked away in a corner whilst the rest of the family sat in places of honour at the top tables. Sharon has never forgiven her sister for humiliating her like that. The point is that the difference between what it means to be common and what it takes to aspire to be posh creates tension within, and can sometimes divide, families. I ask Sharon if it is possible to have nice things and not think that you are upper. 'I 'spose it is possible,' she says. 'But I've never met anyone like that.' Interested in the possibility of working class deference for the monarchy, a royal family who are, by definition, the most upper of all the families in the country, I ask Sharon what she would do if Princess Diana were still alive and were to walk in and sit down on the sofa. To this Sharon replies indignantly, 'I'd tell 'er to get a fuckin' job.' Sharon, then, is the self-appointed common denominator of social class: she is the constant reminder that having nice things, being house-proud and thinking that you are upper, are the achievements of a continuous act of distinction,[1] which is a source of pride and dignity for some, but which also creates tension between friends and within families.

Discussing what I have learnt, about the different attitudes towards being common, with another woman – Kate – who has recently moved to Bermondsey after having grown up in Camberwell, I compare her experiences with what Sharon and Anita have gone through with their siblings. Kate explains that her sister, who has moved to Bromley, also now has the idea that she is posh. When Kate goes out with her sister's friends, she is told to 'behave herself' as the condition for being invited. I ask her what 'behaving herself' means, what should she not do? She tells me that she shouldn't be loud,[2] shouldn't hail her sister out across the car park, and shouldn't 'talk common – the way you would indoors' and of course she mustn't swear. I ask her if she teases her sister about being posh and she says that yes, of course she does; sometimes she breaks the rules she has been given on purpose, in order to embarrass her sister.

What Kate explains to me about her posh sister in Bromley makes me reflect on what I am already learning, which is that common people's humour often exerts a levelling force; it consists, in part, of constantly bringing people 'down to earth'. It is a form of joking that 'takes the piss out of' (teases) pretension and aspiration for self-improvement, and requires that a person be able to take a dressing down in good faith, giving it back in good humour without being disrespectful. It's not easy to do, but it is a lot of fun when it's done properly and of course disastrous when it goes wrong.

Common-as-muck

Moving on from talking about the differences between herself and her sisters, Sharon, referring now to her three daughters, explains to me why even they are not all common in the same way. She describes the eldest, Sophie, as being common-as-muck which is, Sharon says, one step away from being common-as-shit. Sophie, who is within listening distance, fights back against this ascription and insists that she's not as common as her mum is because she thinks that the way her mum carries on, swearing and being vulgar in front of her friends, is too common. Sophie tells me that Sharon is an embarrassment to her and explains that her friends tease her about how common her mum is. When Sophie brings a boyfriend home, for example, Sharon will tease the boy constantly, saying sexually explicit things and bringing into the open the suggestion of what the boy's relationship with her daughter implies. Sophie says she feels that she behaves the way her mum ought to behave in company. While Sophie actively resists Sharon's idea of her, her mother, teasing her all the while, shouts out to me from the kitchen, 'She's common-as-muck really Gillian, when she's indoors every other word's a fuck.'

Sophie and Sharon both refer to the difference between the way a common person is expected to 'carry on indoors' and 'in company', that is, in public or when dealing with the official world that reflects the dominance of posh values. Other common women speak to me about having a 'telephone voice'; when speaking to strangers and official people they are aware that they try to talk 'proper' so as to be taken seriously. Speaking well is like having nice things: everyone knows it's valuable, it's worth something, it counts in the scale of personal value and it gets results.[3] One of Anita's friends, for example, laments that she can't go for the job she desperately wants – as a telephone receptionist – and she explains why: 'I can't speak nicely, I'm too common for that job.' She goes on to tell me about her sister who has worked so hard at trying to lose her common way of speaking and has now developed such a lovely voice that her husband phones her up at work just to listen to her talking nicely. Sharon, on the other hand, wouldn't bother to go for a job where she would have to pretend to be something that she isn't or doesn't aspire to be. She worked as a cleaning lady in a police station until her back was too bad for it and was then out of work following an operation. Now Sharon gets by on 'the social' and her long-term boyfriend[4] who lives with her and is step-dad to the girls, pays the bills. Soon, she says, she might try out for a job at the pie 'n' mash shop where her daughter Sophie works,[5] on the Tower Bridge Road.

Common decency and old-fashioned values

Sharon goes on to tell me about Tracey, her second daughter. Tracey, Sharon explains, is not as common as Sophie because she was her nan's (grand-mother's) favourite and was therefore protected and spoiled. I ask Sharon what she means by 'protected' and she explains that Tracey wasn't 'got at' (brought down to earth) by Sharon and Sharon's sisters in the same way because she spent so much time with her nan (Sharon's mother). By way of example she compares what happened to Sophie: as a child Sophie saw a lot more of Sharon's sisters than either Tracey or Emma have done and when one of their aunts phoned or came round to see Sharon they would tease Sophie, swearing at her as a show of affection. In this way swearing becomes part of an intimate joking relationship between certain kinds of relatives and swearwords become, in this context, terms of endearment. Sharon explains how aunts and uncles bring their nieces and nephews 'down to earth' so that they can't presume to be above their cousins who are their aunts' and uncles' children. The joking relation-ship, which reveals a competitive relationship between siblings, exerts, therefore, a levelling force amongst certain kind of kin, like cousins.

Tracey, Sharon goes on to explain, was protected from all that by her grandparents (Sharon's parents) because she stayed with them a lot when she was little. Sharon then tells me how completely different she is to her mum and how her mum was, therefore, able to exert a different influence on Tracey. 'Me mum,' Sharon explains, 'was born and bred Bermondsey: she '[h]ad old-fashioned values, never spoke about sex, '[h]ated people swearing and 'specially the word cunt.' Emphasising how much her mum constantly held up the value of work to set an example to her children, Sharon describes her mum's job in which she worked for so many years as a cleaning lady in a Bermondsey girls' school, whilst her father worked in a factory making jelly for jellied eels and later for the Corporation of London cleaning public toilets. Sharon explains how, when she left school at the age of 13, she had to get a job straightaway and would have to ask her mum for permission if she thought she needed a day off work. If she lost a job, Sharon knew that she dare not go home until she'd found another one.

The 'old-fashioned values', which Sharon despises because her mother lived by them and which some Bermondsey people still cling to, include, then, a strong work ethic linked to the pride of survival in difficult times. Because of pride about getting money through hard work and struggling against the odds, people who hold 'old-fashioned values' dear are disdainful of able-bodied people who now live on and are dependent on 'the social' (social security payments) expecting 'something [from the government] for nothing'. Accepting charity and borrowing from the Tally Man – the person who would knock on doors in working class areas to offer high-interest loans to poor people – was considered to be something shameful. Many Bermondsey people laugh and tell me stories of how, as children, they were often told by their mothers to tell the Tally Man, when he came to collect payment due on money borrowed, that their mother had just told them to come to the door to tell him that she wasn't in. Other women tell of being asked by their mother to put their father's suit in the pawn shop on a Friday so that there would be money for the weekend; somehow the suit would have to be got back ready for work on a Monday morning.

Leaving school at 13, then, Sharon's first job was in an envelope factory, which her mum didn't mind because at least she was working and bringing in some housekeeping money. Sharon describes how she resolved then never to be like her mum with her own children and she likes to think that to her own children she is a friend in need, but from Sophie's point of view Sharon has gone too far, become too common, knowing no bounds. Meanwhile, Sharon's sister, Karen, who thinks she's posh, is disgusted with and distances herself from Sharon. Karen, Sharon explains, was always their mum's favourite; in their mother's eyes Karen could do no wrong and since her mother's death and with the estrangement between the sisters, the family has fallen apart. Before this when her mother was still alive, Sharon's mother's house was, as tradition would expect, the familial focal point and her mother's brother still lived next door at a time when nearly all of one's family members lived close by in the local area. No one among the sisters has taken on the role that the mother played in keeping everyone in the family together and so the children rarely see their cousins, aunts or uncles who would once have been pivotal people in their upbringing.

At home, Sharon says, she had to 'mind her manners' in a household that was always impeccably clean and tidy. Describing her mother, Sharon presents to me a different kind of working class pride, one that distances itself from vulgarity, licentiousness and above all filth in both language and household. House-proud women, like Sharon's mum, distanced themselves from the grim proximity of poverty, taking pride in their house and its possessions and finding dignity in the face of a past that pressed too closely to the history of Bermondsey's Victorian squalor. As I have already explained, women like this, many of whom spend their working hours cleaning, are often obsessively proud about their own housework. Children, and especially girls of house-proud mothers, quickly learn that doing housework is a way to be valued by their mother and to make easy cash in the future, or, like Sharon, they rebel against the constraints it establishes.

Gettin' it

Comparing our experiences in Bermondsey, Anita's friend Jean, the other Bermondsey outsider from my daughters' school playground at Blackfriars, makes the distinction between 'home-grown' Bermondsey people and those who have to be taught. I suggest that surely it is impossible to teach what 'being Bermondsey' means and Jean replies, 'No it's not, Anita's got it, she's only been here a year and she's gettin' it.' Anita, laughing, affirms this suggestion, 'Yeah, I'm gettin' it' and Jean replies, 'I knew she was gettin' it when she said the kids was wearing new dresses to Tulips[6] tonight and I thought, well that's it, she's 'ere [she's arrived]. 'Cos they always have to look like they've stepped out of a washin' machine – the kids [in Bermondsey].' Anita then explains that the ultimate challenge in Bermondsey is to keep girls in bright whites, tracksuits that are the evidence of meticulous washing skills and mothers' pride in their children.

I begin to appreciate, then, that the pride of Bermondsey women, which is what Sharon's mum stood for and which Anita is now learning about in relation to the women that she has become acquainted with, stands in contrast to all of Sharon's levelling efforts. Being common and taking pride in being decent requires a huge effort; it is an amazing act of determination conjured every day out of the drudgery and sometimes financial hardship of common life. I learn later, however, that many women in Bermondsey are acquiring huge debts so as to be seen to be nicely turned out, have nice things in their homes and keep up with and maintain a competitive edge on their friends, family and neighbours.[7] Older women tell me that there is nothing new in this phenomenon except for the fact that credit is now easier to come by. In the old days they used to put down a woman who was broke and still preoccupied with looking good at the expense of more important priorities; they would say that a woman like this was 'starving behind lace curtains' and nowadays, Anita explains, she would call a woman like that 'all fur coat: no knickers'.

Teenage rebellion

Sharon, then, having 'dragged herself up' and become proud about being common-as-shit, is not a typical Bermondsey woman. She is what proud Bermondsey people might call a 'low-life', but Sharon wouldn't care what they think about her. She rebelled against her mum whom some might describe as a 'decent working class woman' who met the conventions of 'respectable' behaviour, and she rebelled, she says, because her mum wasn't her friend; she couldn't talk to her about anything. 'No one talked in my '[h]ouse,' she recalls, 'specially about sex.' Sharon's teenage years, characterised as they were by the desire for freedom from the constraints of her mother's strict household, distanced her from her mum. What she means, therefore, when she says that she was 'dragged up', is that she was brought up first and hated it so vehemently she determined to drag herself up, with her teenage friends, on the Old Kent Road where Bermondsey standards count for nothing.

Of her mother's old-fashioned values what, if anything, has Sharon retained? Despite her foul language and sexually explicit teasing, what is clear in Sharon's household is that the development of her daughters' sexuality does not and must not threaten her authority as the person who is holding the household together. She is the matriarch that her mother was but in a different way. Sophie's and Tracey's boyfriends must work hard to earn her approval since she places herself at the centre of their world, and to gain approval a young man must call round regularly, spend time in the house while Sharon is there and show respect, consideration and generosity towards family members. He should be able to prove that he is financially self-sufficient so as not to be a drain on the daughter's present and future finances and he must be able to show that he can look after himself in order to demonstrate that he will be able to take care of his girlfriend and her family 'in the right way'.

Because she is so crude, Sharon makes it seem as if there is a sexually liberal atmosphere at home, but 16-year-old Tracey is forbidden to have sex. Sharon begins to tell me about the first time that Tracey brought home her current boyfriend and Tracey explains how Sharon took him to one side and told him, 'If you so much as touch her, I'll personally tie you up and cut yer' fuckin' dick off mate.' Hearing Sharon tell this story again, Tracey laughs and explains that Rick, her boyfriend, is petrified of Sharon. Later, after Tracey and Rick have been going out for about a year, Sharon says she can't very well stop them having sex for much longer since they have shown that they are serious and are now engaged to be married.

Of Sophie, Sharon says that she is old enough to do what she wants and is allowed to have sex with a serious boyfriend in her own bedroom, but what she must not do is fall pregnant. Sharon explains that she has made it clear to the girls that if they get pregnant they shouldn't bother to come home. She regrets having had her own first child at the age of 19 without the father to stand by her. Nineteen is too young an age, she says, for a girl to fall pregnant without being married because, at that age, a girl has had no chance to get started in life and can't look after herself. Sharon perceives teenage, and especially a single-parent pregnancy, as the greatest risk to a woman's productivity, seriously limiting her life chances and, more importantly, disrupting household relations between the girl and her mother. Sharon wants to protect herself and her daughters from this fate. Her strategy is to be open with her daughters about sex, its pleasures and pitfalls. Sophie has been on the pill since she was 13 and Sharon is reassured that the disruption of an early teenage pregnancy is ruled out. She feels herself to be expert at regulating the potentially disruptive influence of her teenage daughters' sexual experimentation and, reacting against her mother's prudish decency, Sharon manages to secure the stability of the household even in the face of the potential fissure caused by the possibility of her daughters' sexual relations outside the home. Young men must pay their respects to Sharon as the centre of the household and their ideas about their own importance in her daughters' lives are, therefore, tempered.

The transition from being a daughter to being a mother in one's own right and having a household of one's own is, in Sharon's eyes, the most difficult thing a young woman undertakes in her life. Sharon may be common-as-shit, much to Sophie's dismay, but she cares about her daughters' futures and couldn't care less about the outward signs of polite respectability. The household and the kin relations in and through which the home is established as a place where the family lives, form the bedrock of what Sharon values. Whilst her own mother lost her to the Old Kent Road, Sharon retains her daughters' affections by trying to be their friend, making a joke out of sex and endeavouring to secure, thereby, her own and their future happiness above all else.

Emma: becoming common: learning how to swear

Of Emma, meanwhile, Sharon says that it is too early to tell how common she is going to be. Responding to this, Tracey tells her mum that when she took Emma out this morning, to get a drink and some crisps, Emma had sworn at some men who had 'eyed Tracey up' (looked her up and down, avariciously) as they drove by. Tracey reports how Emma had called out after the men, 'What you lookin' at? You cunts.' Quick to explain further, Tracey tells Sharon that she had told Emma to shut up and had put her hand over Emma's mouth to stop her from saying anything else. Sharon, on hearing this story, immediately rounds angrily on Emma who is sitting next to me on the sofa in the sitting room. Shouting loudly, she admonishes, 'I told ya not to use that fuckin' word [cunt].'

Swearing, then, is ruled by etiquette. Elderly Bermondsey men tell me that there was a time when men didn't swear in front of women and women and children were expected not to swear at all. Grown men tell me that as a sign of respect they don't swear in front of their mums and dads and that being able to swear with people, just like joking, is a sign of familiarity; it all depends on the social situation. Swearwords are most often used simply and effectively as disparaging adjectives or as markers of emotional emphasis that have more or less force depending on the situation in which they are used. Swearwords also have their own hierarchy, 'cunt' being the most offensive and 'shit' perhaps the least, but it is the feeling behind the words and the situation that matter not so much the words themselves because swearwords (and even the word 'cunt') can be used as terms of endearment. Some common mothers, like Sharon and Anita's friend Jean, swear like troopers in front of their children but don't allow their young children to have a foul mouth. Other children are encouraged by certain family members to swear and celebrate the achievement of profanity as if it is the means by which their distinctiveness as particular kind of people is brought into being.

The celebration of profanity that being common implies extends, in Sharon's case, to contempt for all kinds of supposedly sacred things such as the innocence of children or the piety of priests and religious spaces such as churches. Recounting how she had once been asked, by a priest at a friend's wedding, to leave the church because she couldn't stop laughing, Sharon explains that she can't go into a church because it makes her hysterical with laughter.

'Do as you please'

Rules in Sharon's home are kept to a minimum because it is through her daughters' relative freedom that Sharon feels she gets to see what her girls are really like. Within certain limits she believes that her daughters' happiness depends on her giving them the freedom to 'do as they please', freedom which she couldn't enjoy as a child growing up in a strict household. When her daughters' friends come round Sharon is disdainful if she thinks that they are children who are overly subjected to their parents' rules. She teases them, for example, if she knows that they aren't allowed to have fizzy drinks or sweets to eat as they please and she is disdainful of the so-called scientific knowledge which is cited as the justification for those rules. In Sharon's household the body and its appetites (with the specific exception of sexual appetite) become the location of pleasure, not control. Present desire is not forsaken in the interests of health and future longevity and Tracey and Sophie have been allowed to smoke cigarettes in the house since they were 13 years old.

This cultivation of a lack of constraint makes me appreciate that one of the main differences between my own household and Sharon's is that my children are governed by many more rules and regulations than Sharon's daughters are. As mothers we have very different ideas about what is for our children's good and, because we take our own understanding for granted, each of us thinks that our way of bringing up children is the right one. For example, my children are only allowed to watch television at the weekend and they can only have sweets, chocolate and fizzy drinks on a Friday and Sharon despises me for it. I cook home-made food nearly every day with fresh vegetables and fruit and I am committed to providing a healthy diet for my family while Sharon only gawks at the cost of it. When Emma has to keep going to the doctor because she suffers from stomach pains as a result of anxiety and constipation, I tentatively suggest to Sharon that she try giving her some fresh fruit every day to which Sharon replies derisively, 'What's the point of that? I'd buy a fiver (£5) worth of fruit and by the next day it'd all be eaten.'

School work

Sharon applies the same 'do as you please' philosophy to her daughters' education. She says of them, 'If they want to learn they will, if they don't, they won't and that's that.' Sharon explains that Tracey is the perfect example of the success of this approach because she has done relatively well at school, choosing to apply herself to schoolwork because it pleased her to do so, not because she had been forced at home. I contrast this with my own daughters' experiences: I have high expectations of their educational achievements and have encouraged them all along to do well at school. I insist that a proportion of their day is spent on school-related activities, like homework, but in Sharon's home I begin to think, for the first time, about who my children would become if left to their own devices more.

Elaborating on her mother's point, Tracey explains that when she started secondary school she was in need of remedial teaching, but through self-motivation she has managed to achieve enough to keep her interested in staying on at school until the age of 16 and she hopes for a career in childcare. Her teachers want her to go to college but Sharon says that as soon as she's 16, Tracey must go out to work to bring in a wage and pay her share of the housekeeping. Never having had to pay housekeeping money to my mum in my life, I realise then that qualifications gained through further education are for those people who can afford to forgo money now whilst making an investment on a larger return and greater status in the future. While middle class children learn how to and are expected to become independent of their parents, often, like myself, moving far away from the family home at the age of 18, working class children, like Tracey, learn how to become people that their parents can depend upon; they are much more likely, therefore, to stay close to home. Tracey, then, will achieve adult status at the age of 16, in the full-time pay packet. Then she will learn that the 'do as you please' philosophy does not extend to the way she spends her money; her mother will exercise control over a portion of it and Tracey will appreciate then that work, not further education, is the foundation of working class life. So it is that common values often conspire against any aspiration that a young person, like Tracey, may have towards higher education.[8]

Sharon emphasises that it doesn't matter to her that Sophie left school at 13, as she herself had done also, because this is only evidence to her that Sophie wasn't happy and couldn't get on at school. I ask Sophie if she has any regrets about leaving school so early and she says, 'As long as I enjoy life I don't mind what job I do.' Sophie earns £100 a week from her job in the pie 'n' mash shop, part of which she must give to Sharon every week for housekeeping. Explaining to me the importance of the housekeeping money that a mother gets from her children an elderly Bermondsey woman in her 80s describes how her younger brother was never allowed to marry because their mother wanted him at home. It was, she says, quite common in those days for a woman to keep one among her many children living with her to bring in a bit of housekeeping and look after her in old age.

Family values, education and disposable income

Emma is in her last year of primary school education, but she can barely read and write. Sharon's preoccupation with, and concern for, familial values at home does not extend to an appreciation of the value of formal learning at school. In my household, in contrast, formal learning is part of the way in which I make sense of what caring for my children means. I cannot help but be horrified, therefore, to realise that at the beginning of the twenty-first century a child like Emma is likely to leave primary school unable to read and write proficiently. To me, this is a tragic indictment of Tenter Ground, the school that Emma attends, but it is also indicative of the problems that schools in areas like Bermondsey face with common families in which formal learning plays little part in the way that caring relationships are established in the home.

Because my eldest daughter is not much older than Emma it is impossible for me and Sharon not to compare their respective situations. My daughter, who is a year younger than Emma, is doing exceptionally well at school but her teacher advises me that because the priority in the school is to raise the overall average level of attainment in each class and to focus on special educational needs at the bottom of the class, the most able children are not being stretched to their full potential. He suggests that I should start preparing my daughter to apply, when she is 11 years old, for a scholarship place at an academically selective independent school. Not long after this, however, my partner unexpectedly gains a financially lucrative position as a member of one of the top bands in the country. This means that for the first time since our children were born, we have money to spare. After careful deliberation we decide that, rather than use the money to improve our immediate standard of living, which would mean moving out of our cramped council flat and buying a 'nice house' or flat somewhere, it would be better to consider our girls' long-term future, so we use the money to buy our council flat relatively cheaply, purchase a better second-hand car – an old Mercedes estate (for transporting drums) – and we enter our daughter for a place at one of these fee-paying, academically selective private schools.

Within a week of parking the old Mercedes in the estate car park my partner begins to get comments from male neighbours, such as, 'Nice one mate; you've gone up in the world.' Although we hadn't thought about it at the time it soon becomes obvious to us that the car is the evidence of a change in our fortunes; it is clear to the other men on the estate that my partner must now have access to disposable income. When I explain this to Anita she tells me that when someone on the estates starts to do well for themselves, they have to be careful because the other people, who might really be struggling to make ends meet, might take it 'like a kick in the bollocks.' Every week thereafter, at the same time on a Friday night, one of these men knocks on my door or sends one of his children to knock and ask me, 'Can me dad borrow a tenner

[£10] for the weekend? He'll pay ya back Monday.' Each Friday, from then on, I make sure that I have a tenner ready by the door and every Monday night the man sends one of the children to pay the money back. In this way the chances are minimised of any resentment building up about our new-found prosperity.

When our daughter takes the academic test and manages to gain a place in one of these private schools, we reluctantly remove her from the state education system and commit ourselves, thereby, to a serious financial burden. In so doing, we make it clear to ourselves that we value education, as the key to our daughters' opportunities in the future and as an end in itself, above all else. More than anything this is what differentiates me from Sharon and she makes no bones about mocking me for it; telling me what a waste of money private school is going to be, she speculates about what she would have done with that money. Having a daughter in private school also now makes my anomalous position as a posh woman living in a council flat all the more pronounced. Focusing only on the quality of education that our daughter might receive at private school we neglect to consider the social implications of the decision. Now we become anomalies on both fronts: on Bermondsey's estates we are all fur coat: no knickers and, compared to the upper middle class families at the school, in Dulwich's leafy suburbs, we are out of our financial depth. Most of these people are either seriously posh or seriously wealthy or both, and, not surprisingly, some of them are horribly disdainful. At the same time as I am learning about the various kinds of common people in Bermondsey, I am forced to begin to consider also the differences between all the kinds of posh people in London, England and Britain. Whilst my daughter successfully throws herself into making friends and doing well at school among the children of the upper middle classes, I, paradoxically, am more determined than ever to work out what kind of working class woman I could happily be in Bermondsey.

For Sharon, the difference between our daughters' educational achievements is to do with how clever my daughter is, and she understands this to be a natural and heritable quality, but for me it is to do with the variation in the ways that we are bringing up our children and the difference in our expectations of standards at school. I don't believe for a minute that my daughter has an exceptional IQ; I simply feel that she has learned at home, from infancy, to love formal learning because that kind of learning, for example, through having fun with reading books, conversing and wondering about the world, is a major part of what our loving relationship consists of. For Sharon, in contrast, learning is what should happen at school, but only if the child likes it; it is up to the child. From my point of view, however, the child's attitude to learning is the responsibility of the mother (or principal carer); it is her responsibility to find the best possible education for her child and to teach the child that formal-learning-type activities are not only fun, but valuable too. At school, when Emma talks about not being able to read, she explains, 'My mum never learned me,' and it doesn't occur to her to raise the issue of why the school hasn't 'learned' her either.

Rules and regulations

What is important in Emma's household is that she is learning how to care for others and how to be cared about herself in a way that doesn't require her to do well at school. Formal learning isn't essential to what she is coming to understand about what it takes to be valued at home. In this respect Tenter Ground Primary School has not been successful in providing a point of contrast for Emma between the values she is learning at home and the more general question of how a person comes to be valued in England. Meanwhile, the comparison between Sharon's home and my own reveals to me that no matter how far I go in learning about what it means to be common, I am not prepared to undo some of my most closely held values concerning how I should care for my children. In this light I realise that I can only go so far in becoming common because no matter that I live on a council estate I am still unable to stop myself from bringing my children up to be well educated, 'proper' in their manner and middle class in their aspirations.

At the same time, the contrast between Sharon's household and my own is revealing. I become self-consciously aware that at least on school days, my daughters have to make sense of all the prohibitions and special routines to do with the cultivation of self-discipline: learning how to eat healthily, happily do homework and music practice (not so happily) before relaxing and doing as they please. I realise that this is also what probably makes the transition from home to school easier for middle class children: they are already used to following instructions, doing as they are told and may have some awareness that those rules and regulations are for their own good. Contrasting my household with Sharon's, I begin to wonder, however, whether my daughters are perhaps overly subjected to rules and regulations, which, in extreme cases, is likely to be the source of children's suffering in middle class homes. At my daughter's new school, for example, I become aware of children who have every minute of their spare time, inside and outside of school, filled with structured activities oriented towards learning valuable skills in art, music, sport and drama and so on.

As I begin to observe and become more self-conscious about these pre-viously taken-for-granted rules, I start, to a certain extent, to evaluate their importance, realise how ludicrous some of them are and watch what happens when I relax them. This means that my children get more time to 'do as they please' and they love it; for them it means more time to watch what I call 'rubbish' on television, more time for computer games and all the things that are anathema to middle class parents. One day, coming home from school and pulling up in the car park of our estate, I am approached by a little girl who asks if my daughters can come out to play. I respond, 'Not today,' and she persists, asking, 'Why not?' and I reply, 'Because it is a school day and they've got homework to do.' Smiling, she looks up at me and says, as if she has suddenly understood what is dif-ferent about me, 'Oh, your house has rules.' 'Yes,' I say and ask her in return, 'Doesn't your house have rules?' And she responds matter-of-factly, 'No.' Then, with this perfect understanding in mind, and probably feel-ing sorry for my daughters, she happily rides off to play.

When I talk to Anita about this scenario she explains to me that on the estates you can tell how common a family is by how much they let their children out to play. She emphasises that she doesn't let her daughters out after school either because she doesn't want them to be out with the kind of children who 'haven't got any manners' and who might then want to come into the house to play and then go back and tell their parents about 'what we've got [nice things] indoors'. I explain to Anita that I used to play out all the time as a child and I don't remember it ever doing me any harm. Anita laughs and says mockingly, as if I have still got so much to learn, 'Yeh, but ya didn't grow up on a council estate did ya Gillian?'

Becoming dependable at home and dropping out of school

For Emma, quite often, the demands of learning how to care about her family and especially her mother, results in her wanting to take time off school because she worries when Sharon is ill. These problems have greater priority for Emma than the kinds of difficulties she faces with learning what it means to get along with her peers and do well at school and she contrives, as far as possible, to stay at home as often as she can. During my research in Emma's class[9] at Tenter Ground, the classroom assistant tells me that she had once asked Emma and her friends what they wanted to do when they were grown up. She reports to me, in horror, that Emma had proudly said she wanted to get married and have babies. Based on what I have come to understand in Emma's home, I suggest to the classroom assistant that Emma's ambitions are perfectly legitimate;

after all, a stable marriage and family life is an achievement that often eludes even the most educated of women. The classroom assistant only looks at me in return with disbelief and irritated bemusement on her face: surely, she insists, the end point of education's trajectory is a career, not family life.

It is no surprise to me, however, that one of Emma's principal ambitions is to get married and have children. She lives in a household where those most difficult of tasks – choosing the right man to marry, making a household and having children without disrupting one's ability to care for one's mother – are the primary preoccupations of female kin. To do this legitimately without ruining life's chances or disrupting the harmony of the mother's household would be the perfect expression of Sharon's idea of what makes for a good life. The classroom assistant's retort to my defence of Emma's ambitions is to say dismissively, '[Having babies] – That's probably all she's [Emma] good for anyway.'

The truth, however, is that Emma does have career ambitions: she dreams of being a vet, but it doesn't occur to her that the odds are stacked against the realisation of this dream because she lives in a home where caring counts in a way that formal learning doesn't and she attends a school that has failed her before her education has really begun. The child, like Emma, who is far behind age-related expectations for learning and achievement quickly becomes alienated from schoolwork and naturally feels the pull of the caring and relatively rule-free home as a centripetal force.

This is Emma's problem: often refusing to go to school, she screams about stomach pains if Sharon tries to force her to go and Sharon gets to her wits' end. She takes Emma repeatedly to the doctor to investigate these stomach complaints and is told that apart from a touch of constipation there is nothing seriously wrong. Sharon realises that the school blames her for Emma's problems and non-attendance at school and she then faces the arrival of education welfare officials. 'The Welfare', as Sharon describes them, impress upon her the legal requirement of parents to send their children to school. Meanwhile the school makes no investigation into the specific learning difficulties that Emma might be battling with and she continues to fall further behind as her age/class mates progress apace. Sharon tells me that she has threatened Emma, telling her, 'If ya don't start gettin' into school they'll take ya away from me and put ya in care.'

To me, it seems ironic that Emma should be threatened with separation from a home where caring means everything simply because it is an environment where caring and formal learning are not synonymous.

In the end the problem is ameliorated slightly because in exchange for the time that I spend in Sharon's home, I begin to teach Emma to read. As she makes progress, little by little, her confidence begins to improve and her willingness to go to school increases. I know that Sharon can read because she often uses the Internet on the computer in the living room, but when I ask her if she will read with Emma when I am not there she tells me that she doesn't have the patience for it. She explains that when she used to try to 'learn her', Emma would read a new word in the book and have forgotten it again by the time they turned the page. Sharon says it got on her nerves so badly she had to give up trying. When Emma and I read together, Emma insists that Sharon leave the room so that she can avoid Sharon's constant teasing about her mistakes.

It is clear then, that for those girls, like Emma, who come from common households and are failing at school, it is likely to be, in part, because their mothers are not well-educated and have, therefore, less patience and understanding about how to help their children with their schoolwork. Endless patience for learning is perhaps the most important attribute of an educated mother. In addition, girls from families like Sharon's, are more likely to be preoccupied with the demands that kinship relations place on them in the home than they are to be interested in what they are learning at school. Girls like Emma often take on a caring role towards their mothers who are struggling, for various reasons, with the burdens that common life presents to a woman trying to raise and keep her family together. It is not difficult to see how caring about the family can interrupt the trajectory that being at school implies for a child's, and especially a girl's, future in the world of work.

Sitting by the side of a Bermondsey swimming pool with Anita and some of her new-found friends who are poles apart from Sharon because they are proactive about and ambitious for their children's education and other opportunities, I chat with them while we watch our children having after-school swimming lessons. Taking it in turns to tell about the kind of day each of us has had, I explain Emma's dilemma and the discrepancy I perceive between what it means to be common and what doing well at school requires of young girls. Lisa, one of the mums, responds with enthusiasm. 'Oh, she's spot on there, ain't she? You can't be common and clever.' She explains, 'Me dad used to work up in Chelsea with a lot of posh people and he'd come home and say to me, "Girl, there's nothin' they're doing there that you couldn't do, only you'd never be allowed to do it because of the mouth on you".' Laughing at her anecdote the women discuss how being common often means that you are prevented from taking a role at work where you would be expected to play a part in creating a good impression. Lisa, who is studying every evening after work to take her accountancy exams, says, 'All I want now is respect. When I was at school all I wanted was to get married, 'ave kids and an easy life, but me mum and dad wouldn't allow it. In our family you 'ad to do better than yer parents as they had tried to do better than my grandparents and I expect better things of my girl than I've done for me'self.'

4
Trouble on the Estates

Sharon contrasts what it is like living where her flat is now, in a quiet block in a cul-de-sac street where, as she describes it, 'nothin' ever 'appens', to the way life was when she lived on the huge Canterbury Estate in Walworth: 'It was all right up there, when there was trouble we used to love it, all of us lookin' out [over the balcony] to see what was going on.' To illustrate how she feels about where she lives now Sharon emphasises, 'I said to me mate the other day, "If only somethin' would 'appen."' Sharon then tells me something about her experience of living on other estates in Bermondsey, 'You've got Abbey's Ground and you've got Tanner's Gate and them boys [from those estates] don't mix. They're totally different – Gary[1] [a boy from Emma's class at school] gets bullied a lot by the older boys at Tanner's Gate and then he comes to school and takes it out on the kids there.'

I ask Sharon if it is only boys who get into trouble on the estates and she explains that it depends on the child. Emma, referring to her older sister, then adds, 'Sophie's a trouble-maker ain't she mum?' Sharon elaborates, telling me that when Sophie was 15 she got into a fight with another girl and was accused of grievous bodily harm (GBH). Recounting how Sophie had been having trouble with some girls from another estate, Sharon describes the scene: these girls had come round, in a gang, to wait for Sophie outside the block and below the balcony where she lives. Looking to see what was going on, Sharon had gone out onto the balcony and warned the girls that if they didn't want any trouble they should go away, but they refused to leave. Sharon then told Sophie to go down and sort out the girl who was giving her problems. Because she knew what Sophie was capable of and before Sophie had even got downstairs, Sharon had phoned the police to let them know that they should make their way straight round because there was going to be trouble. Sophie and the other girl agreed that they were going to sort out their differences one-on-one without the girl's gang of friends being involved and the fight began. Sharon explains how the ferocity of Sophie's temper meant that she easily got the better of the other girl; Sophie had quickly knocked her opponent unconscious and then dragged the girl by the hair to a nearby parked car, smashing her head through the windscreen. Not long after, the police arrived.

Sharon laughs because she can see how horrified I am by the story and in a vain attempt to reassure me, she emphasises that girls don't fight as much as boys. I would never have imagined Sophie to be capable of such brutality because she appears, at home at least, to be quite gentle and reserved. Sharon stresses that after that incident Sophie didn't have any trouble on the estates again because she then had a reputation for ruthlessness which protected her against further trouble. I come to understand, then, that trouble is good, not only because it is dramatic and, therefore, entertaining, but also because it usually means conflict of one kind or another and often violent conflict in relation to which reputations are made or broken. Other people's trouble is always better than trouble of one's own because violent conflicts are unpredictable and can be dangerous, but no trouble at all is boring because then it's quiet and 'nothin' ever 'appens.' So far as common girls are concerned they are less likely than common boys to get into fights but the more common a girl is the more likely she is to know how to handle herself in a fight and even to enjoy fighting.

In relation to the territorial conflicts which are meaningful to her mother and sisters, Emma, then, just like me, is learning in Bermondsey all about what it means to become a certain kind of common woman. In relation to all the various aspects of common life that I have explained in previous chapters, and observing the acceptable degree of variation among her siblings, Emma endeavours to make sense of what constitutes an appropriate style of femininity for a girl like her. I begin to realise, meanwhile, that the enjoyment of drama on the estates – looking for trouble, being able to handle oneself in a violent conflict and enjoy the prospect of a good fight – are the antithesis of what femininity means to me and what I want for my own daughters. I am shocked by the prospect of young girls being involved in this kind of trouble on the estates and I begin to appreciate what is especially distinctive about 'ladylike' manners: posh women and girls are not prepared for involvement in and proximity to physical violence; fighting amongst them and especially the prospect of enjoying that kind of violent conflict would be unthinkable to posh women. This means that at the boundary of the distinction between the genders and classes, the taboo against participation in violence becomes part of what distinguishes men from women and boys from girls, but also 'nice girls' from common-as-muck ones like Sophie, and common-as-shit ones like Sharon.

Even though I don't expect my daughters to go looking for trouble, I am aware that they need to learn how to handle themselves on the estates, so I enrol them in karate classes which they enjoy immensely and do well at since they are strong and athletic. Over the coming months, as they move through the grades, they begin to enter competitions and then have to learn how to fight, which means getting hurt and learning how to endure pain for the sake of victory over the opponent. This is not easy for them and neither is it easy for me not to feel horrified when they get hurt. Watching the other Bermondsey mums, however, I learn how to toughen-up myself and observe, in turn, the effect that this has on my daughters. In a major tournament my younger daughter has to fight boys and even though she is doing well and beating her initial opponents, she encounters tougher boys as the competition progresses. I look to see how the other Bermondsey mums are coping and notice one of them shout angrily at her young daughter when the girl is struggling in a fight against a boy. I am shocked to see her lack of empathy and notice that when tears come to her daughter's eyes, her mother responds, not with compassion, but with a battle cry, 'Kill him Tina!'

When my youngest daughter, Fola, faces one of these bigger, heavier, more intimidating boys, I listen to his friends teasing him: from the sidelines, they shout: 'Come on, don't let a girl beat you!' Struggling to endure his ferocious attack, Fola doubles over when she is badly winded by a heavy punch and, with tears in her eyes, she manages to find my face in the audience, silently pleading with me to make it stop. Determined to copy the other Bermondsey mum, however, I harden my face, set my jaw and leap down to get closer to the fighting area. Shouting as loudly and fiercely as I can, not caring now who is watching, I scream at her, 'Kill him Fola!' Taken completely by surprise at my reaction, Fola, in shock, quickly pulls herself together and resumes the fight. Much to the boy's shame and the derision of his friends, she wins it and is elated with her victory. She then goes on to beat every other boy in her age-group category, wins a huge silver trophy and is invited to join the junior team for England. Needless to say, we are both astounded and the other mums are fiercely proud of us both.

As I come to appreciate the value of strength and toughness, I understand that in order to participate effectively in Sharon's household I need to be able to entertain her with talk of trouble on my estate; I need to be able to demonstrate the capacity of my family to withstand threats from the outside and to show that I and my girls can stick up for ourselves. For the first time I begin to feel that the way that I am walking on the street is changing; instead of gliding along, somehow aloof, I feel what it is like to have to assume a stronger presence. I feel the weight of my feet on the pavement and a very subtle change in my stance as I begin to appreciate how the most common of Bermondsey girls come to claim the pavements as their own via the cultivation of a tough, territorial disposition.

I also come to understand how, among some people, in some contexts, violence comes to be conceived of as a social good. Because of the tension implied by the constant threat of violence against oneself in everyday life, it can become a pleasure and a release from this tension to watch other people fighting; therein lies the joy of boxing, a sport which I had only ever before found horrifying. Slowly, in trying to understand what it means to grow up in a predominantly working class neighbourhood, I begin to appreciate something of the history of my partner's upbringing in the East End of London. There, he experienced a similar situation: despite his father's gentle, bookish manner, my partner had to learn the hard way about how to stick up for himself at school and on the street, and having had to prove himself to be an African boy not to be messed with, he was able to survive with his reputation intact. Thereafter he was able to form alliances with Caribbean young men whose notoriety far exceeded his own. With Sharon the fact of my partner's tough East End upbringing is grist to the mill: it counts and gains me credibility as a person in Bermondsey.

'I'm not racialist, but ...'

Moving on from the story of Sophie's violent street victory, Sharon comes back to the subject of Gary, one of the 'trouble-makers' from Emma's school. She teases Emma about him: 'She come 'ome [from school] the other day sayin' she's gotta give 'im an answer 'cos 'e asked 'er to go out with 'im and d'ya know what she says to me?' Sharon, grinning, looks expectantly at Emma and Emma replies willingly, 'I likes to keep me men waitin'!' We all laugh at her precocity and, taking her cue, Emma, who, like me, is permanently on the periphery of the conversation, learning about what kind of talk is valued at home, begins to open up and tells us about the trouble she is having with her friends at school. She mentions her two best friends from her class – Sunita and Sita. These girls are the unrelated daughters of different families of Bangladeshi Muslim origin. One of them, Sunita, lives on an estate just round the corner from Emma and the other lives on an estate not far from where I live. Emma explains how Sita used to be her friend but she hates her now because Sita is 'Always tryin' to steal friends from me and talk behind me back.' Emma then explains in indignant tones how she had once gone to Sita's house, but had never gone back again because she had been accused of stealing something.

Abruptly Sharon interrupts, saying loudly, 'I'm not racialist, but I can't get on with Pakis [Pakistanis].' Shocked at her sudden outburst, I remain silent and when I don't make any response, Sharon returns to the subject of life on the Canterbury Estate. Complaining about how her family could never get rehoused even though they were overcrowded, she tells me of her resentment about the 'Pakis' who were given the four-bedroom flat above where she was living. She recalls how one day that family called the police on Sharon because Sharon had kicked their front door down. She then goes on to explain to me why she had done this: one of their boys had punched Emma in the stomach, accusing her of having written 'Paki' on their front door. Sharon says that she went straight up there to sort it out and the mother of the boy had closed the door in her face, so Sharon had kicked it down. When the police arrived, Sharon says, she said to them straightaway, 'What ya gonna do about these fuckin' Pakis?' She then describes with indignation how the police had tried to explain to her that the family was from Bangladesh not Pakistan and Sharon tells me that she had laughed, saying, 'They're all fuckin' Pakis to me mate.'

Sharon explains that, in the end, the two families were forced to go to mediation but it didn't resolve their differences and Sharon was threatened with eviction for racial harassment. This story, which is told with all the dramatic effect that accounts of trouble-making demand, puts into perspective Sharon's complaint about nothing ever happening where she lives now: she has behind her a long history of trouble-making which has sometimes led to her being transferred from one estate to another. In this light, trouble comes, to me, to seem like a perverse form of neighbourhood recreation and I realise that on Bermondsey's estates it can have to it a specifically racial aspect.

'Our culture': 'our ways'

Sharon continues on the same theme: 'I think they [Pakis] should go to special schools where they 'ave to learn English and learn about our culture 'cos if you come to our country and we've been 'ere longer than they 'ave, they should take on our ways.' Emma interrupts her mum then, and insists, 'Mum, you shouldn't call 'em Pakis.' Sharon ignores her and tells me that when Emma had invited Sita and Sunita to her birthday party at home, Sharon had asked Emma, 'What, should I dress up in a curtain and put a sticker on me head?' Emma, dejected now, stops talking and, like me, makes her resistance felt through her silence. Sharon continues, undeterred by how upsetting it is to Emma, 'If you look at Emma's school photos, there's 'ardly any whites now.' Tracey, Emma's sister, who is sitting with us, joins in the conversation for the first time and emphasises that it is the same at her school. Sharon then tells Emma to go and get her school photos for me to look at. Sharon continues, 'It's like that '[wh]ole Stephen Lawrence[2] thing' and she then looks to Tracey for clarification.

Tracey explains how, in religious education lessons at school, they were forced, following the Macpherson inquiry into the murder of Stephen Lawrence, to do an exercise in which all the white girls had to write an essay in which they had to imagine what it was like to be black girls. They each had to write about how they felt and what white people were like and what white people were doing to black people. They then had to learn about the history of the slave trade. Tracey says, 'I couldn't do it – slag off me own race – and after the lesson all the black girls was comin' out and sayin', "Yeah, we rules and white people are this and white people are that."' Sharon then stresses that she went down to the school and told them that she didn't want Tracey doing that class anymore. Proudly Tracey declares that it was the only lesson at school she ever 'bunked off' (skipped on purpose).

Tracey then goes on to tell me about her friend who looks white but has a 'half-caste' (mixed-race) mum. This girl, Tracey explains, had said to her that even though she looks white she wouldn't do the essay either because, Tracey says, 'She already knew that what they done to Stephen Lawrence was a bad thing and they didn't 'ave to keep going on about it.' Sharon stresses, 'There's already enough white people and black kids with chips on their shoulders, stirrin' it up just makes it worse.' She then tells me that Emma had come home from school the other day saying that she wasn't allowed to say 'half-caste' anymore because someone had told her that she should say 'mixed-race' instead. Sharon bristles then, and says, 'Black people don't like to be called coloured anymore now either, do they?' And I tell her that no, they don't.

Cutting to the chase and, by this point becoming quite irritated with me, Sharon comes to the crunch and asks me straight out, 'Where is your fella from?' I respond without hesitation, trying not to betray any concern that I feel about disclosing my partner's origins: 'His parents are from Nigeria and, as I told you, he grew up in the East End of London.' This information brings the conversation to a complete halt. In that instant my previous silence is put into perspective; Sharon knows that I must, by definition, disagree with her views about black and Asian people and the prospect of a posh cow with a 'coloured' husband and 'half-caste' children is obviously too much for her to bear. Sensing the tension, and as if to prove my worth on a different score card, one which Emma feels Sharon could relate to, Emma quickly picks up my hand and affec-tionately goes through each of my ring fingers, telling Sharon about my rings and which member of my family gave each of them to me. I under-stand what Emma is doing: I know that for common women gold jew-ellery is more than a display of wealth: it is also about the substantiation of familial relations; each item of jewellery is a gift given to the woman by a different member of her family to mark a different landmark in the woman's life, such as a 16th or 18th birthday, the birth of a child or her marriage. The more gold a woman wears, the more gifts she's been given and the more easily she can display the evidence of the esteem and affection in which her family holds her. Emma's strategy successfully distracts Sharon and, saving me from Sharon's wrath for the time being, Emma reminds me that I am supposed to be at her house to 'learn her' how to read.

Reluctantly, Sharon leaves the living room and when Emma and I are reading together on our own, she says to me, 'Me mum is racialist, but I'm not. I 'ate it when people talk about ov[th]er people behind their back. I can't stand it. I go out of the room when I 'ear me mum talkin' 'bout ov[th]er people like that.' I know better than to say anything dis-paraging about Emma's mother behind Sharon's back and so I focus on Emma's reading. On my way home, however, I am reeling: aware of how shocked Sharon was about my disclosure, I am staggered and sickened by how deeply felt her prejudice is against Emma's Bangladeshi Muslim friends and against black and Asian people in general. I wonder how she has come to be so prejudiced and, as a consequence, I wonder too how I have come to be so open-minded. I am reminded, then, that one of the attributes of a middle class upbringing is the cultivation of an open mind and liberal attitude towards difference and I ponder on how ironic it is that that same liberal-minded openness doesn't extend towards the work-ing classes.[3] Middle class people are, for example, much more likely to be tolerant of so-called racial, ethnic and cultural variation than they are of the difference between the classes.

Wondering whether the possibility of my research in Sharon's home has come to an end because of the limit which has been revealed on the possibility of my effective participation, I approach my own home, remembering what Sharon had said to me before, about all the working class people on both sides of the Old Kent Road being the same; they live in the same kinds of council flats; they do the same kinds of jobs for a similar wage and that's all that matters about them. I realise then that the people she was talking about are white people. They are all, in Sharon's eyes, equally common; non-white working class people are, however, a different matter. Because non-white people don't count, I begin to wonder whether, in Sharon's scheme of value, blacks and Asians even count as people at all. Wanting to find out exactly how this evaluation works, I determine to go back to Sharon's home, to learn more.

Breaking taboos

Two weeks pass and I am relieved when Emma calls me on the phone to see if I am coming to the house to read with her. When I arrive, and before we start reading, Sharon and I engage, as usual, in conversation over a cup of tea. She is amicable and friendly, but she is also determined to get to the bottom of the issue which has come between us. She knows that I am conducting interviews with people all over Bermondsey and, like me, she is aware of Bermondsey taboos concerning black people, so she asks me straight out, 'How do Bermondsey people react when they find out your fella [boyfriend] is black?' I explain that so as not to prejudice people against me before the interview has even started, I don't tell them about my partner straightaway. Sharon laughs, scoffing. She says, 'Ya didn't tell me, I 'ad to drag it out of ya.' I laugh back and ask her whether she thinks Bermondsey people would talk openly to me if they knew in the beginning that I was living with a black man. She admits then that she doesn't think they would and begins to explain the situation to me: 'When we was growin' up, we was told: "Keep to yer own!" Ya didn't make friends with, and ya didn't go out with coloured people and that was that; that's what I'm used to.'

Sharon then emphasises that she wouldn't allow her girls to go out with 'coloured' men because, she says, 'They don't treat their women properly.' She illustrates her belief with the example of a Jamaican woman she knows whose husband used to beat her really badly. I point out that my partner is also black, but he has never raised a finger to me. Surely then, I suggest, the issue of domestic violence can't be anything to do with whether or not a man has black skin otherwise all black men would be beating up their wives. I then tell her that a number of white women whom I have interviewed in Bermondsey have told me of how high, in the old days, the incidence of domestic violence was among Bermondsey dockers' families and how, in some families, the legacy of that violence remains. I try to reason with Sharon, concluding that the potential for violence is something that all women have to be wary of – with men in general – not just black men. Needless to say, Sharon is not convinced. My attempts to resist her taboo against relations with black people, and intimate relations with black men in particular, only serves to make her work harder to shore up the boundaries around her own beliefs.

Can't black and Asian people be common too?

As the weeks unfold, the issue of racial and cultural difference comes to dominate our conversations and Sharon's prejudices become more and more vehemently expressed as she struggles to protect herself from what the realities of my intimate and loving relationship with a black man, and Emma's close friendships with Bangladeshi Muslim girls, mean for her own most closely held beliefs. Finally, I ask her the question which, from my point of view, lies at the heart of the issue: 'Sharon, can black and Asian people be common?' Immediately, as if I have hit the nail on the head, she answers in denial, 'No, they can't.' I ask her why and she responds, ''Cos even where they've been 'ere long enough to talk common, they've still got their own f[th]ings in there.' In response, I ask, 'What do you mean by "their own things in there"?' And Sharon tries to explain; succinctly, she declares, as if it was obvious, 'The way their parents talk.'

I understand, then, that Sharon refuses to include non-white people in the category of common people because no matter how common they talk, she feels that she can always hear, in black and Asian people's language, the trace of the way that their parents talk, which is the evidence of a different language from another place, another culture and a different way of life in another country. No matter how common they become on the estates, black and Asian people cannot truly belong in Bermondsey, because, in Sharon's eyes, they are complete outsiders: it is territoriality which is at the heart of the issue. It is all about the question of who controls the territory, who has the right to say how things go there and who decides what the way of life there should be like. I appreciate then that the reason the Stephen Lawrence case has assumed an almost mythological status on the estates is because it marks, for white working class people, an unwelcome shift in the balance of power between black and white people in Britain. Black people are now seen to have the power of the state behind them, a power which they are now often accused of abusing and the white working classes feel, therefore, cruelly overlooked. Ironically, however, despite everything that I had surmised about Sharon's racism, I realise that she is not racist *per se*; she is, in fact, like most Bermondsey people, what I have come to call 'placist'. This means that the defence of the place – the manor – and the way of life of the people in a community formed on the basis of kinship and residence criteria, is everything to them.

The problem with this idea of community belonging is that the definition of who can belong is very narrow. A heavy emphasis is placed on the threat to the basis of community belonging which is posed by outsiders of all kinds. These include white working class people who live in neighbouring manors, like Peckham[4] or Walworth, and those white people on the estates, like me, who have moved in from other manors, but the most extreme and most visually obvious kind of outsiders are black and Asian people. Placism encompasses racism, therefore, as a particularly parochial expression of a much broader and peculiarly English/British historical precedent, which is territoriality. Sharon's preoccupation with solidarity between white working class people across the Old Kent and Walworth Roads is indicative, therefore, of a shift in the idea of community relatedness in Bermondsey: the movement is from a preoccupation with kinship and residence in a narrowly defined geographical area and towards an explicit discourse of ultra-conservative cultural nationalism, which is more broadly defined and racially conceived as whiteness.

Suddenly Tracey interrupts to disagree with her mum, 'Yeah, but there is a Nigerian teacher at my school who is common as anythin'; she swears all the time and everythin'.' Nonplussed, Sharon looks at Tracey in dismay. The disagreement between Tracey and her mother, about which kinds of people can be common, speaks of the generational difference in their experiences: Sharon has more experience with first- and second-generation immigrants who are more likely to be, in their manner and speech, closer to the way of life in their or their ancestors' country of origin. Tracey, in contrast, increasingly encounters, at school and in other places, third-generation immigrants who are more likely to have learned, on the estates, how to be common in the same way as her and the difference a generation makes is significant. Important about their assessment of people of non-white immigrant origin is whether or not these people behave and talk in a way that is more or less common in the white working class sense of the word. What matters to them is the extent to which immigrants are willing to become like them and what is disturbing about immigrants is the degree of their cultural difference and especially their pride in their own ways.

Multiculturalism

Finally Sharon responds to Tracey's point. In a somewhat defeated tone; she explains, 'Bermondsey can't stay the same; it's gotta change. You can't stop your kids mixin' with blacks anymore: they're all together at school.' Her response is indicative of a historical shift; one that is on the majority of Bermondsey people's minds: the increasing presence of black and Asian children on the estates and in the schools threatens the very existence of Bermondsey as they know it. People talk of the death of the community and readily accuse black people of its murder, but rarely do they stop to consider how their own refusal, to incorporate outsiders in general, and black and Asian people in particular, into the network of neighbourly relations has undermined the possibility of social cohesion on the estates.

When I speak to Emma's teacher at school about what is going on in Bermondsey she says, 'I hesitate now to call this area a working class one; it's not that simple anymore because of the arrival of people from different cultures.' The focus now, at school and in the community, is on celebrating multiculturalism, but interesting about this shift is the way that an emphasis on the racial and cultural difference of non-white people eclipses the lack of homogeneity among the white working classes among whom there is a long history of conflict, across the Old Kent Road, for example. Similarly it forces into the background the existence of similarities between black, white and Asian working class people, who are all struggling, under similar constraints all over Bermondsey's estates, to raise their families in difficult conditions. And finally it also ignores the cultural synthesis, which is being forged by young people out of their accommodation to what is different about each other's ways of life.

Meanwhile, in response to the increasing visibility of and support for the cultural difference of black and Asian people in Britain, the white working classes are starting to fight back, making explicit to themselves what they have always taken for granted, which is the idea of their own culture and way of life. In this sense multiculturalism easily becomes fuel for a right-wing political agenda[5] and working class solidarity becomes further fractured as the divisions between the people living on Bermondsey's estates come to be experienced as racial and cultural ones. It is not difficult to see how, in so far as it fails to address this issue in the cultural terms in which people understand it, the Labour Party is in danger of losing its traditional supporters in working class areas;[6] an explanation of the phenomenon requires a more complicated analysis than a straightforward economic or political investigation would allow.

Meanwhile, children and young people in Bermondsey, like Emma, are struggling to make sense of what their own experiences of racial and cultural variation mean for the kind of person they are expected by the older, more prejudiced generation, to become. The way in which Tracey's and Emma's opinions differ from each other and from their mother's reveals how, in Bermondsey, and across southeast London, the question of what it means to be working class and/or common is continuously open to contestation and clearly changing over time.

Cultures of resistance

Interesting about Sharon's contempt for 'Pakis', which exists because she resents their refusal to learn 'our culture' or 'our ways', is how she assumes that 'our [British] ways' are 'her [common] ways', that all common people are the same (which they are clearly not) and that her way of life is better. Having confronted my own prejudices about working class people, I am keenly aware how important it is to be wary of the arrogance that ignorance breeds. I am conscious of the fact that Sharon never stops, even for a moment, to consider that perhaps the reason that Asian children, and Indian ones in particular, are doing so well at school in Britain might be precisely because they are struggling so hard to resist the way of life which defines what it means to be common-as-shit on British council estates. Perhaps they have in mind a different way of being British, one that celebrates their own cultural values but which also fits more closely with what it means to be an upwardly mobile, 'respectable' working or middle class person. Sita and Sunita might, for example, have something to teach Emma about the value of the opportunities which are available to young people in Britain. Perhaps they are exactly the kinds of young people who will become our model citizens; after all, citizenship is the civil idea around which the idea of what it means to be British is currently being modelled.

As for Emma, she certainly appears to be glad of the neutral space of school where it is racism that is the strictest taboo; at school she has the opportunity to broaden her horizons beyond the parochial concerns of the working class neighbourhood and she is able to enjoy the company of black, Asian and mixed race friends. In difficult neighbourhoods, this is what a good education should provide: the opportunity for a common girl to overcome the parochialism of the neighbourhood and become, if she chooses, a different kind of person, a young woman with other ambitions for herself than her parents have led her to expect. Unfortunately, a bad education condemns her to a lack of choice in this respect. At home, through her silence, Emma endeavours to contest her mother's idea that white people should 'stick to their own' and, like her sister Tracey, she contests the idea that to be common a person has to be white. Unlike Tracey, however, Emma doesn't mind that her Bangladeshi Muslim friends are culturally different to her in many ways; as long as they are loyal to her, that is all that matters to Emma about her friends and she enjoys their difference.

It becomes clear, then, that despite the strong influences of their mothers, which lead working class children and young people towards the cultivation of a particular kind of ethical disposition[7] – a specific stance towards the world and others in it – working class girls, like Emma, Sita and Sunita, are continuously comparing and contrasting for themselves – from one situation to another, at home and at school, in their own homes and in the homes of friends – what kind of participation adults and friends require of them and, in so doing, they are, all the time, asking themselves indirectly the following question: what kinds of women is it possible for us to become, here in this council flat, in this block, in this estate, in this neighbourhood, in this school and in this place called Bermondsey – who can we be?

In the next part of the book I focus on the case study of Tom, a boy who is in the same low-ability group as Emma at school. I show why the reasons for boys' educational failure are likely to be somewhat different than for girls' and I explore the specific problems that Tom faces at Tenter Ground – a failing primary school – where he is learning about and resisting the particular form of participation that teachers require of him there.

Part II
Classroom Versus Street Culture

5
Tom at Tenter Ground

Gillian (teasing tone): 'Tom, how did you learn to swear – watching South Park?'[1]

Tom (matter of fact): 'Nah. I learnt to swear in the pub when I was little. Me mum used to take me to the pub and [h]'er friends'd give me a fiver [£5] for every swearword I could say. Man, I was rich in them days.'

Tom is a lively freckle-faced 10-year-old boy; he lives with his mum, step-dad and younger sister in a two-bedroom flat on an old housing association estate just across the road from Tenter Ground Primary School.[2] Like the estate the school has been there since Victorian times. Facing each other at the top of a crossroads and enclosing a narrow cul-de-sac, the two buildings have stood the test of time and many changes. Mrs Waldman, an elderly Bermondsey woman, now in her eighties, remembers growing up on the estate where, as a child, she shared two rooms with eleven other family members.[3] There was only a kitchen and a communal bedroom and residents in the block shared communal facilities for washing clothes, answering always to the strictures of the ever-watchful estate caretaker.

Mrs Waldman remembers how desperately poor her family was and how destitute the children were who got to attend the ragged school[4] which was then housed in a smaller building on the other corner of the crossroads. That building has recently been purchased and renovated to house new offices and as such it has become part of the new Bermondsey regeneration in which old buildings of historical interest, which, having lain vacant and worthless for decades, are now being snapped up by developers eager to capitalise on the property boom.[5] Increasingly fashionable and conveniently located near to the river and central London,

Bermondsey is rapidly becoming one of the most desirable areas for wealthy young professionals from outside the borough to live.

Tom's mother, Anne, is a proud and handsome woman in her mid-thirties; she is well 'turned out' (dresses nicely) and 'keeps a tidy home'. Born and bred in Bermondsey with Irish ancestry[6] on her father's side of the family, Anne still regularly visits her parents, who now live in Kent,[7] which is the destination of choice for Bermondsey people who have made good. Anne's husband Pete is a dustman; he is the father of her second child, Tom's little sister, Mary, who is 7 years old. Anne tells me that Pete is the 'poor relation' in his family since all his brothers and sisters are professional people – accountants and the like – who drive flash cars and live in Kent. They don't like her, she says, because they think she is the source of all the troubles in Pete's life and they worry that she is 'keeping him down' (stopping him from going up in the world). Unlike Tom's father,[8] who was a 'real trouble-maker', Pete is a quiet, law-abiding man anxious only to provide for his family. In order to try and fulfil his ambitions for her to be a stable homemaker, Anne struggles, in response to Pete's influence, to curb her wilder ways. She explains that, like many Bermondsey women, she used to, when younger, 'like a drink'[9] and had then started taking cocaine[10] in pubs and clubs, but she assures me that she is over all that now. Relying on him to save the family from what she now feels is her rather dissolute past, Anne explains that she is pinning all her hopes for the family's future on Pete's good influence.

The street

At home, Tom is a complete mummy's boy, often sitting on his mother's lap for a cuddle while she steals a reluctant kiss from him. They share a joking relationship in which he plays teasing games with her, cheeking her back when she tries to give him instructions and corrections, and he knows how to provoke her as far as he dares before Anne starts to chase him with her hand raised; in good humour she threatens to clout him. Laughing loudly, Tom often runs from the room to escape Anne's clutches and when her nagging gets him down he runs freely outside onto the streets which demand from him an entirely different disposition. Described as mean, inner-city streets are the playgrounds where, if they are allowed to play out, children learn to grow up tough and in this respect Bermondsey is no different. As soon as Tom is on the street his demeanour changes and he begins to bowl: to walk in a way that means business, that shows he can't be pushed around. The street is a place where tough kids rule and these are usually older boys who move in gangs.

When Tom is out of the room Anne tells me that when they first moved to the estate and didn't know anyone, Tom got badly bullied by the older boys to the point that he was often scared to go out. Not being able to stand being cooped up, however, Tom would go back again and again for more punishment. On one occasion someone had run to tell Anne that Tom had been put upside-down in a wheelie bin and couldn't get out. That same night, after Anne had rescued Tom, Pete made Tom tell him who had done it and, learning which group of boys was responsible and who the ring leader was – Shane, a local 15-year-old – Pete went out to look for him. Anne explains that when he found him, Pete took Shane by the scruff of the neck and told him, 'If anythin' ever [h]'appens to Tom on these streets, I'm gonna [h]'old you personally responsible whether you've got anythin' to do with it or not.' Anne emphasises how clearly it was spelled out to the local boys that if any harm should come to Tom, Pete would go straight out to find Shane and kill him. She stresses that with that warning issued, Tom never had any trouble on the street again and I begin to appreciate how, on the estates, the threat of violence can be an effective form of peace-keeping.

Knowing that his parents are fiercely protective of him, a Bermondsey boy bowls because his parents' and older siblings' or cousins' reputations are intact behind him. Tom proudly tells his friends at school one day about what a good fighter his mum is: 'If she ever lost a fight at school,' he says, 'her big brother would wait 'til she got home and beat her up again for losing.' I imagine that Anne toughened up pretty quickly. She shows me Tom's boxing gear that she and Pete had recently bought for him – leather boots and gloves and shiny shorts – and she tells me that the boxing coach above the famous Thomas à Beckett pub on the Old Kent Road had said that Tom had shown promise. Bermondsey boxers are famous; the tough reputation of the men and the area in general is legendary and it is in relation to this kind of reputation that Bermondsey boys, like Tom, must make sense of their developing masculinity. Whilst the women that men desire for their wives are expected by men to be more gentle and peaceable, Bermondsey women are no push-over either. Anne admits that she used to fight when she was younger but explains that once you've got a reputation you don't have to fight anymore: 'You just walk like you mean business and that's enough.'[11] Returning to the subject of Tom's boxing lessons, Anne laments, '[H]'e didn't keep it up; Tom gets bored easily; [h]'e can't settle to anythin'.'

Anne tells me that she's happier now about Tom playing out because he has made friends with Gary, a boy who is a year older than him from the Tanner's Gate Estate. Gary is in Year Six at Tenter Ground; he shares a class with Tom's Year Five cohorts, has a small 'crew'[12] of his own that he moves with outside school and an older 15-year-old brother who is a bod with a bit of a reputation, so he and Tom are less likely to be bothered when they're out and about. Anne's hope is that Gary will be a good influence on Tom; she knows that Tom is restless and wishes he would settle down a bit because she fears that he is heading for trouble otherwise. Thinking about it, Anne laughs and explains how she has had to come down hard on Tom lately because last year he was going too far: 'Bowlin'' down the road with a fag (cigarette) hangin' out his mouth.' When she saw that, Anne says, she took Tom inside and bruised his pride, making him feel bad for 'diggin' out'[13] the family, telling him what an idiot he looked. She is confident that she humiliated him and managed to convince him that it's not 'big' for kids to smoke. Despite his young age, however, Tom is already aiming for manhood; he knows how to hold himself, how to 'act big', and is full of self-confident bravado in the place where his charisma comes into its own – on the street.

The difference between boys and girls

A boy like Tom needs a firm hand and knows how to put on his best manners when it suits him, but he can also be free of his mother's restraining influence as often as he pleases. Anne speaks hopefully of Tom's friend Gary's step-father because sometimes he takes the boys fishing. The problem, she says, is that there's nothing for the kids to do on the estates and so they easily get into trouble. Despite her best efforts to contain Tom, Anne does not have the kind of relationship with him in which finding constructive things for him to do – like boxing – is enough to distract him from the fun he can have with his friends – making trouble – on the street. Trying to maintain a consistent vigilance over young boys is a full-time job for mothers in Bermondsey and the commitment to keeping them 'on the straight and narrow' (out of trouble) requires unceasing resourcefulness and devotion. At the same time, however, boys are encouraged to be tough; they enjoy a teasing relationship with older boys and men in which mock fighting plays a large part in what is seen as the necessity to toughen a boy up.

In general, things couldn't be more different for girls.[14] Tom's sister, Mary, is not allowed to play out unless she is safe in the garden square at the back of the flats and she is quieter and more serious than Tom, spending more time at home playing close to Anne and Pete's company. Immaculately turned out with waist-length, straight brown hair, which Anne lovingly tends, Mary is what's called a 'nice girl': well mannered, nicely spoken and extremely feminine. Mary enjoys reading and writing and is at least three years in advance of Tom's reading ability even though she is three years younger than him. Commenting on the difference between her two children, Anne explains what differentiates them: 'Tom's common-as-muck; [h]e's got a mouth on [h]im no doubt about that: [h]e's like me really, not like Mary; she's gentle, like 'er dad and well spoken.'

I ask Anne if Tom's story is true: the one in which he had explained to me how he learnt to swear in the pub when he was little, and she confirms the veracity of his tale. Telling me the story of Tom's christening, Anne goes on to clarify further about what kinds of early influences Tom was exposed to. She explains that Tom was already 5 years old when he was christened; during the ceremony his uncle – Tom's own father's older brother – told Tom that he would give him a fiver if he was brave enough to go up to 'the man in the black dress' (the priest), and call him a fucking cunt. Needless to say, Tom did as he was told and was well paid for it. Just as I would have expected, Tom's uncle's sense of humour exerts a levelling force on any ambitions that Anne and Pete might have for Tom's future – as a 'good', christened child – or, for that matter, anything else that might make them feel that he is a boy to be valued above others. Anne's story is confirmation of my observations in previous chapters in which I describe how being a certain kind of common person involves, in part, the cultivation of irreverence for what is supposedly sacred – priests and the innocence of children, for example. I draw attention to this aspect of what it means to be common because I want to highlight the discrepancy between the ideas that common parents have about their children and what teachers assume should constitute suitable behaviour in children. There is nothing to suggest, for example, that common children, like Tom, don't grow up in a language-rich environment, but the way that they learn to talk and what they learn to value as an appropriate contribution in a conversation with adults may be miles away from what 'posh' teachers expect of children at school.

Mary, however, is significantly different to Tom. In part this is because she has a different kind of father than he does; she has not been 'got at' (levelled)[15] and made common-as-muck by her mother's friends and sisters and her father's siblings in the way that Tom has been. Anne explains, for example, that her sister teases her when she hears Mary talking nicely, saying, 'Blimey Anne, where'd she learn to speak like that?', and Anne emphasises how she protects Mary from such taunts, telling her that there's nothing wrong with speaking nicely. Mary is proud to be her teacher's favourite at school and often teases Tom at home because she can read better than he can, and whilst she is a 'good girl', he is always in trouble at school.

Learning and caring

The time that I spend in Tom's home is subsequent to a year's fieldwork in his class at Tenter Ground School. I visit Anne to conduct an interview in her flat and we agree that if I come to the house once a week to help Tom with his reading then I can also spend some time with the family.[16] Anne is glad of the offer, telling me that she has tried to help Tom with his school work but she despairs, she says, because she knows that she doesn't have the patience for it. Anne explains that when Tom gets things wrong she loses her temper; they always fall out and so she feels as though it is no good her trying anymore. Because I have made a good relationship with Tom at school he is keen for me to come to his house and is excited about my visits. As I did in Sharon's home (see Part I), I begin my visit by having a cup of tea and chatting with Anne. Tom and I then begin to read. We start with reading material which is aimed at 6-year-old children and Tom insists, because he is embarrassed about making mistakes, that both Anne and Mary leave the living room.

Always the confident and extrovert personality, Tom reveals, in private, another, much more vulnerable side to himself. In the safety of his home he allows me to get to know the insecure 10-year-old boy, the one who knows that he is no good at school work; the boy who worries that he can't do it because he's dumb (stupid or 'thick') and who, in class, has to cover his fear with complicated avoidance strategies. Over the following weeks Tom applies himself well to reading and I have the opportunity to observe what his precise problems with reading are. Firstly, his concentration span is very small; he has never learned how to sit still in order to apply his energies to mastering symbolic work with letters and numbers. His problem is not just that he can't read the words; he doesn't know how to read in the sense of sitting still with someone and enjoying the pleasure of their patient attention whilst they show him how to appreciate the book's story. Secondly, Tom's confidence is low; when the words are too difficult he gives up completely. Easily feeling defeated and quick to pretend, then, that it's boring, Tom readily asserts that he doesn't even want to learn how to read. Thirdly, Tom doesn't know how to work with the alphabet phonetically and he cannot, therefore, tackle the basic principles of reading three-letter phonetic words such as j-u-g. As he begins to master this skill his abilities quickly improve and his reading vocabulary gradually expands. Tom is lively and quick to learn so that, week by week, he starts to make progress through the series of books that I have chosen for him, and gradually he begins to feel pleased with himself.

One Saturday morning, when I am at Tom's house, Pete, his step-dad, comes home from work early to find Tom reading to me on the sofa. Pete sits down quietly and watches us. Tom doesn't dare ask Pete to leave the room[17] and so Pete listens and observes, hearing me encouraging Tom and witnessing Tom's application to the book. When we have finished, Pete tells me that this is the first time he has ever seen Tom sit down with anyone to read a book cover to cover without getting bored or having a temper tantrum. He calls Tom over and pulls him proudly onto his lap, filling him with praises. Pete tells me that he's really happy about Tom's reading and he calls Anne in from the kitchen to reinforce to her how proud he is of Tom.

Anne then tells me that Tom has got, on his shelf in the bedroom, a boxed set of classic children's books; she asks Tom to run and get them. Tom brings and shows me the set of books which has titles in it like *Treasure Island*, and he takes a book out to show me. He emphasises how small the print is, how big some of the words are and how the books have no pictures: Anne explains to me that every now and again Tom gets the books down and says to her, 'Mum, why can't I read these books?' and she says it breaks her heart because she knows that he thinks boys of his age should be able to read them. Presenting to me the challenge of what they feel he ought to be able to achieve, Anne and Pete look expectantly at me to see what I can do for Tom. I turn to him and stress that if he practises enough he will soon be able to read these books, but I emphasise that he would have to practise reading every day and not just once or twice a week when I am there.

Later, when he has left the room, Anne explains that Tom won't pick up a book unless I am there. I am reminded then, that in the beginning reading is an interpersonal skill; it is internalised as a pleasing and self-preoccupying activity only after a degree of trust has been gained both in the other person who teaches the child to read and in the idea that reading is an enjoyable thing to do. Thereafter self-confidence with appropriate reading material is reached over time. Even children as young as 12 to 18 months can reach this stage of self-preoccupation with books; given the right encouragement they will readily repeat back to themselves the words they have memorised during the time spent on their parent's or carer's knee and soon become absorbed in the world they can conjure out of the book's pages. Other children, like Tom's sister, Mary, discover this delight at school and bring it into the home as a pleasurable activity to share with a willing parent. Unfortunately, for various reasons that I will discuss later in chapter seven, Tom and I never have the chance to get him to the stage of being able to enjoy reading as a self-preoccupying pursuit.

Parental expectations

Anne and Pete's reaction to Tom's initial progress in reading reinforces what I learn in almost every home that I visit during my research: the majority of working class parents want more than anything for their children to do well at school because they know only too well that it will lead to a better livelihood in the future. In this respect Sharon (see Part I), with her 'do as you please' philosophy, is the exception that proves the rule. Some children are encouraged, whether they want to or not, to continue with formal learning activities at home and this is especially the case in first- and second-generation families of West African origin.[18] Even in families where the mother speaks little English and has, even in her own language, only a very basic education, which is often the case in the families of Bangladeshi origin, the mothers nevertheless push their children towards education as the source of future opportunities in Britain. The important point to note, however, is that, depending on the level of their own education, rarely are working class parents actually engaging with their children in activities that would constitute formal-learning-type tasks. For example, children may regularly be told to, 'Go and pick up a book!' but parents aren't necessarily likely to sit down with their children to show them how to read and enjoy it and to build, thereby, an intimate relationship with the child on the basis of that shared enjoyment.

In common households, like Anne's, then, an appreciation of the value of formal learning is less likely to take the form of shared activity during the early relationship of caring between mother and child in the home. Formal learning and caring are not considered to be synonymous and, therefore, the ability to learn and do well at school is not usually thought to be a social skill that parents can influence and encourage directly. 'Cleverness' is more likely to be considered to be a heritable quality; the child is thought of as being either 'naturally clever' or not. When, for example, I interview the mother of a particularly able girl who is in Year Five at Tenter Ground, I am intrigued to hear her say of her daughter: 'I dunno where she gets them brains from 'cos me and her dad are thick as shit.' Nevertheless, the same woman also emphasises how pivotal a role the girl's grandmother has played in her upbringing; the grandmother constantly played interactive games with the girl when she was little, took her to the park and often rounded on mothers who didn't make time to play and interact with their children. The point is that if a working class child does well at school, parents tend not to take the credit themselves; they are more likely to undermine their own abilities and, at the same time, underestimate the extent of their own influence over the child. If a child, like Tom, fails to do well his parents usually feel that there is little they can do about it except to try their best to enforce the value of education and hope for the best.

Gender, school and the street

My suggestion, then, is that common children, like Tom, are usually well cared for at home but they are not necessarily well prepared there for the kind of participation that formal learning at school requires of them. They are more likely, therefore, to resist it. On the other hand, we also need to be able to account for the fact that there are children, like Tom's sister, Mary, who also come from common households but who are, nevertheless, doing very well at school. Tentatively, I propose that these children are more likely to be girls because girls, unlike their brothers, do not usually have the same degree of freedom to play on the streets. Girls are less likely, therefore, to participate on the street in peer groups in which being tough, looking for trouble and resisting authority are ways to gain a respected reputation. Gender differences are, therefore, always going to be educationally significant in schools in areas where boys enjoy a large measure of freedom to compete, often violently, for prestige on the streets.

My proposal is not, however, to suggest that everything that we need to know about boys' educational underachievement[19] will be explained by an analysis of the difference that gender makes. Whilst working class boys may be very different to their middle class peers, it is also clear that not all working class boys are the same: some are more protected than others from the influence of the street. By implication, those boys who are not allowed to play out and who are not, therefore, likely to be contenders in the tough boys' rankings, are, just like 'nice girls', more likely to do better at school. This is because they are not so likely to be as torn, as tough boys often are, between the different ideas – tough boy on the street versus good boy in the classroom – of what it means to become valued as a child. Similarly, those common girls, like Emma's sister, Sophie, who are allowed to play out and who are more likely, therefore, to develop reputations for fighting are, just like common boys who develop a taste for trouble, much less likely than 'nice girls' and 'good boys' to do well at school. An adequate analysis of the reasons for school failure must, therefore, account for gendered differences between children but it must also account for how those differences intersect with social class distinctions. And it must also take into consideration how, even in one family, each child's attitude towards what it means to be common may vary. For example, in a family where all the children are boys and the eldest of them has become a notorious trouble-maker who fails at school and enjoys a tough reputation on the street, there is no inevitability that his younger brothers will follow in his footsteps. The history of how each child comes to be socially positioned in the family is unique and any of the younger boys may well be protected, either at home or at school, from what it means for a boy, like Tom, to become common-as-muck: 'givin' it large' (becoming a big man) on the street.

When things go wrong at school for Tom and he fails, for various reasons, to learn what is appropriate to his age group, his parents worry a great deal, but they lack the confidence in their own education and necessary skills to successfully challenge the school or rectify the problem at home. The kind of intervention that I was able to make with Tom was possible only because I was prepared to visit him at home. I am doubtful, however, whether the extra reading work that we did could have been achieved at school because, in the eyes of his peer group, Tom would have been shamed by his need and desire for special reading assistance. Even if Tom had been amenable to the idea, the school is rarely in a position to either give or afford the individual assistance which children like Emma and Tom require if they are to overcome their learning difficulties. By the time the problem has become chronic, as it had in Tom's case, it is usually too late to do very much about it.

Tenter Ground Primary School: its reputation, Tom's teacher and fellow pupils

In the mornings, then, when Tom runs across the road to school, he leaves behind him a loving home where he is apparently safe to be a vulnerable 10-year-old boy. At school, however, he adopts the posture that his developing reputation demands and he bowls into the playground to meet his peer group. Some of these are boys and girls he knows and hangs out with on the street and others he meets only at school. Here are different sets of boys in relation to whom he can test his mettle, but the school is not like the street: Tom cannot run out of the classroom when he is sick of the teacher nagging him and so his freedom to seek the street when he pleases is limited. At the same time, however, the peer group counts for a great deal at school, not the way that it does on the street, but certainly in a way that it never can at home. On the street children quite often form groups of disparate ages within a range of a few years either side of the average age for each group, but at school classes are formed on the basis of mixed gender and same age-set groups. At Tenter Ground School children begin school in the nursery class at age 3 and formal school proper starts in the class of 5 to 6-year-olds who progress together through primary school year by year until, at the age of 11, they make the transition to secondary school.

At the school gate the care of kinship relations gives way to the cama-raderie and competitiveness of the peer group, the importance of which is mediated now by the teachers' responsibilities for the social organisa-tion of school life. Perhaps the most important social difference about school, compared to the home environment, is that the adult-to-child ratio is massively reduced. At home children may relate on a one-to-one, two-to-one, three-to-one or perhaps four-to-one basis with their principal carer, but at school the ratio is more likely to be thirty-to-one. For chil-dren who have already embodied an understanding of the kind of par-ticipation which is required for formal learning this ratio may not pose a problem, but for children who have no idea what to expect and who find what is required of them at school massively different compared to what happens at home, this low adult-to-child ratio is more likely to pose a sig-nificant problem. In schools where the majority of children are unpre-pared, at home, for formal learning, teachers will be spending a large proportion of their time trying to instil in the children an understanding of the social skills which are required for school-based learning.

Tom is in Year Five at Tenter Ground Primary; he shares a classroom and teacher with the older and less numerous Year Six children. Christine, his teacher, is a woman with local roots who grew up in Peckham and who has Bermondsey connections in her grandparents' generation. Even though she now lives in the leafy streets of Richmond in order to be closer to her partner's workplace and could claim middle class status if she wanted to, she will, she says, always think of herself as a working class woman. Christine is one of education's success stories but she refuses to turn her back on the struggle of her parents and grandparents: being true to and respectful of their struggle is what being working class means to Christine. Speaking fondly of the working class community in which she grew up, Christine explains how much she misses the camaraderie among women and men who, when she was young, all pulled together to support one another and have a laugh in the face of common difficulties. She can recount the history of her family's involvement with the now defunct economy of the docks and associates herself with, and is proud of, the resilience that surviving and overcoming poverty entails. Part of her relationship to her background means that teaching in a school where she will encounter the children of working class families has become a personal commitment. Christine says of the children, 'I understand them; I know what they're going through.'

Christine explains that Tenter Ground School has a bad reputation: prior to the beginning of my fieldwork, Tenter Ground had been labelled, by Her Majesty's Inspectors, as a school with 'serious weaknesses'. This means that in many respects it is a failing school, what people call a 'sink school', where children are, by implication, going down the drain. This doesn't say much for the prospects of the pupils' education and reinforces the metaphors which associate working class people with waste products. Because it is a school which doesn't get good results, Tenter Ground School does not attract any of the more ambitious parents in the local area and for this reason, Christine emphasises, it isn't considered to be a typical Bermondsey school. Most Bermondsey people wouldn't even consider sending their children to Tenter Ground; even though they might not have done well at school themselves, Bermondsey mothers still have high aspirations and want the best for their children. They are more likely, therefore, to favour the stricter church schools which have reputations for better discipline, greater formality and neat uniforms. Even if they have to attend church once a week out of the instrumental desire to secure places for their children, Bermondsey mothers will do what is necessary to give their children access to available advantages in the competition for success at school.

Tenter Ground pupils live mostly on the surrounding council housing estates but not many of them, with the exception of a few like Emma, Tom and Gary, know much about the legacy of Bermondsey's exclusive past.[20] Anne, however, emphasises that she doesn't instil in her children any sense that they are 'Bermondsey'. 'I don't,' she says, 'put any religion or culture on them. I just let them get on with life', and Pete points out that the closely knit community that Bermondsey once was is dead and gone anyway. He suggests that what I see at Tenter Ground is more like the future, more like what Bermondsey is to become, which is a multicultural place. Although Anne was thoroughly schooled by her parents in what she understands to be the conventionally prejudiced Bermondsey views about not mixing with 'coloured' children, she refuses to try and enforce the same prejudices in Tom and Mary. She is not 'racialist', she says, because even though her parents were against outsiders of all kinds, she went to school with 'coloured' children and thereby got to make her own mind up about different kinds of people. She tells me that if she ever hears the children being 'racialist' she comes down hard on them and she emphasises how distraught Tom was when he was forced to leave his old school because he had to leave a boy he was really 'tight with' (close to) – his best friend Max – who is a 'half-caste' boy.

Compared to those few who are born and bred Bermondsey children, the majority of Tenter Ground's pupils travel from further afield in South London, from the Elephant and Castle, Nunhead or Peckham, for example. Many of them are the children of first-, second- or third-generation immigrants: eight out of ten children in Year Six, and thirteen out of nineteen children in Year Five, are the children of first-, second- or third-generation non-white immigrant families. This doesn't include the children of parents who are first-, second- or third-generation immigrants from Ireland, but anyway, the point is that white children are clearly in the minority at Tenter Ground School. Boys also predominate, with a ratio of just over two boys to one girl. Christine suggests that this is the result of the head teacher's policy of accepting boys, like Tom, who have been excluded from other South London primaries.[21] The head feels that she can hardly turn boys like this away since she is trying to secure funds for the school, but because these boys are, for one reason or another, usually trouble-makers, the school has become trapped in a vicious circle from which it is difficult to escape. Over the years, parents reluctant to keep their children, and especially girls, in a deteriorating and increasingly troublesome school environment, find places for them elsewhere, usually in the church schools to the north of the borough.

Christine explains how badly the school is affected by a lack of confidence amongst parents in the local area: Bermondsey people would be likely, Christine stresses, to say that only the children of parents who don't know any better, or who, for some reason, can't get their children places at other schools, are to be found at Tenter Ground. The principal effect of this bad reputation is that children in Year Five and Six have to share one teacher and classroom because there simply aren't enough children to make a single age-set class. Because funds are allocated to schools on the basis of pupil numbers there isn't enough money to pay for one teacher per year group.

So, the school that Tom runs to in the mornings is not a straightforward place to be. It is blighted by low educational standards, has a reputation for troublesome boys, a lack of funds and, therefore, low teacher/staff morale. But no matter, Toms knows little of these things; he runs in because this is where he can have fun and find his place in the peer group. Occasionally he is reluctant to go to school because there has been too much trouble for him to handle either with other boys or with the teacher because of his behaviour. Every now and again, for example, he is suspended from school which means that he is forced to stay at home because the head teacher is unprepared to keep him in class while he is misbehaving. This always means that he's then in trouble with his parents too and will probably be 'grounded' (prevented from going out to play on the street).

Whilst Tom certainly has more freedom to do as he pleases at home where, like most boys of his age, he spends a lot of time on his Sony Playstation, he is nevertheless constrained by having to share a small bedroom with his sister. Like many children, and especially teenagers, who spend a lot of time on the street, Tom does so, in part, because he is seeking space from overcrowded housing. When he is suspended from school and confined to the flat, a sociable boy like Tom quickly gets bored and lonely; he is always keen to get back to school where his friends are. So why does Tom get into so much trouble at school and how does he fit into the boys' peer group there? To answer these questions it is first important to understand how the classroom is organised socially, to appreciate what values are established for children by the form of participation that adults require of them there and to gain a sense of what the discrepancies are between this form of participation and what boys expect of each other in their peer groups. These issues are the subject of the next two chapters.

6
The Classroom and School

Tom's school day begins in the playground, which is reached by entering the gate in the walls that mark the school grounds off from the streets and surrounding housing estates. Playing freely whilst they wait for lessons to begin, children congregate in the playground five or ten minutes before school begins at 9 o'clock. Parents and carers stay with the younger children until the bell sounds, which signifies that it is time for parents to hand responsibility for their children over to the teachers until the school day ends at half-past-three. Older children often make their own way to and from school, sometimes having responsibility for younger siblings too.

Whilst children are synonymous with play, their youth is also associated with the desire and necessity to learn. The problem at school, however, is that tension is continuously created between the different ways in which children's learning is organised at various times and in the various spaces of the school. Informally, in the playground, for example, children are expected to learn through self-guided play. The playground is a place for free play, loud noise, rapid movement and games where, within certain limits, children can run about and do as they please. A large concrete area dominates the outside space, with a football pitch marked in white lines and a goal at either end; there is also a basketball pole, a roofed but open-sided shed for shelter and a large garden area which is restricted for educational purposes only. Some small climbing frames and other fixed objects cluster close to the nursery and infant classrooms; these are for the sole use of younger children between the ages of 3 and 5 who, at this young age, are still expected, throughout the school day, to learn through self-guided play rather than formal instruction.

As they mature, however, children are increasingly expected to transcend the need for playthings at school and because they are expected to create their own forms of amusement, there are very few objects or structures provided for older children's outdoor play. In the playground, when there is no ball to play with, there is just the empty concrete space out of which the children have to conjure a distracting game. They have only their bodies to work with, but it is amazing how preoccupied they become with playing chasing games, clap songs and so on.[1] Children are not supposed to bring playthings from home into school, but they often smuggle in small things in their pockets. Girls might walk about chatting in small groups whilst boys play football with a smuggled-in tennis ball or, surreptitiously, act out WWF (World Wrestling Foundation) wrestling bouts. Younger children, and some older ones too, play make-believe and bring to life in the playground scenarios and characters from favourite television programmes and cartoons. Fighting and bullying are prohibited in the playground, but they happen nevertheless.

In the classroom also, the use of objects for play becomes increasingly restricted as the children get older. Eventually they should be prepared to preoccupy themselves only with task-based work using pens, pencils, rulers and other equipment required for formal learning. Access to fun objects for play in the classroom is, for older children, restricted to free-time/free-choice periods only. Whereas in the playground children get to learn through moving about and doing, in the company of their friends, more or less as they please, in lessons they are required to be still, quiet and attentive to the teacher and their work, not to each other. Children are expected to concentrate carefully on working through designated tasks within a specific time and good behaviour in this respect signifies their application to formal learning. Distinctive about the social organisation of classroom-based learning is the specific spatio-temporal rhythm which arises in relation to the timetable of lessons and activities and also the teacher's attempts, within those periods of time, to manage the children's behaviour.

Disruptive boys

Just as children's movement and language are constrained at school, so they learn in time what kind of participation is required of them at particular times in specific spaces. This requirement is first of all a bodily disposition, a restraint that embodies order and readiness for concentrated application to work which demands conceptual thinking.[2] As opposed to practical learning, conceptual thinking involves mastery over language and abstract symbols, like letters and numbers, through which the child gains access to a whole new world of significance. The bodily restraint required for conceptual thinking is, however, difficult for some children to achieve and this is clear to see in the frequent interventions of the teacher who devotes a large measure of her energies to trying to manage children's bodily comportment.

It is significant that the children who have most difficulty with this kind of restraint are boys, and those particular boys who are among the worst offenders are quickly labelled as 'disruptive'. Their refusal or inability to participate appropriately in the classroom means that these boys are immediately treated as a problem. When they are eventually referred for special educational needs assessment they are often labelled as having emotional and behavioural difficulties. It is the individual boy who is said to have a problem; his behaviour is rendered pathological while the formation of the disruptive boys' peer group, as a social phenomenon, is never considered. Neither is the effect on children of the highly specific form of classroom participation taken into account. The discrepancy between this and the kinds of participation that children, and especially boys, require of each other is never subjected to critical scrutiny. It becomes impossible, therefore, within the parameters of school life, to conceive of what a normal child is without thinking of the child who behaves well and learns successfully. By implication, those children who resist the constraints which are placed upon them at school are considered to be abnormal and the chance is lost, thereby, to consider how extraordinary are the restraints which children must learn to accommodate to at school. Observing what children choose to do when they are free of these restrictions, which is to play, move about, interact freely and competitively with each other and with objects of their choice in the immediate environment, making lots of noise as they go about it, I come to appreciate that the more exceptional phenomenon is not the child who resists formal learning, but the child who comes, early on in life, to adore it.

The whole of the school day, as it unfolds in the various spaces of the building, becomes a virtual battle ground in which the fight to inculcate in children a disposition towards formal learning is waged against their more fundamental desire to play, move about a lot and interact freely and noisily. The extreme expression of this conflict is witnessed in the teacher's outbursts of irritation and anger when she is distracted from teaching in order to have to continuously focus on managing the comportment and misbehaviour of the most disruptive boys. Tom is by no means the worst offender, but he struggles to get through a school day without getting into trouble and the amount of time he devotes to learning anything through school work is minimal. In periods of forty-minute lessons Tom might only settle down to five minutes of work, whilst the rest of the time he spends amusing himself with his friends in the work group to which he has been assigned. As a result of this lack of focus Tom is far behind the age-related expectations for academic ability in his class and he finds himself in the lowest ability group for both numeracy and literacy.

Because children's schooling is organised on the basis of age-sets, children of a similar age move through the education system together regardless of whether or not they have achieved the expected level for their age group. This means that a child, like Tom, who has not yet mastered some of the most rudimentary academic skills, like reading, falls farther and farther behind as his peers progress apace. His learning difficulties are not adequately addressed at home or at school and, meanwhile, his peers in higher ability groups move farther and farther away from his level as their understanding of the curriculum develops in each new academic year.

Children's comportment

Out of the apparent chaos of playtime, the order of entry into the school buildings is marked by the arrival of teachers who take designated places in the playground, expecting the children to line up in single-file class-sets. When each line is orderly and relatively quiet, the teacher leads the way into the classroom through the corridors and up the stairs of the huge and ageing Victorian building. From the freedom of play to the relative restriction of orderly conduct, movement and noise are constrained further and further until stillness and silence are achieved under the watchful gaze of the teacher who waits for the children to settle down on the carpet ready for registration. The surveillance of children's comportment is at its most pronounced when they must gather together like this, under the teacher's eyes, either for registration or instruction in the classroom, or for whole school meetings in the assembly hall. In these moments, by virtue of her ability to hold the children's attention, to keep them still and quiet, the teacher's power and authority to impart knowledge is recreated on a daily, if not hourly, basis.

Those children who fail to attend to what the teacher has to say because they are more interested in interacting with those sitting next to them, or in moving about and making noise, are punished first through verbal admonishment and then by increasing degrees of spatial exclusion from the group. If these measures are insufficient to quell disruptive behaviour then the spatial exclusion is further emphasised and a disruptive child will be sent to the deputy or head teacher's office. In extreme cases a child might be suspended from school for the day, which means that his or her parents will be called to come into school and take their child home. Exclusion from the group is supposed to induce shame and encourage conformist behaviour in children: if they want to be part of the group they have to accept the rules of participation; if they do not learn to do as they are told they will suffer exclusion and isolation at school and bring shame on themselves and their families. Ideally, when a child misbehaves and, in extreme cases, is suspended for a day or two, what is brought to the foreground for that child and, by implication, for all the other children, is the realisation that parents want their children to be at school to learn; that parents support the teachers in their disciplining of children; and that parents want their children to learn successfully and do well. Apart from the force of the law, which requires children between the ages of 5 and 16 to be at school, the permanent background of the school's authority to teach and discipline the child is given by the parents' support for the teachers.

Sometimes, however, a suspension has the opposite effect and serves only to highlight the child's parents' opposition to the school's authority. Conflict between parents and teachers then ensues and education welfare officials might be called in to remind parents of their legal responsibilities with respect to their children's education. In addition, the necessity to temporarily suspend a child from school can stand, in parents' eyes, for a failure of the school to adequately discipline a child within the school. Compared to parents, however, teachers are limited in the means which they have at their disposal for enforcing their authority: they can withdraw privileges, but since they are forbidden to use physical force of any kind, exclusion from the group is, in effect, their only weapon of restraint. Often having no problem controlling their children at home, parents are often frustrated about teachers' inability to discipline their children at school.[3]

The pecking order of disruption

The opposite of the learned disposition that teachers require of children in the classroom is the playful, rowdy, intimidating, sometimes violent, apparently frenetic movements of particular boys. During and between lessons they assert their presence to each other and to other children in ways that enable the reconstitution, on a daily basis, of the pecking order of their physical, as opposed to academic, dominance. The dynamic of this volatile process works alongside and periodically interferes with the pace of the teacher's rhythm for curriculum delivery. She must then intervene to restore order to the learning process. Each child in the classroom is preoccupied every day with trying to accommodate the demands of the different dispositions required for play, peer group and classroom interaction. Some boys manage to do well in their work and be part of the pecking order of disruption whilst others behave beautifully, draw no attention to themselves and still struggle, nevertheless, with the learning tasks assigned to the class. However, because quiet children pose no disruptive threat to the rhythm of the teacher's timetable for curriculum delivery, they are much less likely to command any of the teacher's attention and their learning difficulties are more likely, therefore, to be overlooked. The obstacles they face in their learning are, however, often no less serious than the problems facing badly behaved boys.

Meanwhile, a large measure of the teacher's and children's emotional and physical resources is preoccupied with the heightening tension which is caused by the disruptive boys' challenges to adult authority. Whilst Tom's case appears to prove the point that streaming of ability within school classrooms can cause children to become subversive – children react against the demeaning position ascribed to them – it is also true that the worst offenders among the disruptive boys in Tom's class are some of the most able academically. When the climate amongst them is one of ruthless domination, it is often the brightest amongst the tough boys who quickly become peer group leaders. It is not simply a matter of brute force; it is also to do with the combined skills of daring and personal charisma and Tom's friend Gary excels in this domain.

Observing Tom's class, it soon becomes clear to me that the really difficult challenge which boys face, in schools like Tenter Ground, is how to work relatively well in class when it suits them and still be able to demonstrate their subversive edge to peers when need be. In Year Five/Six there are a few of these kinds of boys; they tend to be the boys of West African origin who are trying to strike an acceptable balance between their parents' high educational expectations and what is required of them if they are to be valued in the disruptive boys' peer group at school. Even though they are academically capable of it, these boys will often not excel at school because, as a result of trying to strike the necessary balance between concentrating in class and disrupting their own and others' learning, they lack the required focus for excellence. They tend, however, to do well enough to get through the system, keeping their parents and teachers reasonably happy.

Other boys, like Gary, who could do well academically if they put their minds to it, appear, from an educational point of view, to self-destruct. They play the game of peer group leader all the way to its final conclusion, spending many days either absent from school to try and avoid trouble or suspended by teachers because of bad behaviour. Additional problems then arise because boys like this then have to struggle to catch up with missed work. Because he is one of her favourites, Gary is relatively protected at Tenter Ground by his teacher, Christine's, support; she knows, however, that he will not be cosseted at secondary school where, she says, boys like him are quickly and permanently excluded from school.[4]

Gary is one of her favourites, Christine says, because, like the other disruptive boys, he is a rebel. He stands out as a strong individual who dares to resist conventional expectations; he has charisma and refuses to just do as he is told, but his energies and intelligence are misdirected. Christine feels sure that under different circumstances Gary would be a creative and strong leader and she watches, in vain, as his leadership skills are put to less constructive uses than she imagines for him. Anxious not to alienate him, Christine determines to win Gary's respect and confidence in order to try to persuade him of education's possibilities. Meanwhile, Rochelle, who is Christine's assistant in the classroom, is often furious about Christine's soft spot for Gary; she knows that Gary has health problems and she is aware that Christine attributes a lot of Gary's behavioural problems to his struggle to come to terms with his illness, but Rochelle is, nevertheless, constantly infuriated by Christine's failure to take the hard line with Gary that she feels he deserves. Many of the classroom assistants, who have less authority than teachers and who are, therefore, less respected by the disruptive boys, bear the brunt of Gary's influence at school and they have little sympathy for any problems he might be struggling with in or outside of school. So, it seems that, after all, Tom's mother's hopes for Gary to be a good role model for Tom will not come to fruition. On the contrary, Gary is more likely than any of the other boys at Tenter Ground to bring Tom closer to trouble.[5]

September 1999: preparing for SATs[6]

Within the first two weeks of the school term, children in Year Five/Six face the realisation that their formal learning abilities are to be tested and quantified in relation to their attainment in the government's Standard Assessment Tests (SATs) (Level 2). It is according to the results of these tests that children's abilities and the performance of the school are measured.

Christine sits on her large comfy chair overlooking the large carpeted area in the Year Five/Six classroom; she waits for the children to come in and sit down for morning register. Year Six children, who are aged between 10 and 11, are distinguishable because they sit around the carpet on wooden chairs whilst Year Five children, who are aged between 9 and 10, sit cross-legged on the carpet. Christine addresses the class:

> 'Right, only one person let us down coming up the stairs. I'm not going to say who it was, but it's not fair when everyone else is trying so hard. Someone is talking [irritated pause]. Excellent: everyone in and everyone on time.'

Christine takes the register, greeting individual children by name and each child replies, 'Good morning Christine';[7] she then notes down their attendance. Christine explains to the Year Six children that they have to start preparing for their SATs and she informs them that they will be doing sample tests all morning so that she can assess how much work they are going to have to do during the coming year. She instructs the Year Six children to sit at the tables with four or five children at each cluster of tables of which there are five in the classroom. Meanwhile the Year Five children are given Year Four's assessment tests to work through so that Christine can assess their current level of attainment. Staring menacingly at a boy who is moaning loudly about the tests, Christine fixes her attention on him[8] and the boy, realising that her gaze is upon him, stops complaining.

Christine makes it clear to the children that she cannot give them any help because they must learn to work under test conditions; she explains that they have forty-five minutes to do as many questions as possible. The majority of the boys react to the test with sulky looks and slumped body postures. Heads often held in hands, they struggle to get through the questions in time. For the most part, however, the children manage to work in silence, which is punctuated only by Gary's persistent requests for Christine's help. Christine repeats loudly and clearly that she cannot give advice to anyone, and eventually Gary quietens down.

The test conditions set a benchmark for the children's ability to work individually and in complete silence, and despite their depressed demeanour it is significant, even if they don't finish all the questions, that the boys are able to sit through and apply themselves to the test. This capacity for completely focused attention exists at one end of a spectrum that encompasses the different ways in which children work in the classroom. Silent, individual concentration is rarely seen except on the occasion of tests, and the ability of the children to meet examination conditions is testimony to Christine's authority in the classroom. Christine is the only member of staff who can induce this class, with its high proportion of disruptive boys, to apply itself to school work for any length of time. Her authority is a function of the trust that she has nurtured in her relationship with the children in this class in general, but in particular she has managed to gain the respect of the core group of badly behaved boys.

Observing the boys' antics, which are so often disruptive of the aims and objectives of classroom-based learning, it is easy to see how a teacher might form an antagonistic and resentful attitude towards them. Christine, however, is quick to defend them, remarking that the boys are extremely sensitive to the dislike for them that many members of staff have developed. She explains that hating the boys does nothing to remedy the situation since their own anger and resentment is only inflamed which results in increasingly insubordinate behaviour. One young male teacher, for example, refuses to tolerate the disruptive boys' behaviour; he has become their worst enemy and consequently they go out of their way to make his life at school very difficult indeed.

Acceptable levels of distraction

Generally speaking, the children don't work individually in silence in the classroom; they work in small groups, five or six at one cluster of tables, and as long as they appear to be getting on with their work, a permissible level of good-humoured chatting prevails on non-test days. In reality, however, children take advantage of the acceptable parameters governing noise levels during lessons so that they can furtively engage in the kind of interaction that largely distracts them from their work. This doesn't necessarily get them into trouble: background distraction takes many forms from messing about with the few permissible objects on the table – pencils, pens and so on – to talking with friends about football, computer games, television programmes and other things to do with life outside school. Unless the distraction escalates into too much noise or movement, like that involved in getting out of seats at an inappropriate time, tussling, fighting or obviously talking loudly about things other than the work, then the children's surreptitious disruption of formal learning goes largely unnoticed. Christine endeavours, meanwhile, during any given task, to focus on as many children's individual needs for assistance as possible.

When the tests are over Christine praises the children for the sensible way in which they have approached the test and she then instructs them, table-by-table, to line up in single file by the door ready for assembly in the school hall. Although this automatically entails an increase in levels of noise and movement, the children are orderly enough for Christine not to have to intervene. This is the kind of transition from one activity to another that teachers expect children to be able to manage amongst themselves such that their behaviour facilitates an orderly progression of the class through the spaces and times of the day. The older children in Year Five/Six are expected to set an example to the younger children in the school, but much to Christine's dismay, a consistent level of application to the work in the classroom and orderly conduct in and through the other spaces of the school, such as the stairs and lunch hall, are a rare occurrence for her class.

Self-control

As the children file, class by class, into the assembly hall, Eileen, the popular deputy head teacher, watches sternly over them. The smallest children are organised by their teacher and classroom assistant into a neat row facing Eileen and the classes of older children fall in, row by row, behind them. Eileen waits for all the children to settle down and she then confidently tells the teachers and classroom assistants that they don't have to stay. Relieved, the staff members leave the hall for a break in the staffroom. Eileen's ability to hold the whole school's attention is a function of the security of her authority and she turns to me, welcoming me, inviting me to stay and impressing upon the children what she expects of them, 'I'm sure you [Gillian] will be impressed by the way the children are able to behave sensibly during assembly.' She then begins to tell the children a story about Mohammed and spells out for them what the moral lesson of the story is: it is all about learning to resist the temptation to do things that are wrong.

All assemblies are about moral instruction of one kind or another; lessons are taken from a variety of religions and once a week certificates of achievement are given out to individual children who have either done especially well in a particular subject or otherwise made significant improvements in their work or behaviour. Probably the most important thing that children learn, however, during this collective time together, is how to attain a level of self-control over their bodies in order to meet the conditions of the highly specific kind of participation which is required of them when they assemble as a group. Not surprisingly, Eileen's story is punctuated by the necessity for her to have to manage individual children's comportment:

'Sit up and behave yourself!'

'You don't talk in assembly!'

Eventually one child is excluded from the gathering and told to go back to his classroom and wait for the teacher. As he leaves Eileen calls after him, 'I'm ashamed of you.' Angrily, she turns to the assembled children and emphasises what she expects of them:

'Show me you know how to sit please, everyone should be sitting legs folded, arms crossed, looking at me.'

Eileen then explains to the children what she wants: rather than having to show them her miserable face, she would like to be able to give them some of her smiles which, she says, mean, 'I'm pleased with you.' She then singles out individual children that she is really pleased with and demonstrates to them the 'big smiley face' which she wants to give to them as a gesture of her pleasure.

Children's learning about what constitutes appropriate participation at school is inseparable, then, from the development of their social relationship with the teachers. As children learn what is expected of them they come to know what makes teachers happy: children are required to behave sensibly at the appropriate times and demonstrate, thereby, their preparedness to learn from the teacher. In this way the effort to try hard, participate successfully and please the teacher can become, in time, a source of the child's own happiness. Education is, then, not just an intellectual achievement; it also depends on the successful development of a more or less happy relationship between teachers and pupils, which involves a reciprocal emotional engagement between them. A problem arises, however, when there are a minority of children who don't care about doing what's considered to be appropriate in order to please the teacher; preferring to please themselves, these children struggle to find joy in formal learning and it is difficult, therefore, for them to build a positive and happy relationship with the adults at school.

Observing the whole-school assembly, which is an extraordinary situation in which upwards of a hundred children are expected collectively not to speak unless they are spoken to, to sit cross-legged, keep their backs straight, arms folded and their eyes forward, I am reminded that children's appropriate participation at school depends, firstly, on them learning to accommodate themselves to what is considered to be a correct bodily disposition for formal learning. This disposition, which signifies that the child has internalised the teacher's authority as a form of bodily self-control, is what teachers take as the sign of children's readiness to concentrate. Depending on what kind of learning children are expected to be engaged in, the degree of self-control required of them changes at different times in various places of the school.

Disruptive boys, in contrast to 'good' children, constantly resist the bodily constraint that appropriate participation requires of them. They rebel continuously, asserting their own form of participation, which challenges the teacher's authority and leads to deterioration in their relationship with other children, who are trying to be good, and with the teacher as she becomes displeased with the disruption to learning that a lack of appropriate self-control presents. Disruptive boys' parents, just like any other children's parents, also become increasingly concerned because quite often they want more than anything for their boys to do well at school and they don't understand why things are going so badly wrong. In time, good children begin to try to manage each other's comportment; they tell tales on offenders and react against the infringement by others of rules they have themselves learnt to accommodate. And, meanwhile, those unobtrusive children, the ones who behave well but struggle to learn anything, continue quietly to demonstrate the fallacy that good behaviour means effective learning. Their lack of progress highlights the cost to the whole class of the teacher's continuous focus on trying to manage the behaviour of disruptive boys.

Special educational needs

After the break for outside play the children return to the classroom and Christine explains the next test they face, which is English comprehension.[9] Before she can begin to get the children organised for the test, David, the independent child psychotherapist who works in the school, comes in and asks if he can just have five minutes to explain to the children how the service that he offers works. He tells the children that they can come to him and talk about anything that they might be unhappy about, but he emphasises that whatever they talk about will be just for him to hear and he won't tell anyone else. If they want to come and see him, he says, they must put their name in the book and then come and see him on either a Tuesday or Wednesday lunchtime.

The presence of the psychotherapist in school suggests that children who are unhappy do not learn well; misbehaviour is taken as just one sign of unhappiness,[10] but not a single one of the disruptive boys ever goes to see David by choice. The only ones he gets to know are those who are forced, as a result of the head teacher's interventions, or as part of a process of assessment for a special educational needs statement, to 'talk over their problems' with the psychotherapist. David explains that he rarely makes any kind of progress with these boys and members of the psychotherapy team are often seen to be trailing one disruptive boy or another around the school after one of them has decided to abscond from a compulsory psychotherapy session.

David's interruption of the literacy test creates a distraction; not surprisingly, the children take advantage of the situation in order to begin talking and interacting amongst themselves. Each distraction from formal learning always leads to the same consequences: control is momentarily lost and Christine is then repeatedly forced to manage the children's comportment until order is restored. In this way, in relation to children's movement in and out of periods of more or less concentrated application to formal learning, a spatio-temporal flux is created in the classroom. It goes like this: degree of control (still, silent attention on the teacher or one's work) and then relative freedom of constraint (noise, movement and interaction with peers and objects in the room): degree of control (still, silent attention on the teacher or one's work) and then relative freedom from constraint (noise, movement and interaction with one's peers and objects in the room) and so on throughout the day; like a living thing in its own right, the social structure of the classroom ebbs and flows. Children at school are seen, then, to be in a constant state of flux between what the institution demands of childhood and what being a child means to children themselves.

In this way children's application to formal learning becomes inscribed, over time, in a particular bodily disposition, which formal learning requires, and that free time easily undoes. This is a disposition towards work that lends itself to the preparation of the child for the future world of adult labour. Children by this age know all too well that they must go to school and learn otherwise they won't be able to get good jobs in the future. The problem, however, is that learning well at school is easier said than done. The same is true of teaching well: the behaviour of the disruptive boys places untenable levels of stress on Christine and as the year progresses this stress begins to take its toll. She must plan her lessons, organise an ideal strategy for curriculum delivery, make it look good on paper and all the time she knows that only a fraction of the knowledge that she wishes to impart will be learned by the children in her class. It is a farce: the level of disruption that Christine has to endure undermines the possibility that she will fulfil her plans and meet the formal requirements of her job.[11] Despite the existence of a special educational needs policy, many of the children at Tenter Ground and in Year Five/Six in particular, including those disruptive boys and other children, like Emma, who haven't even mastered basic numeracy and literacy skills, will be leaving primary school without a formal statement from an educational psychologist. Budgetary constraints and the high level of commitment required by the SENCO managers conspire against the children to prevent their problems from being formally recognised and addressed. Meanwhile, teachers like Christine and her dedicated colleagues struggle vainly on. They endeavour, day by day, to contain classrooms of thirty children, in which at least six children might pose a permanent threat of violent disruption to their own and other children's learning.

Christine's class is particularly difficult to manage because apart from the fact that the range of abilities and needs within the class is so disparate, there are two year groups in one. There is also a disproportionately high number of boys. Acknowledging that Christine faces the most difficult challenge at Tenter Ground, other teachers also complain, however, of similar kinds of problems in their own classes. Staff morale is very low and teachers feel unsupported by, and lack confidence in, the senior management and especially the head teacher. The deputy's power to instigate changes is limited by the power of the head teacher, and the discretionary power of the governing body is impotent in the face of their ignorance about the day-to-day realities of school life. The main discrepancy between teachers and senior management arises because management staff members have little or no teaching responsibilities and it is impossible, therefore, for them to empathise with, understand or do anything about the impossible task that teachers face in the classroom. Effective support strategies either for staff or children remain, therefore, unforthcoming.

'Good enough parenting'

Christine speaks to me often of her desire to leave Tenter Ground. She imagines moving to another school where there might be less stress: somewhere that she would be able to do her job, which is to teach the curriculum and not to teach children the social skills required for learning. Christine is, however, loyal to the overwhelming needs of the disruptive boys and so she perseveres. She wonders what will become of them and, like other education professionals in the school, she interprets their failure to behave and to concentrate in class in terms of an emotional deficit at home. David, the psychotherapist, explains his interpretation of the problem as follows: 'The problem in this school is that children don't get good enough parenting.'[12] Christine agrees, explaining that she thinks of herself as the boys' surrogate mother. She imagines that the boys' own parents are failing to establish an adequate parental relationship with their sons and that this is the reason why the boys don't know how to behave. She feels sure that what the boys lack is consistency in their familial lives and, lacking this constancy, they are then unable to trust adults. Having to fight for their needs to be met, they crave attention whilst pretending that they need no one. Christine does her best to provide what she feels the boys need, which is a firm and fair relationship to an adult that they can depend on, and having given herself this role she is loath to withdraw from the stress that being their teacher places on her.

Interesting to me about the education professionals' interpretations of the disruptive boys' misbehaviour is the way that children's problems at school become synonymous with problems at home. According to this kind of interpretation the blame for so-called deviant behaviour is placed squarely on a lack of responsibility and appropriate emotional and moral guidance on the part of the boys' parents. The assumption is that if only the boys' families could be put right then the boys wouldn't misbehave at school. Other staff members go so far as to assume that the real reason for the disruptive boys' behaviour is a pathological deficiency in their individual psychologies and even in their brains. In despair, a classroom assistant tries, for example, to explain to me the reasons for the disruptive boys' behaviour: pointing conclusively to her temple, she says, 'They've got something wrong: up here.'

Good enough schooling

Of course, I too am horrified by the disruptive boys' behaviour. I cannot imagine my daughters having to attend a school like this one and I can only imagine how different the learning environment is in the classrooms of my daughter's new private school. Like the teachers, my first instinct is also to blame the boys' parents and, in private, before I begin my fieldwork research in the boys' homes, I too speculate about their family lives. As my research progresses, however, I begin to realise that it is important to be wary of jumping to such easy conclusions about the reasons for disruptive boys' behaviour. It is true that learning how to sit still and be quiet in order to attend to what the teacher wants children to learn about is the first and most important social skill that children at Tenter Ground have to learn. It is important, however, as I have already stressed, to realise that a physically passive child is not necessarily any more likely than a disruptive boy is to be disposed towards formal learning.

In the light of a more thorough social analysis of the realities of these disruptive boys' lives in and outside of school, the pervasiveness of the projection, by teachers and staff, of boys' misbehaviour in school onto a deficiency in their homes is arguably short-sighted. Despite the fact that Her Majesty's Inspectors had, at the time of my fieldwork, recently labelled the school as having 'serious weaknesses', staff rarely if ever held the social organisation of the school and/or the way that the education system itself is organised, to be responsible for the failure of individual children to learn successfully. Even though Tenter Ground has a tainted reputation both officially and unofficially in the local community, the authority of the head teacher and the legitimacy of the school as a national institution suffice to conceal a multitude of problems. Poor results and boys' behavioural problems are projected onto the unseen damage that poverty is said to inflict on families, and as long as inadequate learning at school implies inappropriate care at home the implications of the school's failings needn't be seriously considered. The problem with this, however, is that the following question never gets raised: what about good enough schooling?

In the same way that homes are not necessarily good places for children to be cared for, schools are not, by definition, good places for children to learn. The problem is that formal learning and caring are posited as inseparable variables in the equation that education establishes for child development, and when children fail to learn this failure is blamed on inadequate care. Because the domain for the care of children is thought of principally as being the home, teachers easily blame parental deficiencies in the home for children's misbehaviour at school. But when parents and carers hand over the responsibility for their child's education to teachers and other staff members every morning, they also expect their children to be well cared for.

A chaotic school in which a minority of disruptive boys dominate proceedings is a high-adrenaline environment where both children and staff have to cope constantly with the threat of disruption, intimidation and violence. This is a far from caring atmosphere for children to be in and, at times, school can be an exhausting and dangerous place, both emotionally and physically. One boy – Tunde – for example, who is 8 years old and the son of first-generation Nigerian parents, is renowned among staff at school for his angry and aggressive disposition which often leads him into confrontations with other boys at school. It is true that at school Tunde is constantly frowning and always on the defensive, ready to fight and often actually fighting. When I visit him at home, however, I discover that there, Tunde lives under the ordered and strict discipline of his mother and older siblings and in that context I see nothing from him but boyish charm and very good behaviour; there isn't a trace of the boy he is at school. Whilst the teachers assume that an angry and aggressive boy is the result of a difficult home life and a disturbed psychology or impaired brain function, it becomes clear to me that Tunde's angry disposition might be little more than a necessary tool for his survival in a failing school where aggressive boys are allowed to rule. The point to emphasise is that Tunde's school-based aggression is a situationally specific, social skill. If we pathologise his behaviour we miss the opportunity to analyse, as a social phenomenon, the formation and effects of disruptive boys' peer groups at failing schools like Tenter Ground.

Accountability

Her Majesty's Inspectors supposedly represent the requirement for schools to be held accountable, but what parents and teachers can do about inspectors' findings is limited. After all, parents rarely ever get to find out exactly what actually happens beyond the school walls. Neither do inspectors ever get the full story because, prior to an inspection, there is a lot of impression management. For example, during the week of the last inspection before my fieldwork ended in December 2000 all of the disruptive boys are strategically suspended from school so that disruption to formal learning is minimised and a better impression created. There is, therefore, no legitimate way for the reality of teachers' experiences in the classroom to be objectively witnessed; their urgent need for support is then missed and the failures of senior management are effectively concealed by the naïve collusion of the governing body.

Because my inclination is to shout this injustice from the rooftops, I struggle to maintain my silence and when I ask Christine why she is prepared to go along with this kind of deception, not telling the inspectors exactly what goes on at Tenter Ground, she says that the failure of the school's inspection wouldn't do the children any good. If the school was demoted from 'serious weaknesses' to 'special measures' it would then have to be run by outside agencies. In Christine's opinion this would only make matters worse and the school would eventually be forced to close. She emphasises that the teachers' first commitment is always to the children and, unfortunately, in the face of the paramount power of the head, there is little that teachers can do to effect positive changes in the way that the school is run. If, for example, they were to go so far as to bring in the unions, which makes morale amongst teachers even worse and the relationship between teachers and management deteriorate further, it would, Christine suggests, make little difference to the children. Change, she explains, can only really come about as a result of a change in the head teacher and the review of management procedures that follows. Meanwhile, as dedicated teachers like Christine endeavour to stay the course, staff turnover at Tenter Ground remains exceptionally high. Time after time, new teachers are alienated by the impossible task of trying to balance behaviour management with having to deliver a carefully prescribed curriculum.[13]

7
Who Rules the School?

Christine is the only member of staff in the school who can control the disruptive boys in Year Five/Six. Most of the time that she devotes to their problems is spent on sorting out the trouble which they have caused during periods of time when they are not under her supervision. The problem is that whilst her authority over the boys is relatively secure in the classroom and their behaviour manageable under her watchful gaze, they immediately start to mess about in the other spaces of the school where different teachers and other kinds of staff members are responsible for supervising them. Almost all of the severe disruption that Christine faces in the classroom is the result of ongoing disputes between the boys which started much earlier in the day – on the stairs, at lunch play in the playground, at wet play in the classroom or at lunchtime in the dinner hall. The problem, Christine explains, is that she cannot be with them every minute of every day. In each period of time that follows their time away from her she is left to pick up the pieces after incidents that have occurred under the supervision of members of staff whom the boys have no respect for. These staff members are usually the classroom assistants whose job it is to supervise dinner time in the hall and lunch play in the playground whilst teachers retreat to the staffroom for their breaks.

23 September 1999: wet play

At lunchtime play it is raining, which means that children's time for free play must be constrained and instead of going outside to the playground the children have to remain in the classroom. Whilst Christine leaves to go to the staffroom for her break, a classroom assistant comes in to supervise the children. As soon as Christine has gone, the levels of noise and movement rise dramatically. This is the children's free time so they are not expected to be still and quiet anymore or to focus their attention on the adult members of staff in the room, but they are, nevertheless, expected to behave reasonably sensibly. Fatema,[1] the Year Four classroom assistant, is in charge; nervously she looks around to see what the children have decided to do with their freedom. Instantly the classroom divides along gender lines: some of the boys sit down at one table to draw, play noughts and crosses or hangman and a large group of girls sit down at another table to draw too. Relatively speaking the girls are generally quieter than the boys in the classroom; they move around less and focus more readily on their chosen activity.[2]

At another table a group of boys take out the construction bricks and begin to make guns with them. Once their guns are completed the boys run around the room chasing and shooting each other and Fatema gets up to intervene, 'Don't play guns! You don't have any other work to do? You have work to catch up on?' Ignoring Fatema's attempts to make them settle down to focused activity, the boys continue to chase and shoot each other; they certainly aren't interested, during their free time for play, in following her suggestion to catch up on school work. Compared to teachers the classroom assistants have very little status at Tenter Ground. Although they have the option of training courses, they do not have teaching degrees and they need have no formal educational qualifications for the job. Usually the classroom assistants are either older women, perhaps grandparents of children in the school, or they are young mothers glad to find locally based, flexible work that fits in with their children's school hours. These women are most often assigned specifically to the group in the class which is in most need of special educational support, but they do not have any training or specific qualification to prepare them for the particular difficulties of this kind of work in a school like Tenter Ground which has, among its pupils, several boys with very challenging behaviour.

Often disgruntled, the classroom assistants frequently complain to senior staff about children's behaviour, but their protests carry none of the weight of teachers' grievances and their differential status is thus reinforced to the children. It is not surprising, therefore, to see that Fatema's increasing attempts to control the children during wet play are frustrated and the disruption that is typical of wet play begins to escalate out of control. Fatema takes the self-styled gun from one of the boys and he, breaking the spatial boundary of control which the classroom space is supposed to imply, then runs out of the classroom. He disrupts, thereby, the surveillance made possible by children's containment in the classroom space. Fatema responds angrily, 'Not outside the classroom please.' She then attempts to praise other children who are behaving appropriately.

Trying to set a good example to the disruptive boys by focusing on those boys who are doing something constructive, she calls out loudly, 'Very good Anthony, Anthony's doing something creative, he's making a dinosaur,' and Anthony replies defiantly, 'Yeah, a dinosaur gun!'

Meanwhile, on the carpeted area, Gary and Tom begin to play kick touch. The idea of this game is to avoid being kicked by the other person; it is boisterous because they are kicking hard and moving fast to steer clear of each other within a small space. Fatema instantly forgets about the other boys with the pretend guns and goes over to the carpet to intervene. She pulls Gary by the arm, forcing him to sit down on the carpet and she turns to Tom, saying, 'You are pushing it; I am not smiling.' Whilst the general level of movement and noise increases those children who choose to concentrate quietly continue to do so; they are adept at ignoring the disruption. Some other boys, who have made paper aeroplanes, start to make them fly around the room. Great hilarity ensues amongst all the children when one plane suddenly gets stuck on the pipe that runs high along the ceiling. Periodically the disruption caused by the disruptive boys becomes a source of entertainment for other children in the class and the worst of the boys are then spurred on to perform more daring pranks.

After lunch, Christine, who, as usual, has had her supposedly relaxing break spoilt by a bad report about Year Five/Six's behaviour, admonishes the offenders. Privately she explains to me that she is frustrated because classroom assistants cannot control the children. Classroom assistants, meanwhile, are nearly always enraged, both with the disruptive boys and with teachers and senior staff who ignore their pleas for a unified network of support calling for stronger discipline backed by the head's authority. Without this support, in all the moments of the day where classroom assistants are in charge – at lunch, in the playground and at wet play – the potential is high for levels of disruption to escalate out of control.

28 September 1999: supply teacher

The following week Christine is away and a supply teacher has been brought in[3]; Gary is also off school. As the children come in and sit down on the carpet the supply teacher, Helen, who has probably been warned that this is a difficult class, nervously attempts to use positive behaviour management techniques: 'Well done; it's Richard isn't it? I like the way Richard is sitting this morning, that's another name on my [good children] list.' Helen soon realises, however, that her attempts are in vain. As she attempts to take the register the behaviour of a key group of boys becomes increasingly silly and Rochelle, the classroom assistant, attempts,

in Christine's absence, to take a more authoritative tone. Helen introduces and explains the numeracy task for the morning and, anticipating
the disruption of their movement to the tables she finishes, 'I wonder
how quickly and quietly the three maths groups who sit at the table can
go and sit down.' Not surprisingly, the children's movement is neither
quick nor quiet. As the morning proceeds movement and noise in the
classroom escalate and fights between certain boys begin to break out.
Helen intervenes and sends one of the combatants, Martin, to go and
explain himself in another teacher's classroom. Martin, a chubby boy,
who is no favourite among the disruptive boys, is often bullied: he is
teased for being 'fat' and for being a 'mummy's boy' because he still walks
to school with his mum and has no shame about holding her hand on
the way. Vehemently, but not very successfully, Martin constantly
attempts to fight back and to defend himself; he is often in trouble
because he refuses to be submissive in the war zone which the disruptive
boys constantly create for him.

As the prospect of Martin's humiliation before the supply teacher is
raised, Ade, who is another among the most troublesome boys, along with
his relatively quiet, but willing accomplice, Mark,[4] leap up from their
seats and move swiftly across the classroom to endorse Helen's decision
to exclude Martin from the classroom. Even though Martin is now outside
the classroom, Ade begins to taunt him, trying to wind him up further.
Martin, meanwhile, who has been hurt in the fight, begins to cry outside
the classroom door where he has taken refuge from the boys' laughter
and the teacher's admonition. The sight of Martin's tears sends the boys
into a frenzied, victorious uproar and Helen claps her hands declaring
emphatically; 'All eyes are to be on me!' Furious, she ignores Martin and
gives curt instructions for tidying up the classroom. The numeracy task
disintegrates, then, into full-scale chaos which is punctuated by Helen's
vain attempts at behaviour management. Ade, feeding on the heightened
tension in the room begins to rant, 'Martin's a fucking bitch, man. Martin's
a fucking bitch man.' On and on he repeats his chant; Mark giggles and
another boy tells Ade to be quiet.

Helen asks each table of children to line up by the door and then,
because Ade and Mark continue to disrupt the class with their antics, she
calls them all back to their seats. Laughing, Ade and Mark collapse into
their chairs and Ade starts rapping: 'In' it [isn't that right] nigger? In' it
nigger?' Using the language of black American gangster rappers, he leads
himself into a fully rehearsed rap. All is chaos now as the other children
attempt to line up, purposefully falling noisily over each other. Eventually
Helen manages to get the children out of the classroom and into the

assembly hall where Eileen contains them relatively quickly. Waiting for the children to settle down she exclaims:

> 'That took about ten minutes; I had to turn the music off because it was so noisy. And still people carried on talking.'

Eileen asks a persistent offender to move to the edge of the hall. When the children are relatively settled she begins to tell another story about Mohammed and how the world was made.

Literacy

After outside play and during the chaos of the children's progress up the stairs, Martin, for some reason, thumps one of his friends, Kevin, hard in the groin. Kevin, who is one of the quieter, better-behaved boys in the class, struggles to hold back the tears whilst he tries in vain to catch up with Martin and vent his vengeful fury. It is soon clear to see that the disruption of the morning has spilled into playtime and is to be prolonged and extended throughout the day; one incident after another leads, among the boys, to an escalating cycle of revenge-seeking behaviour. Helen, the supply teacher, resorts again to positive techniques for behaviour management and at the same time she endeavours to explain the literacy work. Much to Rochelle's fury, Ade ignores Helen and continues with his disruptive antics. Helen ignores him and continues to introduce the literacy task, which is to make up riddles that describe objects. Well-behaved children ignore the continuing disruptions and when Helen has finished explaining the literacy task the children move to their tables.

I join table five where six children are sitting. This group has some of the lowest ability children in it: two boys, including Tom, and four girls including Emma. The task is written on the table on a sheet of paper and all of the children, except Kevin, ignore it. The children begin to talk about who their worst enemy is and they all agree that it is Martin. Because I empathise with the impossible task facing the supply teacher, I try to engage the children, asking them about the first part of the task in which they have to think of an object and describe it in riddle form for others to guess.[5] With the benefit of my focused assistance, the children on table five settle down for a little while to try to think about the task and I begin to engage one-on-one with Kevin. Working happily, he begins to write his riddle in his literacy book, but as soon as the other children see that my attention is on Kevin, they stop thinking about their work and continue to discuss who their worst enemy is. Tom declares, 'Martin needs to get beat up today.' Kevin, who had been punched by Martin earlier replies, 'In' it [isn't that right] though.' Emma says, 'My worst enemy is a knife.' This idea rapidly becomes incorporated into the enemy scenario and the children all talk about how Martin ought to be stabbed. They begin mock stabbing each other's hands with hastily sharpened pencils and Tom suddenly shouts across at Martin, 'Watch out! After school I'm gonna break your nose.' I ask Tom why Martin is his worst enemy and he says, "Cos '[h]e said bad things about my little sister; '[h]e kicked her.'

Martin feigns fear in response to Tom's threats and says, 'Ooh, I'm so scared.' Tom continues, telling the girls about his intentions towards Martin, 'I'm gonna to beat '[h]im, bash '[h]im after school,' and the girls reply enthusiastically, 'No, no, do it in PE [physical education].' Tom shouts across the room again, 'Martin you've got no friends at school, 'cept for infants and they can't fight.' Kevin, meanwhile, has finished his first riddle and moved on to another one; the other children at his table still haven't even begun. Tom asks the girls to take it in turns to arm-wrestle him and then he calls out to Martin again, 'What are you lookin' at you little fat pig, you look like your mum, innit?' At this the girls all throw their hands up in horror and cry out in unison, 'Ooh!' All the children know that cussing (putting down) someone's mum is the worst possible disrespect that children can show to each other; it is an unequivocal provocation to a fight. The girls then begin to plot how they can get hold of Martin's pencil case and one of them suggests, 'He's probably so fat he can't get in the car.' Distracted for a moment by the pencil case idea, Emma opens her own one and proudly shows me all the pretty pencils, pens and rubbers in her pencil case and, meanwhile, Tom calls out to Martin again, 'Oi! Fat Boy Slim.'[6]

Finally, unable to tolerate the disruption any longer, Helen, the supply teacher, tells Tom to stop shouting out and he replies defiantly, 'I'm not shoutin' out man; I dunno know why you're gettin' on at me.' Ignoring Tom's defiant behaviour, Helen calls all the children to the carpet to mark the end of the numeracy task before lunchtime play. Everyone on Tom's table, except Kevin, managed to mess about for the whole forty minutes that the task was in progress. Waiting for the children to settle down before she lets them go outside, Helen threatens to cancel PE (physical education) if their behaviour doesn't improve after lunch.

PE

Compared to the physical constraint required for classroom learning, freedom of movement is always a welcome relief to the children. For the disruptive boys in particular it presents an opportunity for them to let off steam. In the playground, getting ready for PE, Helen asks the children to sit quietly and calmly on the bench ready for instruction. She quickly becomes infuriated, however, as boys begin to ignore her and fall to the floor tussling and fighting. Immediately Helen makes all the children line up again and some of them begin to follow her lead to go back upstairs to the classroom. Amidst the widespread rebellion that her decision provokes, some boys begin to fight at the back of the line. Ade pushes another boy who pushes Ade back and they fall on to the ground, which forces Helen to come back and separate them. Finally all of the children manage to line up in single file behind Helen and they walk towards the door that gives entry to the school building and the stairs to the classroom. All, that is, except for Martin: unnoticed, he remains behind, crying out of sight in the sheds. He makes no effort to be seen by anyone, but I have seen him there. Quietly I go back to him and ask cheerfully whether or not he is going to come upstairs with us. He replies, 'No, because I am sick of these boys picking on me and they keep picking on me and I don't know why.' I respond carefully, telling him that I have noticed how they pick on him; I reassure him that when Christine returns things will settle down, but Martin tells me that he just wants to go home and I don't blame him: Tenter Ground is rarely a safe place for Martin to be. Aware that he is in need of protection and trying again to reassure him, I ask if it would make any difference if he could sit next to me in the classroom; readily he agrees to come with me back to the classroom and we make our way back inside.

Imaginative boys

On the way up the stairs Martin stops at the boys' toilets to wash his face so that the boys cannot witness his tears as the evidence of his defeat. We enter the classroom together, sitting down quickly and trying not to draw attention to ourselves. The other children, meanwhile, are working at another literacy task. On the next table two of Martin's friends, Anthony and Adam, are whispering together in animated discussion. Boys, like Adam and Anthony, are often reprimanded for not concentrating on the learning task that has been assigned, but they do not form part of the disruptive boys' peer group. Via drawings and imaginative conversations, boys like this distract each other by conjuring for themselves characters from the fantasy worlds of television and films that they enjoy so much outside school. Even though, compared to the disruptive boys, boys like Anthony and Adam are relatively good, their interactions with each other fall, nevertheless, within the range of distractions that interrupt the flow of concentration which formal learning requires. Frequently the self-constraint that formal learning requires is punctured by the children's overwhelming preoccupation with things to do with their lives outside school: their toys and pastimes, favourite television and cartoon characters, sports teams as well as other concerns like arguments they have had with their siblings or exciting things they are going to do with their parents.

Meanwhile, the other boys working at the same table as Anthony and Adam, who are normally distracted by Gary's antics, have nearly completed the literacy task because Gary is away from school today. Anthony and Adam continue with their drawings, enjoying each other's commentary about them; together they spin a detailed yarn that involves James Bond, famous footballers, Superman and Jackie Chan, but they never get round to actually writing anything down. Anthony and Adam are two boys in a friendship group of three which includes Kevin and sometimes incorporates Martin. In their demeanour and physical disposition they oppose everything that the disruptive boys take to be valuable about a boy. Anthony and his cohort are what I call in my notes 'the imaginative boys'; they are hopeless at football, no good at fighting, brilliant at drawing and often lost in their daydream world of dinosaur and other kinds of creature fantasies. The imaginative boys are not embarrassed to act out their cartoon adventures in the playground and, as a consequence, they are often at the receiving end of taunts and jibes from the disruptive boys about their 'babyish' behaviour.

Surviving this kind of attention from the dominant boys requires that the weaker boys become skilled at strategies of avoidance and submission which keep them out of trouble. All those boys, like the imaginative but relatively weak Anthony, Adam, Kevin, and the overweight and often bullied Martin, are defined, in relation to the disruptive boys' pecking order of violence, as less than boys should be. They are demeaned as being more like babies, girls, 'bitches' and 'gays'. Meanwhile, these physically weaker and more gently disposed kinds of boys, whose peer group coheres around a different kind of participation than that of Gary and his crew, do their best, like girls do also, to just ignore the oppressive and disruptive antics of the violent boys. The imaginative boys cultivate the appearance of physical submission and, taking care not to draw attention to themselves, they learn how to survive at Tenter Ground.

Among his close peer group Martin, then, is the exception; he is overweight and cannot, therefore, diminish his physical presence. He gets picked on all the time and so, fighting back both physically and verbally, he defies the openly aggressive onslaught that is waged continuously against him. In turn, Martin learns how to expertly cause a violent disruption in the classroom, but this never endears him to the other disruptive boys; he is only isolated further when they are disdainful of his antics. At the same time Martin regularly vents his fury on others, even his so-called friends, like Kevin, and he also picks on younger and weaker children in the playground. This kind of behaviour breaks the older boys' code of conduct which protects younger boys and all girls from their violence. Martin is, therefore, further alienated from many different sections of the school population and no one is ever impressed with his violence.

10 February 2000: supply teacher

When I enter the playground one cold February morning, there is a rabble of Year Five/Six boys outside the steps leading inside the school; some of them are wrestling on the ground. Gary is among them but not Tom. I presume that the rest of the class must have gone inside because it is already after 9 o'clock and the playground is otherwise deserted. I approach the boys and ask, 'What's up?' They explain that Christine is away again. I ask them what is going to happen and Nathaniel[7] responds, moaning and groaning, telling me that the class will probably be split up as usual and divided between other teachers' classes.

I manage to persuade the boys to come upstairs with me and on our way up we meet Baqir, who is crying, and being comforted by his best friend Basim. Both of these boys are the sons of first-generation Bangladeshi Muslim families; they have plenty in common with the disruptive boys because of their passion for football and computer games, but just like the imaginative boys, they are rarely involved in instigating any of the skirmishes which preoccupy the disruptive boys. Even though they are valued by the disruptive boys for their goal-keeping skills on the football pitch, Baqir and Basim are, nevertheless, quite often on the receiving end of their team mates' violence. I stop on the stairs to ask Baqir what happened and he tells me that Victor (another boy of West African origin who is a serious contender among the disruptive boys) kicked him in his bad leg. I take Baqir by the arm and lead him up the stairs, distracting him from his tears by talking about his number one passion, which is Manchester United football club.

We reach and enter the classroom where Mara, the head teacher, has just finished taking the register. She is explaining to the children that they are going to have a supply teacher for the day and while they wait for the teacher to arrive she begins the numeracy hour with some mental maths challenges. Mara fires times tables questions at individual children whom she calls by name. As soon as she does so, levels of movement and noise amongst the children begin to increase and the boys start to taunt each other when they get their maths questions wrong. Mara stops the questions to manage the boys' behaviour and when they take no notice of her she responds, shouting loudly, 'Shut up!' All the children find Mara's rudeness hysterical and some of the boys cover their mouths, feigning shock. Mara then gives up on mental maths and tells the children to go to their numeracy tables where the numeracy task for the morning is written on sheets.

Suddenly Tom saunters in, fifteen minutes late; Mara notices him but makes no comment.[8] For the duration of the numeracy task I join table one where Nathaniel, Gary, Daniel, Kevin and Anthony are sitting. Daniel, like Tom and Gary, is a Bermondsey boy; he lives with his father who is devoted to and protective of him. Daniel, like Nathaniel, skirts around the edges of disruption and sometimes finds himself at the centre of trouble as he tries to impress Gary. Making good the opportunity that Christine's absence presents, Gary is intent from the very beginning of the day on having a laugh. He tries to distract Nathaniel who has started working on the numeracy sheet. In a tone indicative of their friendship, he repeatedly calls his name to try and get his attention, 'Nat, Nat,' and Gary begins to jibe Nathaniel, attempting to stop him from working, 'Don't start Nat, you're just copyin' that lot.'

Then, without warning, the supply teacher walks in. He is a small and slight man, about 30 years old, dressed formally in suit trousers with shirt and tie. Every teacher knows that the impression they create on children is formed within the first few minutes, if not seconds, of their entering a classroom and this teacher looks scared. Mara introduces him to the class. His name is Chris; he is Australian. Gary immediately takes up the bait and begins to entertain the boys at his table, 'Kray, did he say Kray? Yeah look at '[h]im. He looks like one of the Kray twins, don't he?[9] Is it Ronnie? Is it Reggie?' Chris ignores Gary and reinforces the numeracy task that has been while Nathaniel makes a vain attempt to manage Gary's behaviour; showing his irritation he mutters, 'Just get on with your work man.'

Soon after Chris arrives, Mara leaves the room. Immediately the levels of noise and movement begin to rise. Ade gets out of his seat and comes over to Gary's table. Gary says to him, 'Chris is coming; you scared in'it?' Mark then joins them and begins to jibe Nathaniel, 'Nat, you better give me the rubber, man.' When they manage to get the rubber away from Gary, Ade and Mark go back to their table. Gary gets up and follows them, saying to Ade, 'Give me the rubber you fat head.' Ade playfully refuses. Gary goes on taunting Ade in a teasing tone, 'Just give me the rubber before I bang your face in.' Changing tack, Gary adopts the Jamaican accent that he has been trying to perfect, 'Hey! Rasta!' Mark calls across the class to Nathaniel, taunting him, adopting a mock fighting posture, 'Nat, Nat, just watch out right!' Kevin responds sarcastically, doubting Mark's credibility, 'Oh right Mark!' and Daniel joins in the tease, 'Nat, he's gonna stab ya.' Daniel then turns on Kevin – one of the imaginative boys – who has taken the risk of making his presence felt and asks him accusingly, 'Do you believe in Santa Claus?' Kevin ignores him. Daniel then attempts to get Gary's attention out of having teased Kevin, 'Gary, I just asked Kevin if he believes in Santa Claus and he just stared back at me.' Gary responds, 'Yeah course he does, that's why he puts his milk out and prays, "Please Santa".'

Gary continues to taunt Ade, posturing and making mock fight challenges. Then he turns to Kevin and says disdainfully, 'Get a life.' Kevin retaliates quietly, under his breath, 'I've got a life' and he continues to focus on his work, keeping his head down. Ade approaches Gary's table again, 'Give me the rubber!' Gary replies, teasing Ade still, 'Go away dog! Don't start boy!' Ade walks away, swearing under his breath. Gary flicks the numeracy task paper and declares, 'I'm not doing it anymore.' Daniel leans back on his chair and Gary turns on Anthony, 'You're a baby man, you even cuss babyish.' He then turns to Nathaniel trying to provoke him and says, 'Anthony said you know a slut and it's your mum.' But at that moment Gary and Daniel are suddenly distracted by Martin who is making loud sheep noises on the other side of the classroom. Astounded, Gary joins in even more loudly and he and Daniel collapse into giggles. Nathaniel, meanwhile, is still trying to concentrate on his work. Gary picks up some pencils and starts to throw them across the room at other boys. Kevin, sensing the ensuing chaos, says calmly, 'Where's that man, Chris?' and Anthony replies, 'Probably being beaten up by Winston.'[10] Gary states matter of factly, 'Ronnie Kray? He's a legend,' and then resumes throwing pencils across the classroom, which finally descends into chaos.

Victor, who is good at gymnastics, is doing a handstand in the book corner. Anthony and Kevin get up and leave the table; trying to avoid the trouble they attempt to join a different table, but Rochelle sends them back. Suddenly, Obi, who is the latest contender in the disruptive boys' peer group and most recent addition to the class from Nigeria, is up out of his seat and fighting with Victor. Obi looks more like a boy of 13 or 14 years old rather than 10 or nearly 11 and he is physically intimidating; violently he pushes, shoves and attempts to punch Victor, and as they tussle, they bump into other children, tables and chairs, causing mayhem around them as they fall fighting to the floor. Rochelle attempts to separate them but can't manage it; Chris intervenes and manages to get the boys to sit down. Kevin, resolute now in his need for self-protection, retreats to the book corner and sits alone reading. Astonishingly, Nathaniel is still trying to complete the numeracy task.

Meanwhile, the tension of Gary and Ade's slowly developing and teasing exchange suddenly erupts into another full-scale fight. Hysterical, Daniel picks up his chair and raises it threateningly over his head. The noise of the children's shouting attracts Fatema from the neighbouring classroom. Rochelle tells her, 'All hell is breaking loose in here.' Fatema tries without success to calm the class down. She raises her voice in angry tones, trying to shame the children into behaving properly. Attempting to make them feel guilty, she reprimands individual children and threatens them with exclusion from the class. Noise and movement subside while they listen to her tirade and as soon as she leaves the room it explodes again. Finally, a teacher from another class arrives to reassure Chris that it is time for assembly and he assists him in getting the children out of the class into the assembly hall and from there to outside play.

Literacy

After play time, during literacy hour, a similar chaos ensues: Gary gets up, and, without permission, leaves the classroom. He climbs up on the gym equipment which is stacked outside the classroom and he bangs on the windows at the top so that everyone can see him through the glass. Ade, Winston and some other boys immediately run out to join him. Chris sends someone to get Mara. Gary and the other boys run off to hide somewhere in the school and Mara comes back into the classroom. She reprimands the children about their behaviour and threatens to tell their parents; she then tells the boys that football club has been cancelled because of their misbehaviour. Mara explains to the other children that Gary is going to be sent home and she leaves the class again. Tom starts up a chant, 'We want Christine. We want Christine,' and several children join in with him. Rochelle confronts Tom about his behaviour, but she is now at her wit's end. She tells Obi to be quiet and in exasperation and close to tears, she tells Tom and the other children on his table that there is no point in her telling them how to behave when this is what they get up to as soon as Christine is gone. She reminds them that they've got SATs in a few months' time. Rochelle turns to me then and tells me that she feels like walking out of the class; she is outraged because the supply teacher gets paid £100 a day, is completely hopeless and still relies on her to try and get the class under control.

Who rules the school?

During lunch break in the staffroom, Alison, the Year Three teacher (in a class of children aged 7 to 8), sits despondently in her chair moaning to another teacher and to Mara that it is impossible for her to teach her class because she spends 20 per cent of her time teaching and 80 per cent dealing with behavioural problems. She says that the children do not respond to any of her strategies for reinforcement of positive behaviour and she just doesn't know what else to do. Mara looks at her glumly and offers no encouragement. Eileen, the deputy, comes in, listens to Alison's complaints and offers nothing in the way of either solace or practical suggestions of support. Alison remains in her chair looking increasingly distressed and uncomfortable.

Finally, because no one else among the staff speaks, Chris, the supply teacher, tries to address the issue; he says that because he is a supply teacher he is used to this level of disruption in classrooms and he explains that even though this morning was a nightmare he has taught in schools in Hackney that are far worse. He says, matter of factly, 'Being a supply teacher, you are basically a zoo-keeper.' Steve, the SENCO manager, responds, saying that he thinks the problem in the school is the dominance amongst the boys of 'alpha males'. Interesting about these remarks is the way that when formal learning breaks down and the boys' contention for control of the classroom is successful, boys are likened to apes and wild animals. It is impossible for teachers to conceive of the idea that normal human children could behave like this; disruptive boys must be other than human – more like animals. The idea that children are capable of struggling for and competing violently for prestige and influence in an environment that is supposed to be controlled by adults, is both frightening and demoralising for teachers. Such disruption threatens the very idea of what it means to be a child and is subversive of every value that education holds up to children. Whilst it is telling, Chris's desperate analogy between schools and zoos does nothing to reassure Alison, and she walks out of the staffroom, unsupported.

No wonder then, when the boys discuss amongst themselves who is the ruler of the school, Obi dismisses Mara outright. I listen to them arguing about which of them rules the school and Gary tries to dismiss Obi's desire to be a contender for leadership by saying, 'You're tough Obi, but you haven't really got any friends.' Being the ruler is not just about being the toughest boy; it is about using toughness as one means to integrate a group of boys within a hierarchy of fraternity. That is why so much good-humoured teasing precedes the fighting and why the fighting might possibly be more about a display of bravado than it is about actual bodily harm. The boys make trouble and, in so doing, they fight their friendship into existence; it is fun – they enjoy it. When I ask Obi why he keeps picking on other boys in the classroom, he turns to me and smiles; in his thick Nigerian accent he explains, 'It's sweet for me – like honey.'

In the face of Gary's dominance, Tom's antics recede into the background of classroom disruption. When Gary is at school and Christine is away it is Gary who leads the escalating cycle of exchanges between the boys that leads to the intimidation of weaker boys and fights amongst the bravest and strongest. Via these exchanges the disruptive boys' peer group is constituted and a particular kind of participation is established as valuable amongst them. He who dares wins and Gary's daring supersedes that of other boys. Gary opposes and challenges the tranquil participation that being a child in a classroom implies and, in Christine's absence, he destroys the authority of Mara, Rochelle, Fatema, Kofi and Chris. On this day at least, Gary rules the school.

Disrupted mothers

Over the next few months Gary and Tom fall in and out of friendship and Anne despairs of Gary's parents who, she says, allow him too much freedom to do as he pleases. She worries that Gary is leading Tom into trouble. By the end of the school year Gary has to report once a week to the local police station because he has been in trouble on the street once too often. No stranger to trouble herself, however, Anne begins to share with me some of the problems that she is facing. I come to understand, then, why she clings so desperately to the possibility of stability which Pete presents to her: he is a 'decent' man who wants nothing more than to be able to earn a living and have a peaceful home life, but Anne struggles to 'mend her ways'. Having taken cocaine in the past, Anne reveals to me that she had decided, during the past year, to become a small-time supplier to friends just as a way to make a bit of extra money to buy nice things for the kids. She was, she says, sick of not being able to get them what they wanted; it had been Tom's birthday coming and she had wanted to get him a new bike.

Only selling drugs while Pete was at work and when the children were at school, Anne had kept her plans and her dealings secret from the family. She had, however, been unable to resist sharing again the pleasure of using the drug with the friends to whom she was supplying it. Unable to afford the cost of the cocaine she was using herself, Anne had soon got into debt to the supplier and couldn't repay him. Calling in a debt he knew she couldn't afford, the supplier had demanded instead that Anne bring in a shipment of drugs from Amsterdam. Desperate and scared, Anne had then been forced to tell Pete what she had done and, in horror and desperation himself, because he had no spare money of his own with which to repay the debt, Pete had then given Anne a final warning. He would help her bring in the shipment to repay the debt on condition that she 'go straight', come off the drugs, stop drinking and start to 'behave herself' for the sake of the family. Terrified about her predicament, and with no alternative, Anne had agreed.

Thinking that their troubles were over, Anne and Pete naively brought the shipment in. Little did they know that the supplier had 'grassed' (informed the authorities) on Anne to customs so that he could create a diversion and use it to bring in a much bigger shipment. Pete and Anne were arrested and Pete did what he had promised to do which was 'take the rap' (take the blame) for Anne if they got caught. This meant that Pete was waiting, even as he had been listening to me reading to Tom on that Saturday morning, to hear about a date for his prison sentence. No wonder he had been watching Tom read with such a sense of hope and admiration; he wanted better things for Tom than he had to face up to himself.

Anne explains to me that because it was Pete's first ever criminal offence and the drug in question was marijuana and not heroin, she was hoping for leniency and no more than eighteen months inside for him. And when Pete did eventually go to prison, to 'do his time' (serve his sentence), Anne began to spend every weekend with the children at her parents' house in Kent; it became impossible, therefore, for me to read with Tom anymore. Six months later, however, I bump into Anne in the road near Tenter Ground and she has a letter in her hand. As soon as she sees me she bursts into floods of tears. 'What is it?' I ask anxiously. 'What is the matter Anne?' Tearfully she explains that she is on her way to post a letter to Pete telling him that she can't take him back when he comes out of prison. She is distraught because she knows that it isn't right: Pete is doing time for her and she can't bring herself to stand by him. Anne struggles, through her tears, to explain to me that the woman Pete is trying to encourage her to be isn't the person that she is and she can't pretend to him anymore that she is going to change. I try to comfort her as best I can and, feeling helpless, I ask after Tom and Mary.

After this day I never see Anne again. A year later I am told that when Pete came out of prison Anne had tried to take him back, but it hadn't worked out. Consequently, on Mother's Day, Pete, who, it was said, couldn't live without Anne, had hung himself in the flat. Anne came home and found him there. Punished beyond measure, she had then taken the children out of school and moved out of Bermondsey to live again under her parents' care in Kent. Tom's story ends tragically then, and many people will say that disrupted and irresponsible mothers are obviously the cause of their children's misbehaviour at school. But I would persist with my argument and suggest that disrupted mothers are still only part of the story. Despite the fact that all of the most disruptive boys in Year Five/Six have mothers with disrupted lives, many of the girls in the class, who face similar difficulties at home, don't misbehave and don't find themselves in trouble at school in the same way. Tom's sister Mary, you remember, is as good as gold. What the most disruptive boys do share in common, however, is an unusual degree of independence, what Christine describes as an 'unhealthy' level of independence. Some of them, by the age of 11, are reaching for manhood already: they know how to fend for themselves, often on the street, in a way that girls rarely have to because girls with that much responsibility are close to home, either keeping their mothers company or looking after the home and younger siblings. Focusing only on the disruption in the boys' family lives ignores the developing relationship between gender and prestige-seeking behaviour that those boys, like Tom, must accommodate to in common households, on mean streets and in sink schools as they struggle to make sense of their developing masculinity. Teachers, who cannot conceive of children, and especially boys, as aggressive and intimidating prestige-seekers, ignore the violent dynamic of peer group formation amongst these boys at their peril. Feeling sorry for their family circumstances is enough to enable a teacher to persevere in the most stressful classroom situations, but it is not enough to get the problem that disruptive boys pose under control.

Understanding trouble-making and violence as forms of social good

The problem at Tenter Ground then, is twofold: if these disruptive boys have a genuine special educational need, as teachers and other staff suggest that they do, then it is a travesty that the will and the funding are not available at Tenter Ground for them to get statements of that need prepared. Without those statements no relevant support can be put in place before the boys leave primary for secondary school where matters will only get worse. If, on the other hand, as I suggest, the problem of disruptive boys is a social one, to do with peer group formation in a school where adult authority is weak and disruptive boys are allowed to rule, then the focus alters. We need to understand how it is that at school, particular kinds of boys find the opportunity, which they may not get at home, but that they may have become accustomed to on the street, to compete for power and influence.

In failing schools, boys like this have the opportunity to establish amongst themselves a form of participation that is completely at odds with what teachers require of them and therein lies the source of their subversive and charismatic power. All the other children, and especially other boys, have to learn how to accommodate themselves to this disruptive influence in one way or another and in so far as their behaviour goes unchecked the disruptive boys dominate. Rather than making their behaviour seem pathological, my proposal is for research that might help us begin to understand how it is that young boys in certain kinds of social situations, like on the street and in failing schools, can come to structure their relations with one another in such a way that troublesome, violent and intimidating behaviour becomes a social good. Only in this way will we be able to understand how, at schools like Tenter Ground, boys are inadvertently given the opportunity to cultivate an ethical disposition which is embodied as an oppositional, surly, aggressive and intimidating stance that is entirely contrary to what didactic practice intends to establish for children.

At school it is easy to see how thrilling to them and efficacious is the competition for boys to violently seek prestige in relation to peers, to antagonise teachers and eventually get used to the idea that they are going to disappoint their parents. It is true to say that as boys like Tom feel the pressure of adult opprobrium they begin to suffer because, despite their best intentions, they become caught in the cycle of turn-taking pranks and revenge-seeking scuffles which define not only their daring and their reputation, but also their friendship with one another. To strongly resist the form of participation that disruptive boys demand is to risk losing their friendship and, therefore, their protection. Only rarely does a boy find the courage to dare to get on with his work and resist another's idea of what constitutes an appropriate style of subversive masculinity for boys. The question then is: what kind of boy can a boy, like Nathaniel, become if he starts to do well at school?

Because the principal dynamic of group formation amongst the disruptive boys is aggressive competition, there is little impression, from the outside, of solidarity amongst them.[11] What friendship there is between the boys at school has, as its background, a tension born of the high adrenalin, antagonistic and potentially intimidating physical exchange. What arises is a competitive system of disruption, without formal or written rules, which new boys discover in the classroom and that they must choose to either resist or participate in. If they feel themselves to be contenders, they declare, via their ability to fight back effectively, their eligibility to be incorporated into a peer group which is established on the basis of often violent acts of subversion. Success in this inevitably implies the destruction of a boy's chances of doing well at school and quite often jeopardises the opportunities that being at school presents to his better-behaved peers. In the end, however, a disruptive boy's resistance has no effect on the value system that education establishes for children because, treated as an individual, the most disruptive boy is usually excluded from school and often claimed by the street. And so, for as long as failing schools are protected from proper scrutiny and disruptive boys are treated as individuals with emotional and behavioural difficulties, the basis of the formation of their peer groups is neglected as a social phenomenon, and the cycle goes on. It is a bit like *Lord of the Flies,* only without the desert island, and plenty of adults are looking on in vain as, everywhere, danger looms.

In the next part of the book I consider Gary's case study more closely. I describe the process of social transformation through which it becomes possible for me to get to know the disruptive boys better and, in so doing, I show in more detail, (a) how the various boys' peer groups are formed in contradistinction to each other and (b) how it is possible to transpose the aggressive conflict which rages amongst them into more constructive forms of competition. I move away from an analysis of verbal exchanges in the classroom to consider the medium of object exchange and object-specific physical competencies outside the conventional learning environment. Demonstrating how such exchanges facilitate the creation and transformation of value, I elaborate further upon the theory of participative learning. The ethnography describes the Pokemon phenomenon and leads, via new case studies of children's learning outside school, to an analysis of the inseparable relationship between masculinity and territoriality.

Part III
Creating and Transforming Value

Figure 2   Pikachu. ©2005 Pokemon/Nintendo TM and ®Nintendo

8
Pokemon and Peers

Gary is not an easy boy to get to know. He, like many of the boys, is sulky, reticent and reluctant to be in the classroom where application to school work is expected. The boys' reluctance raises the problem of my own participation. I am careful not to involve myself in the classroom in a way that renders me like a teacher or her assistant and yet I am obviously not a child either. So what do the children make of my presence? For the first three months I am largely an adult person who observes and makes notes. I do not challenge bad behaviour or tell on children to the teacher and it is easy, therefore, for the children to ignore me if they choose to do so. In particular, I struggle to find a legitimate periphery from which to get to know the disruptive boys better. For obvious reasons I cannot participate in the pecking order of disruption, which dominates social relations in the classroom, and I cannot play football, which is the boys' main preoccupation in the playground.[1] I am, therefore, a marginal and largely irrelevant person to them. Gary is particularly surly: he resists any attempts on my part to get to know him: I smile at him, he ignores me; I greet him, he ignores me; I am insignificant to him and he is intimidating to me. All of this changes, however, on a single day in December. Just before the children break up from school for the Christmas holidays, my status in the classroom transforms dramatically.

16 December 1999: Pikachu

The children have endured a week of inspections in which they have been expected to be on their best behaviour. Christine is proud of them because they have tried really hard and she takes this effort as a sign of their regard for her; the children knew that it was important to Christine that they behave well and work hard during the inspection. She laments that the inspector didn't get to see any personality in the children, but at least disruption was minimised, so Christine is pleased. The good news is that the school hasn't been demoted from 'serious weaknesses' to 'special measures', but it remains a school with serious problems and the stress that an inspection creates has taken its toll. As a reward for good behaviour Christine suspends formal learning for the whole day and declares that the children are first going to do fun tasks followed by free time in which they can choose what they want to do. The children are excited and in jubilant mood.

In the morning the children begin by helping to make the backdrop for the infant classes' Christmas nativity; they work at their numeracy tables in small groups. I join table one where Gary, Anthony, Kevin, Nathaniel and Daniel are sitting. The task is to draw stars on card and to cut out the best one to make a stencil. This stencil is then to be used to make lots of stars from silver paper. The boys are dissatisfied with the wonky stars they have drawn and I show them how to make more uniform ones using two regular triangles. Anthony, who is the most competent artist at the table, is not interested in my assistance since he is taking great pleasure in making his stars as irregular as possible; their lack of uniformity delights him. Gary, seeing the stars that Daniel and Nathaniel have managed to make with the stencil I made for them, reluctantly accepts a stencil from me for himself and all of us begin to make silver stars together.

Every now and again I write a couple of notes down on my pad. Suddenly Gary turns to me and, engaging me for the first time, asks inquisitively, 'D'you 'ave to write everythin' that we do down?' and I respond, 'No, I just try to write down as much as possible that I think is interesting about the way that children learn.' He then asks me if I am going to be in the classroom with them until they leave for secondary school and I tell him that I am. Suddenly animated, he asks, 'Ain't it that Pilgrim's[2] is a rubbish school?' I feign ignorance, pretending to know nothing about the school so that I can find out what their impressions of it are. Gary looks at Nathaniel and teases him, taunting him about Pilgrim's because he knows that it is one of the secondary schools which Nathaniel has applied to.[3] I ask Gary which secondary schools he is applying to and he replies abruptly, 'I dunno, I ain't even filled in a secondary school transfer form yet.' I ask why that is and he says, "Cos of me mum, I've asked my dad but he just ...' and he mimics the way his dad mumbles into his chest. Looking dejected, Gary gives up trying to explain and we continue with our stars.

Later, Gary points to my notes and says to Nathaniel, as if he is feeling left out, 'She never writes anythin' 'bout me in that book.' I turn the book towards him and show him where his name is: 'Look, your name is written down there more than anyone.' Seeing that it is true, Gary asks, 'Why?' and I tease him saying, 'Because you do the most talking, that's why.' Gary smirks and concentrates on his stars again, happily singing the lyrics to the latest chart topping songs as he works. Anthony works quietly on his own, every now and again directing conversation towards Kevin. During the star-making activity, as with any task in the classroom, there is constant comparison between the boys of how each of them is coping with the task and a running commentary on the various conversational exchanges that take place between them. Nathaniel, who is pleased with the stars he is making, addresses me for the first time in three months by my first name. I am surprised to hear my name after having been ignored by the boys for so long and I am pleased that the relaxation of formal learning has allowed the terms of engagement between myself and the boys to shift, if only slightly. Gary, noticing these signs of developing familiarity, looks up from the star he is making and scrutinises me, staring closely. I ignore him, continue making stars and wonder whether he is feeling encouraged or threatened by these signs of budding intimacy between himself, other children and me.

As we work, Kevin and Anthony begin talking about Pokemon. Kevin brings out of his pocket a small poster with about thirty cartoon characters that I have never seen before, drawn on one side. On the other side a single character takes up the whole page. This, they tell me excitedly, is Pikachu. I ask the boys who these characters are and they introduce me to Pokemon. These are creatures they have become familiar with through watching television cartoon programmes on Friday afternoons and Saturday mornings.[4] Abruptly, Gary interrupts, changing the subject and attempting to engage me again on his terms; he asks, ''[H]ave you got a car?' I let him know that I have and he asks me what kind. 'A Mercedes',[5] I tell him and he's impressed, 'Rah [wow],' he says and this sparks off a conversation amongst the boys about what cars they like and what cars their dads have got. Anthony, bringing the conversation back to himself again, then tells Kevin about his birthday, which was the day before and he lists some of the things he received as gifts. He speaks proudly about the ten-pound note he was given and tells Kevin that he's going to buy two Pokemon toys with it. He lifts up his school shirt to show Kevin his Darth Maul[6] Star Wars T-shirt that he is wearing underneath his uniform. Kevin admires it and Anthony goes on to talk about the Action Man[7] things he received. Daniel intervenes then, saying disparagingly, 'Hello, which planet d'you come from if you still like Action

Man?' Gary joins in and starts teasing Anthony about how childish he is because he is also still 'into dinosaurs'.

Noticing this differentiation, that Gary and Daniel emphasise, between the kind of things Anthony is passionate about and the things they like to discuss, such as cars, I come to Anthony's aid. Distancing myself from Gary's disparaging remarks, I ask Anthony if he has been watching the *Walking with Dinosaurs* series on television and he has, so we talk about the awesome sea dinosaur that it features. Losing interest and probably disgruntled because I resisted the humiliation of Anthony that he and Daniel were trying to effect, Gary gets up and leaves the table. He joins some other boys who are now playing board games in the book corner.

Having engaged the boys for the first time about things that are nothing to do with school work, I realise that the problem I face in the classroom is one of how to interact with Gary, as one among the more dominant boys in the class, without having to participate in what he does to gain influence which, in part, involves intimidating and antagonising other apparently weaker boys, like Anthony. Some boys, like Daniel, for example, face the same difficulty and, in trying to impress Gary, they often participate in intimidating and antagonising behaviour which then gets them into a lot of trouble. Witnessing the constant challenges Gary makes to boys whom he perceives to be either a threat to his dominance or to be weaker and more childish than he is, I resist the temptation to protect the weak child and to antagonise the bully back. This is the route that many members of staff have taken with Gary but I am not here in the school to discipline children, but rather to understand how social relations between them are formed in the classroom and school. Of course I am continuously pushed against my own ideas of what constitutes acceptable behaviour in children and it is difficult to observe disruptive boys without becoming infuriated. I note the ways in which Gary attempts, on a daily basis, to wield his influence in the classroom and also how other children, like Anthony for example, skilfully resist this influence. What emerges is a constant state of flux: the various peer groups are seen to be in a constant process of formation and transformation, from moment to moment and over time. The problem for me is how to participate in these complex relations in a way that takes me beyond the more passive observations of the past three months.

As Christine approaches our table Daniel tries to tell on Gary because he abandoned the task and went to play games. Daniel does not dare, as Gary does, to do as he pleases in class, so he is disgruntled. Coming to Gary's defence, Christine tells Daniel that Gary probably got bored with making stars. She instructs them all to finish the star they're making and then to choose what they want to do. Daniel quickly finishes his star and then goes to join Gary and the other boys in the book corner. Kevin and Anthony ask Christine if they can stay at the table to do some drawing, and when she agrees, I stay with them. Martin joins us and sits next to Kevin. I decide to do some drawing too. I ask Kevin if I can borrow his Pokemon poster. He agrees happily and, using a black felt tip pen on A4 white paper, I start to copy Pikachu. After a few seconds I realise that Anthony is staring at me. Focusing intently and with complete surprise on my drawing, which is an almost exact replica of Pikachu, Anthony pulls Kevin by the arm and tells him to look at what I am doing. Within seconds all the boys have been alerted to my achievement. Suddenly the table is crowded with boys who are praising my drawing, 'That's bad man [excellent].'[8] 'Rah man, that's bad,' 'She's a good drawer man,' 'Can you do one for me?' 'Can you do one for me?'

Realising, with amazement, what a stir I have caused with my Pikachu drawing I stay calm, as if it is nothing, and say, 'This one is for Kevin, but I could photocopy it for other people.' Suddenly and without warning the Pikachu drawing is hot property, everyone wants a copy, and, for the first time, this means that I am the focus of the boys' attention. When Anthony sees the reaction from all the boys he teases Daniel, 'I thought you said Pokemon was borin' and now you're carryin' on like they're bad.' Unwittingly, and to Anthony's surprise, I have created something that is of specific significance to all the boys, not just to Kevin and Anthony's imaginative and creative friends; I am as surprised as Anthony is by the immediacy of the social effect my creation has.

Subjects and objects: popularity and friendship

Astounding about this moment is how much it reveals theoretically: objects are obviously crucial to the way that social relations among children are both formed and transformed.[9] Because of what I demonstrate that I can do and what I reveal that I am able to produce – this object, a drawing of Pikachu, and a specific form of physical competence, being good at drawing, that matters to the boys – I become for them, in a single transforming instant, a person of significance. This is not a note in my fieldwork diary, about which they couldn't care less; this is a drawing of Pikachu about which they care a great deal.

I understand, then, how the objects which children attend to (as well as the physical competency that relating to the object requires), become the bridges over and through which they encounter and make sense of each other in particular ways. This means that if we are to understand children's social relations we have to find out, in any situation, which specific objects and practices mediate peer group formation. It is an understanding of the specificity of those objects and practices that gives us the key not only to discovering what the significance of peer group relations is to children, but also what the potential is for us to transform these relations. Particularly interesting about this observation is the analysis that it makes possible of how, in the process of learning how to participate appropriately, children are simultaneously coming to appreciate how the value of subjects and objects becomes mutually specified, created and transformed, in social practice, over time.

I have found, for example, quite by accident, a way to participate that makes a difference to the boys and which makes me, therefore, instantaneously a person of value and, thereby, a person worthy of incorporation into the various peer groups. Suddenly the boys are all calling my name, asking each other if I am an artist, and dominant boys, who up until now have been physically removed and reluctant to engage me, push closer. They shove other boys out of the way so they can sit next to me at the table and watch me draw. Even Mark, Ade's sidekick, who never speaks to me and is often silent and withdrawn in the classroom, asks me quietly and politely if I will make a copy of the drawing for him. I experience directly then, what I have already begun to appreciate from observation alone: popularity and indeed friendship among children is predicated on a shared and finely differentiated physical mastery towards objects of specific significance. It is children's bodily competence in relation to specific objects in certain environments that makes the difference between them.

In the playground, for example, Gary and the other disruptive boys are differentiated from the girls and imaginative boys by their preoccupation with and physical competence in relation to the game of football. To be incorporated into this game a boy first has to know what form of participation is required. It is in relation to that one specific object – the football – and via the particular physical competence that controlling a football requires, that a boy begins to build his relationships with other boys in the team. Without these skills, a boy is, on the football pitch, a non-entity and he will be treated with derision. It matters not whether a boy has just arrived from Nigeria, Jamaica or Bangladesh, whether or not he can even speak English is irrelevant to the boys; if he can play ball a boy can earn respect among his peers. The beauty of this simple example of football, in which language is relatively unimportant, is that it helps us to understand how the social structure of the boys' peer groups is formed: it emerges out of the ongoing and dynamic processes of participation in and through which the boys are continuously making sense, in practice, of their relations with each other.

On the pitch, during the game and in the boys' analysis of the game thereafter, there is a continuous comparison amongst the boys about their differing ball skills. Each boy competes to be as good as the best of his peers. The structuring dynamic is, therefore, one of competitive equality. This often leads to fights amongst the boys when conflict arises over the interpretation of whose fault it was that a game was won or lost on either side and arguments develop about who was the player of the match. The likelihood of fights erupting leads to another comparison of physical competence among the boys relative to each one's ability to hold his own in a fight. The most popular boys can both play football skilfully and stick up for themselves when under attack. With respect to football, then, the disruptive boys' peer group depends, for its integrative force, on the embodied accommodation which each boy must learn to make to these highly specific kinds of participation that have nothing whatsoever to do with school work.

What it is possible for the boys to do at playtime in the playground may not be considered appropriate in the classroom and so, from one situation to another, the boys are constantly working out amongst themselves, and in relation to adult expectations, what counts as valued participation. It is the same in all the children's peer groups, except that in each group the form of participation varies. It is important for us to understand, therefore, that against the background of what classroom participation requires of children, children are, all the time, trying to make sense of each other on their own terms. It is as if they exist in parallel worlds: children are constantly making sense of what adults require of them in various situations but they are always also preoccupied with trying to accommodate to what they expect of each other. In many situations it is clear that adults have no idea of just how vast the discrepancy is between what they expect of children and what children require of each other.

The emotional significance of social transformation

Startled by the dramatic change in my popularity, I promise the boys that I will try to photocopy the drawing at lunchtime. I make my way to Eileen's office to ask for permission to use the photocopier, but I am wary because I worry that she might refuse my request since it has nothing to do with school work. Keenly aware that the seal, which formal learning places on children's interests outside school, is now punctured, I worry that it will be me now who is perceived by the teachers as being disruptive.

Outside the office I find a gaggle of boys waiting for me. Persistent and not to be put off, they ask if I have copied the picture yet. I tell them that I haven't and I knock on Eileen's door. As I go in, Ade, as if he has picked up on my reticence, follows to check and make sure that I won't let him down. I explain to Eileen that we have done some Pokemon drawings and ask her if she would mind if we photocopied them. She notices the boys crowding eagerly round the open door, smiles and gladly agrees. At her favourable response the boys rush into the office and crowd around the photocopier. I make twenty-four copies, one for each child in the class, and I thank Eileen.

Filled with excitement now, the boys and I rush back to the classroom together and I feel, for the first time, the thrill of the camaraderie that competitive access to a difficult peer group grants me. I understand then, that the real reward of the social process of learning how to participate effectively, in any situation, is the change in one's feelings as one's sense of value in relation to others transforms. Learning always has, therefore, emotional implications. This means that the failure of the disruptive boys to learn successfully in the classroom might be more to do with their reaction against the way that formal learning makes them feel than it is to do with learning difficulties *per se*. If formal learning doesn't make them feel good, we need to ask: why not and what, if anything, can we do about it?

Reaching the classroom and having to settle down again for the register, I begin to appreciate how irksome is the restraint that classroom participation places on other kinds of interaction between children. Exchanging excited glances and gestures, the boys are eager to get their photocopies and find it difficult to concentrate on afternoon registration. Having taken the register and sensing the excitement, Christine allows us to go on drawing in the classroom. Boys rush to sit next to me at the table and I give out photocopies to the sea of hands; the girls, seeing that something is being given out, become interested for the first time and take their copies gladly.

Immediately the boys differentiate between the value of the original drawing and the photocopies. The original becomes the hottest property and I give it to Kevin because he let me copy his poster. Christine asks us if we would mind moving to the library (adjacent to the classroom) because she needs to get some children that she can trust to continue to work quietly, in the classroom, on the large backdrops for the nativity. She leaves Rochelle in charge and joins me to supervise the disruptive boys in the library. She is amazed, however, to see how focused the boys are on colouring-in the Pikachu drawing and quietly she asks if I would mind her leaving me to get on with it while she goes back to the class-room. Astonished myself by the change in the boys' behaviour, I agree to be responsible for them for the first time.

As we colour Pikachu in, Ade gets frustrated because he looks at my colouring-in and can't make his look the same. My Pikachu is dark yellow, with strong vibrant colour and even tone; his is pale, uneven and dull. He moans and is despondent. I show him then how to affect the tone by pressing harder or lighter with the coloured pencil and advise him to work on small areas at a time. He applies himself, manages to make progress and is momentarily pleased, but he is also impatient; he wants immedi-ate results and makes incessant demands of me, even if I am in the mid-dle of helping someone else. The other boys ignore Ade and continue to concentrate on their own colouring-in. The competition amongst them to achieve something and to complete a task happily rather than trying to disrupt it or to endeavour sulkily not to have to engage with it makes a welcome change. The boys' smiling happy faces make all the difference. Significant about this moment is the realisation in me that these boys are indeed capable of cheerful, still and quiet concentration on a task, but for it to be enjoyable it has to be a task that is meaningful to them. The question I then start to ask myself is: why are formal-learning-type tasks so meaningless to the boys?

Gary's colouring-in is the best; it is neat, vibrant and carefully done so he is pleased with himself; he begins to show off, but not without also encouraging the others.[10] As we colour in, concentrating happily, I begin to realise what Christine knows already, which is that to judge the boys on the basis of their brooding, sulky dispositions in the classroom would be to misrepresent them. Their personalities, suppressed during formal learning in order to meet the requirements of classroom participation, emerge all of a sudden, not gradually but in a single transforming moment of significance. Most important about the change in the boys is the dif-ference in their emotional state and, therefore, their bodily disposition: the surliness is gone. This is not numeracy or literacy which appear to be abstract and, therefore, tiresome skills for the boys to have to learn. Pokemon means something to them and they are happy to learn from me how to draw, colour in and bring to life for themselves charac-ters from the world with which they are passionately engaged outside school. Nathaniel takes photocopies for Victor who is off school today and beaming at me, he says, 'Victor's not gonna believe it when '[h]e comes back.'

Significant about the Pikachu moment then, is that it marks the point at which the bind of formal learning is removed in order to allow the terms of participation, for me and the boys, to change dramatically and, in this case, quite by accident. The problem, however, as Christine is all too well aware, is that a classroom teacher doesn't have time to devote to trying to reach out to the disruptive boys and also to do what she or he is getting paid to do, which is to deliver a curriculum to a classroom of thirty children. Ideally, the disruptive boys should, Christine suggests, be removed from the classroom and taught within the school in a separate classroom, where there would be, at most, a one-to-six adult-to-child ratio with a specialist teacher focusing not on curriculum delivery, but on the more complicated but necessary task of learning how to build relationships with these boys. After this, at the point at which the boys have made the necessary accommodation to what it means to relate to a teacher at school and to begin to understand something about the form of learning that classroom participation requires of them, the boys should then be gradually reintegrated back into mainstream classes. Christine emphasises how much she would relish such a task, but she knows that there are no resources in the school for this kind of support. Without it, however, she knows that boys like Gary and Tom are doomed to fail and, in the process, they will continue to jeopardise other children's learning and test their teachers' patience to and beyond the limits.

Commonality and conflict

After Christmas the emphasis on formal learning is firmly established again. With the prospect of SATs tests looming Christine is determined to deliver as much of the curriculum as she can manage. Feeling the pressure now, all the Year Six children voluntarily attend the booster club after school that she and Eileen organise to give them extra assistance. During the usual school day, however, the disruptive behaviour of particular boys continues to thwart Christine's best intentions. Without the freedom to choose what we do, and with the constraints of task-based work in place again, my participation in the classroom reverts to a balancing act between observation and assistance as children who now know me better are eager for me to help them with their school work.

   The only free time that I now have to continue with Pokemon drawings is in the playground where I can bring out my pad in the shelter of the open shed. Each day a large gathering of about thirty children of all ages crowds round to watch me draw. Classroom assistants, who supervise playtime, look on curiously. Disruptive boys, who are preoccupied, as usual, with playing football,[11] send emissaries over every now and again to find out which Pokemon character I am drawing. If it is a Pokemon that they are particularly interested in, they then all rush over together, pushing and shoving through the crowd to have a look and heap praise upon me. In this way I begin to understand which Pokemon character it is that the boys value above others: the aggressive fighting potential of individual Pokemon is what makes a difference to them because, just like the boys, Pokemon are fighting creatures permanently poised to do battle.

In return for my gifts of Pokemon drawings, I am increasingly incorporated into the children's various peer groups and have the opportunity, therefore, to learn more about the differences between them. Gary, for example, makes a point of differentiating his interest in my Pokemon drawings from what he sees as Anthony and Anthony's friends' childish obsession with Pokemon in general. I observe then, how similarities between children within one friendship group are emphasised in contrast to the various preoccupations of other kinds of children in different groups. Whilst Gary emphasises toughness, adult computer game competence and knowledge of other, specifically adult-like and male concerns in his peer group, he excludes babyish, child-like, weak, soft, girl-like, cartoon- and dinosaur-loving boys like Anthony.

As for Anthony, he has no desire to be like Gary, or to be part of his group, and he is able, therefore, to effectively tolerate and ignore Gary's continuous and aggressive character assassination. He is physically submissive in the face of Gary's antagonising antics, but his persistent affirmation of the kind of things that he is preoccupied with and the world which he enjoys, is an effective form of resistance. Not seeking to be a contender in Gary's pecking order of toughness, Anthony rarely comes to physical blows with Gary; each is the antithesis to the other of what it means to be a 10-year-old boy. Observing the way that boys' peer groups are formed at school, I begin to appreciate how, within any friendship group, the structure of social relations emerges with respect to twin processes of participation: both commonality and conflict are implied. Gary's friends have things in common but they are also competing, within this concern that they share, for toughness in fights or skill in football, to be the toughest and the best; they compete against each other, but only within the parameters of their shared preoccupation. Because a balance is constantly being struck, in any peer group, between these processes of commonality and conflict, there is inevitably a degree of tension. The boys' ability to manage this tension determines the extent to which they can remain friends, continue competing for equality against each other and not fall out irrevocably, for example over fights that have gone too far.

At the same time, depending on the specific form of participation that is required within each group, boundaries are continuously negotiated on the basis of who can and who cannot be included. There is, therefore, conflict arising within the group, over the competition for equal competence in relation to the specific form of participation required and, from the inside out, there is also conflict with those who are excluded from belonging to the group. This conflict with outsiders then becomes another thing that group members share in common. These boundaries, formed against those who cannot belong, can be quite fluid and open or else they can be ruthlessly defended and breached only by physical assertion as when a new boy at school proves himself to be a good fighter and, therefore, to be a contender for leadership among the disruptive boys. It is in relation to this ongoing and dynamic tension between processes of commonality and conflict that I begin to appreciate what is so appealing to the disruptive boys about Pokemon characters: Pokemon and Pokemon battles symbolise perfectly the conflict in which disruptive boys are continuously competing amongst themselves to establish a hierarchy of fraternity.

Participation as exchange

At home, meanwhile, I learn with my daughters how to play the Nintendo Pokemon Game Boy games. This is essential because otherwise I cannot take effective part in the dialogues which boys are constantly having at school about their relative progress and strategy in the games. At first I struggle because I find the medium of hand-held gaming difficult to get used to. The screen is tiny and the graphics are in black and white and, without instructions, it is difficult to get a sense of what the game consists of. However, once I get hold of the Nintendo Pokemon game strategy magazine the game becomes comprehensible and enjoyable and I begin, then, to experience the obsessive pleasure of interactive computer gaming. Much to my partner's dismay, I am happy to devote hours at a time to competing against myself to try and complete the challenge which the game sets. As a result I am soon able to engage with Martin, at school, in animated conversations about the challenges we have met when playing our Pokemon games and together we happily obsess about the finer points of our fighting experiences.

This focus on the specific kind of competencies that I must acquire in order to continue to be a person of significance for the boys, makes me begin to focus on what exactly the process of building these relationships consists of. Whether on the football pitch or in a fight, whether drawing or when talking about experiences with objects that they possess, such as computer games or Pokemon toys, for any boy, learning how to participate effectively in the peer group always means working out what constitutes an appropriate relation of exchange. Exchanges can be verbal, physical, or, in terms of actual objects, like photocopies of Pokemon drawings, they can involve a trade in objects.

It is because an ongoing process of exchange is involved that the social dynamic of peer group formation is always observed, in practice, as a spatio-temporal flux. This is because the formation of friendships, as much as the making of enemies, is never finally achieved; it is a continuously emerging social process in a specific material environment and it depends on children's evolving understanding about how best to participate in particular relationships of exchange. Without exchange relations there can be no social participation and, without exchange relations there can, therefore, be no learning: learning is an exchange phenomenon. To become valued a person or child has to understand, in any situation, among any group of people, what kind of exchange – in language, gesture or object – ought to be made in order to demonstrate the capacity to participate effectively. It is, therefore, in and through the process of exchange that the value of both subjects and objects is created and transformed, mutually specified over time.

This means, to a certain extent, that the social structure of the disruptive boys' peer group, and within it, any boy's social position vis-à-vis others, is always defined by the question of who has enough influence to define what constitutes an appropriate exchange for the group and, by implication, who is able to place a limit on the question of who will be allowed to make those kinds of exchanges. At school the battle between teachers and disruptive boys is all about who has the authority to decide, for children, what constitutes appropriate exchange relations at particular times in specific spaces. The problem is that there is a huge discrepancy between adult ideas about what constitutes a legitimate exchange for a child to be making and the kinds of exchanges in which certain kinds of boys are working out amongst themselves, at school, at home and on the street, what counts for them as appropriate participation. Perhaps what is anathema to these boys, then, about the particular form of classroom participation is the specific sphere of exchange in relation to which it is established what it means to learn how to be valued and to be good at school. My suggestion is that if we are to stand a chance of explaining why the kinds of exchanges entailed by formal learning in the classroom are so lacking in meaning to disruptive boys, we first need to understand what *is* meaningful to the boys about their own forms of participation. Without this understanding we lose hope of ever brokering the difference.

Girls, games boys play and football

Of course, the social processes which I describe above do not pertain to the formation of disruptive boys' peers groups alone. The difference between what it is to be a boy and what it means to be a girl is similarly constituted on the basis of an ongoing differentiation in relation to specific forms of participation. Although I focus in this book on the formation of boys' peer groups at school, the question of what is different about the forms of participation that girls expect of each other is a pertinent one. What kinds of things do girls care about? What are the distinctions between kinds of girls' peer groups? Are any of the things that are significant to girls the same as for boys? One girl in Year Five/Six – Sally – for example, has grown up with older brothers and developed a love of playing football; her brothers have taught her well and she is relatively good at it. This makes her competent in football skills that boys expect girls to be hopeless at. As a consequence, Sally is not excluded from the boys' football teams at playtime; her ability to participate appropriately outweighs the fact that she is a girl.

Similarly, the more competent I become in terms of the kinds of exchanges that are valued by boys, the greater the expectation among them becomes that I should also know about football and other kinds of things that they are preoccupied with. Out of the blue, for example, Baqir declares in class one day, 'I like you Gillian. You can draw Pokemon. Will you be here forever?' Before waiting for me to answer he immediately asks me which football team I support. Not wanting to betray my naivety in this respect, I hastily fix upon Liverpool, which used to be my team of choice as a child. Baqir is a big Manchester United fan so he tries, then, to engage me in playful rivalry about who the good players are, which games have been won and lost and which is the better of the two teams. At a loss, with little to contribute to the conversation, I resolve to watch the football on the television at the weekend. For the first time in my life, and much to my partner's (he is a football fanatic) surprise, I begin to engage with and try to understand the reasons for boys' passion for football.

At lunch play Baqir, who is often chosen by the disruptive boys to be their trusty goal keeper, asks me to play football with him and the other boys. He looks at me, his face full of cheerful anticipation, but I am terrified of failing miserably and of jeopardising, therefore, the respect which I have worked so hard to earn from the boys. I am athletic and supple but the specific skills that football requires are a daunting prospect to me so I postpone the challenge, assuring him that I will play next week. Significant as Pokemon are, I realise then, as I watch the boys play on without me, that there is no object or physical competence quite as important to them as being able to play football. Whilst I sit and try to make sense of the rules, which I have never understood, some younger girls run over to sit down next to me. Complaining hard, they protest to me about how unfair it is that boys don't let girls play football. I try to explain that it isn't because they're girls, it is because they don't know how to play and need to practise their skills, but the girls are neither interested nor convinced; they just want me to stop watching football so that I can draw more Pokemon for them.

I resolve then, to force myself at the weekend to watch a game of football on the television and, much to my partner's amusement, I even make time to go to the park with him and our daughters to have a go at playing football. Dreading having to expose how woeful my skills are and wondering if this is how the boys feel when their skills in numeracy and literacy are about to be tested, I begin the school week filled with trepidation. The first thing I discover is that morning playtime has been suspended for Year Five/Six children because the level of violent behaviour at playtime is out of control. It is causing so much disruption to other children and staff that letters are to be sent home to the boys' parents. The letter from Mara reads as follows:

Parents of all boys in Year Five/Six
Dear Parents

I have been very concerned lately about the great amount of violent behaviour on the part of boys in this class. Several boys have had short exclusions recently for hurting other children. We have now changed playtimes so that boys in Year Five/Six have more opportunities for physical activities, but bad behaviour at lunchtime is continuing to be a problem. I have now decided that if these older boys, who should be giving a good example to the younger ones, cannot behave in a civilised fashion at lunchtime, we have no alternative but to ask you to have them at home at lunchtime. Please talk to your son about the seriousness of this.

This suspension of outside play means that the Year Five/Six children have to stay inside during morning break. Lunchtime play, however, remains a problem because conflicts begun between the boys at this time then continue to spill over into and to disrupt classroom activities for the remainder of the afternoon. To compensate for playtime missed in the morning Year Five/Six do, however, get to go outside on their own in the afternoon. Their isolation from the other children in the school makes them more manageable and it is Christine, their teacher, rather than a classroom assistant, who then supervises their play. The majority of the boys take advantage of this time to play football. Without interruptions from younger boys a more focused game can happen and the boys are pleased because usually they are continuously pestered by younger boys who want to join in. It is these younger boys, who, if they can't meet the standard of skills required, risk being violently bullied off the pitch,

Christine cannot stand football but she appreciates how important it is to the boys and wishes they could manage to play a single game without it descending into conflict. Sally and I stand with her by the side of the pitch wondering what to do with ourselves. The boys, who are choosing their teams, want to play five-a-side football but they are short of two boys. Catching sight of Sally and I, they hail us, urging us to join in. I look at Sally with some trepidation, but she is keen and encourages me to have a go so we agree to make up the numbers. Quickly we are allocated to the teams and immediately the game begins. There is no time for nerves, however, because the ball is moving too quickly from one boy to another down the length of the pitch and I can't even remember who is on my team or which way my team is shooting. I shout out to Nathaniel for instructions and eventually I work out who my team mates are.

Two minutes into the game the ball comes my way, moving fast through the air for what could be a perfect header. Terrified, but having just watched Tom execute a perfect header himself, I try to do just the same thing and miraculously I pull it off; the ball moves accurately down the pitch towards the next player. Tom, who is even more surprised than I am to see that I can head the ball successfully, laughs out loud, and even though he's on the opposing team, he comes running over to heap praises on me. I am laughing too and so is Sally, who also runs over to congratulate me, telling me how much she hates headers. The game continues, but our team is being demolished, largely as a result of the brilliance of Victor's (on the opposing team) considerable talents. Sally begins to moan to me that the boys on her team won't pass to her and I agree, secretly glad that I'm not seeing much of the action. Without warning, however, the ball is suddenly coming my way again and I'm close to the goal. I take my chance and before I know what has happened, and kicking the ball as hard as I possibly can, I score. Tom comes running over, fit to knock me over this time, with his hand raised high in the air for a high-five hand slap. Delighted with me, he affirms, 'Nice one Gillian!' Sally and I laugh out loud; I can't believe my luck. We both know that it was sheer enthusiasm and not skill which placed that ball in the goal.

Now that I have proved myself to be at least minimally capable, however, Winston begins to regularly pass the ball down the left side of the pitch to me, but I am hopeless at tackling the other players and cannot retain control of the ball when I've got it, so I decide to stay out of trouble near the goal, where Gary waits, up front. Setting up goals for each other once other more capable boys have won possession, we make a good partnership and two more goals follow in quick succession for Gary. Once the game is over, the boys let me know how thrilled they are with my first attempt and I have to confess to Christine that I haven't had so much fun in years; I feel elated. No wonder boys love football so much; it really is a beautiful game. For me, it perfectly substantiates my new-found theoretical appreciation of how, via particular forms of participation, social relations between people come to be structured in specific ways. Each social situation is characterised by distinctive spatial and temporal constraints – in football it is a pitch where a game unfolds for ninety minutes – and in each situation any person's social position vis-à-vis others emerges competitively, in relation to a shared but also finely differentiated physical mastery with respect to particular kinds of exchanges. These exchanges are always mediated by specific objects – in the case of football it is beautifully simple because there is only one object and it is a ball, which has its own special physics-related qualities, and which moves from player to player, but is never ultimately possessed. The fact that there are two teams playing against each other only makes it more perfect because the twin processes of participation – commonality and conflict – are then posed in constant tension both within each team and against the opposition. In football this structuring process is very physical, very fast and often furious; therein lie its thrilling qualities.[12]

On the way back upstairs to the classroom, Gary and Tom argue about the validity of Gary's team's victory. Tom, who is proud and not to be outdone, refuses to acknowledge that Gary's team is the better side. Christine asks them to leave the conflict outside and threatens to suspend afternoon football if they don't desist from arguing. Sweating and dehydrated, filled with excitement, we find it more difficult than ever to then settle down to what being in the classroom requires of us. All afternoon, during lessons, Gary surreptitiously takes the opportunity to wind Tom up about the defeat of his team.

Unlike Pokemon and other crazes that will come and go, football is an enduring preoccupation for the boys, one that will probably last into manhood either as a sport that they play or as entertainment which they watch on television. It is a fast-moving, exhilarating and physical game which is perfectly suited to boys whose social life is already oriented around the development of a pecking order of toughness and violent intimidation. Most of the disruptive boys dream of becoming Premiership footballers earning six-figure salaries and they know full well that most footballers didn't have to do well at school to be chosen to play for Premiership teams.[13] The world of football sets them an example, which reminds them that the tough qualities that they admire in each other, which are anathema to those necessary for what it means to be good at school, are highly valued and can be developed elsewhere than at school. The challenge is to convince the boys that the skills their teachers want them to learn in class and the skills which they value on the pitch are not necessarily mutually exclusive: it is possible to be clever, well educated and good at football.

Objects of desire

In the week following my first triumphant game of football, Gary is suspended from school again; this time for a week. At lunchtime I see him outside; he is sitting in the front seat of his parents' car. I go over and ask him what's happening and we have a chat. He tells me that his mum has come in to have a meeting with Christine and Mara because he has been excluded and told that he can't come back to school until Friday. I ask him why he got excluded and he says that it was because he was laughing in Mara's assembly. When she told him off, he explains, he carried on laughing. As he tells the story Gary hangs his head, blushing, half-ashamed, but at the same time smirking in amusement. I ask him what it's like to be excluded and he says, 'The teachers think it's a punishment but it's not; you get to stay at home and play Dreamcast[14] all day.'

Gary then takes out of his pocket and proudly shows me his brand new, shiny blue, mobile phone. I appreciate that this is a sign of things to come; after Pokemon, there will, before long, be new and different objects of desire to learn about; kids will, I'm sure, soon all be carrying mobile phones. Gary passes his phone to me. I look at and admire it and privately I think to myself that it is no wonder that Gary has so much influence amongst the other boys: apart from his skills in football and fighting, his daring and charismatic resistance to the figures of authority at school, there is nothing his parents will see him go without. No matter that he misbehaves at school, he still gets what he wants and getting his own way gives him influence among his peers.

After a few weeks, some of the boys begin to bring into school, surreptitiously smuggled into their trouser pockets, collections of Pokemon stickers, which cause a whole new wave of excitement. Every pack of stickers contains one shiny sticker; the graphics are bright and colourful so it is not surprising that the stickers quickly become highly valued objects. At every opportunity, Gary, whose collection is held together in a thick wad by elastic bands, shows his stickers off to me and others. He allows me the honour of going through his collection one by one whilst other boys lean over my shoulders, crowding round and uttering praises when they see the Pokemon which they hold in high esteem. Snatching moments where there are no teachers or other staff members around, the boys frantically swap their stickers. The rarest are the shiny ones and Gary has many of these. Since the children are not supposed to bring such playthings into school and there is always the risk of having them confiscated by the teachers, we have to be careful where we look at the stickers.

At the boys' instigation I begin to develop my own collection of stickers and experience the thrill of tearing open the top of the packet to pull the stickers out and see which shiny Pokemon it contains. Gary and I discuss how we feel about this particular pleasure and he admits then, that when he is colouring in his Pokemon drawings his heart beats faster because he is so worried that someone is going to nudge or jog him and ruin his picture. Demonstrating how much he cares about his Pokemon drawings, Gary shows how proud he is of his colouring-in and I am aware that via the medium of this specific exchange between us, as well as a degree of camaraderie on the football pitch, a fragile friendship is beginning to develop between us. I am reminded then, that significant exchanges between people – of words, bodily gestures or objects – can facilitate emotional transformation and such exchanges hold, therefore, substantial integrative potential.[15] Getting to know someone is, then, all about trying to work out what counts for them as a meaningful exchange; with any luck the process is reciprocal and a mutual curiosity begins to develop. Only in this way does Gary finally start to seek my support: tentatively he begins to ask me for help with his school work in class and I am only too glad to help out. Slowly he begins to experience the parallel pleasure that I have learned in his world; taking pride in occasional pieces of school work that we have focused on together in class, he hesitantly makes his way across the classroom to show it to Christine who happily heaps praises upon him.

Meanwhile, remembering the Pokemon trading cards that I bought back in December when Anthony and Kevin had first suggested that I go to Toys R Us to buy some Pokemon things, I bring them into school to see what the boys make of them, but they are not interested; they are still completely preoccupied with their drawings and with swapping stickers. Whilst the boys persevere at school, trying to confine their enthusiasm for Pokemon into the snatched time that unsupervised spaces allow them, I am introduced to the joys of Pokemon card trading elsewhere, by the children who hang out on the estate where I live.

9
Place and Prestige

On my way into school one morning I bump into Baqir and his cousin, Chetana. They are the children of first-generation Bangladeshi immigrants who reside in the block of flats opposite where I live. Both Baqir and Chetana are pupils in Year Five/Six at Tenter Ground School. Between their flat and mine is the garden square which is enclosed by three blocks of flats four storeys high; each block contains about forty flats. These blocks form part of a much larger estate comprising other garden squares of which there are approximately five or six in total.[1] As we walk to school together, Baqir offers to carry my bags. Eager with reciprocal gestures because they are pleased with the gifts of my Pokemon drawings, boys who are not preoccupied with trying to look tough often offer to carry my bags when they see me coming into school.

As we walk Baqir asks me, 'Do you know why we don't come into your area [to play after school and at weekends]?'[2] I tell him that I don't know and he goes on to explain that it is because of a girl called Jenna and other kids who live in my block. Baqir outlines how these children won't let him and Chetana come into what Jenna and the others call 'our area [where I live]'. He goes on to describe how kids from Jenna's area chase him and his cousins away, telling them, 'Stick to your own area!' Fervently Baqir tells me about the time when Aamir, Chetana's younger brother, was hit on the head and made to bleed by a stone that had been thrown by kids from my area. He details another incident in which Aamir was injured so badly on the arm that he had to go to hospital to have it stitched.

I ask Baqir why he thinks this sort of thing is happening and Chetana interrupts to explain how it all started at school. She says that Jenna, who is 9 years old and has two younger brothers, used to be their friend but then she started telling lies, picking on them and getting the older boys in her block to gang up on them. I know exactly which children Baqir is referring to: during the period of my fieldwork all the children from my block who play out regularly are white kids; included among them are four older boys, aged between 10 and 14, who all hang out together. Three of these boys do not attend regular school: one receives a few hours' weekly tuition at home because he was so badly bullied at school that he refuses to go back; one goes to a special school for children with emotional and behavioural difficulties; and another never attends school at all. Ian, the youngest, but most dominant amongst them, is the only boy one who attends school regularly.

Again, I ask Baqir and Chetana to explain what they think are the reasons for them being chased by Jenna and the other kids out of my area. I am surprised when they make no mention whatsoever of it having anything to do with them being Bangladeshi Muslims. I am aware that white families' prejudice against 'Pakis' is high on the estates. I am also aware that white families are not the only ones to hold racial, ethnic and cultural prejudices of all kinds. In my block, for example, all the Bangladeshi Muslim children live with their families in flats that occupy the ground floor of the block. They are the youngest children to be seen outside, playing near to their doorsteps. When their mothers are not watching, the little Bangladeshi Muslim girls spit at my daughters as they walk by. Looking like butter wouldn't melt in their mouths, they call out at my daughters: 'Fucking Pakis.' This only makes my daughters, who are so much older than these little girls, shriek with laughter at the irony of it all: these girls have learned that 'Paki' is a good insult to throw but they haven't yet learned that it pertains only to a certain kind of non-white people of whom they are members. The conflict between Baqir, Chetana and the white kids in my block may, however, have nothing to do with so-called racial, ethnic or cultural differences; I know that territorial conflicts between children and young people living in different blocks are common even when the children in those blocks are all white.

Interesting about the blocks of flats is the way that the patterns of residence reveal how patterns of immigration are changing over time. During the time of my fieldwork, there are, living in the most desirable first- and second-floor flats in my block, mostly white families with children between the ages of about 6 and 14. There are two long-standing white tenants: these are women – widows or divorcees – who have lived in the block for forty years or more and brought up all their children here. On the ground and second floors there are also two long-standing black, and specifically Jamaican, tenants who have also raised their children here and are now retired: Caribbean families were often the first to become established in Bermondsey followed later by Bangladeshi Muslims and more recently West African families.

On the second and third floors there are two mixed-race families, one of which is my own. My daughters are of an age to play out but they don't hang out with Jenna and the other kids very much and not at all after school. As I explained in Chapter 1, children and families on council estates are differentiated, in part, on the basis of whether the children are allowed to play out or not. When my daughters do play outside, they tend, at first, to keep their own company, roller-blading or playing on their scooters and occasionally this develops into a game with the other kids. Usually, at weekends, we tend to go out as a family on different excursions, to the park or the sports centre, or to visit friends and family and this also differentiates my daughters from the other children who spend longer periods of time confined to the area, making their own amusement outside. The older boys in the block – those between the ages of 10 and 14 – are differentiated from the younger children and from girls by virtue of their freedom to move, usually on their bikes, beyond the immediate area of the block further into the estate; there they explore the main roads and make forays into other unfamiliar areas.

Learning how to stick up for yourself

Baqir and Chetana continue to describe how they are excluded from playing in my area and fearfully they describe the violence which this exclusion entails. Once, Chetana says, Jenna and the others followed them back to where Chetana's family lives and threw stones at Chetana's flat, breaking her mum's kitchen window. Chetana tells me that her mum is scared and wants to move away. She says that her family needs more space anyway because four of them have to share one small bedroom and Baqir sleeps at her house[3] too. Her mum wants a proper house, Chetana says, where she can grow plants in the garden. She then tells me that her dad works in a carpet shop in Whitechapel and, going on to make spontaneous kin associations, Chetana describes her family in Bangladesh.

Baqir, eager to get back to the point, interrupts and tells me that Chetana's dad has phoned the police twice because of the kids in my block. Each time, he says, the police tell them to 'stick to their own areas'. But, he thinks to himself, Jenna and the other boys don't stay in their own area so why should they? As we arrive at school, Gary and Daniel see us and come running up to greet me. They overhear Baqir, Chetana and me talking about the troubles they are having and I ask Chetana if her dad ever does anything about the trouble himself. Emphatically she says, 'No, it would only makes things worse.' Daniel interrupts to disagree; loudly and forcefully, he says, 'You 'ave to stick up for yerselves else they won't stop.' He then tells us how he had to punch someone once because he was being picked on. Eagerly, Gary agrees. Understanding what Gary and Daniel already know, about how reputations work to secure protection for family members on council estates in Bermondsey, I suggest to Baqir and Chetana: 'Tell Jenna and the others that you know me and say you are coming into my area to knock for my daughters. If they try and stop you or give you any problems then let me know and I'll tell my boyfriend.' Gary quickly picks up on this idea, asking me enthusiastically and with excitement, 'Is your boyfriend tough? Can he fight?' Emphasising that my boyfriend knows how to handle himself, I tell them that he grew up in the East End of London, which I know will mean something to Gary. Whilst Gary and Daniel are excited by the prospect of a violent confrontation, Baqir, who is obviously afraid of Jenna and the older boys, begins to look nervous. He is not a tough boy, and his uncle is patently not a fighting man either, so he quickly changes the subject. He asks me if I watched the Lazio/Chelsea football match the night before and luckily I did, so we are occupied with discussing Chelsea's poor performance until we get up to the classroom.

Territoriality

A few days later, watching from my balcony, I observe how Ian, Jenna and some other kids from my area run to hide behind the outside refuse bins when they see Baqir, Chetana and her brothers coming along the path that separates the blocks. At the last moment, having great fun with their campaign of terror, Jenna and the others jump out to frighten and chase the intruders away. I realise then, how children can come to claim the spaces and areas that they live in as their own: the distinctiveness of their peer group, as one which is identified with a particular area within any one estate, arises from their ability to define and physically defend the space from children who are outsiders. For them this is obviously one of the most exciting games they can play outside. Unlike the objects which mediate peer group interaction at school, space is a more abstract form of material object, but nevertheless it is the stuff with which, when children have little to do outside, they are crafting their sense of themselves as particular kinds of children.

In my area, and on most estates, there are actually very few amenities for children's play. For the most part children are not allowed to go out of the area – to the parks, for example, where they would be out of their parents' sight – and they do not, therefore, have access to the local playgrounds. There is a garden at the back of the flats which is a communal area but the children rarely use it because people allow their dogs to mess there and there is no provision for safe disposal of the faeces; sometimes in the summer the boys play football there. Those children who are allowed to play out usually make their own amusement in the car park at the front of the flats where they can still be seen by their parents. Out of any discarded items of furniture – old mattresses, bits of wood and other items – the children quickly conjure a game that occupies their time until their mothers call them up for dinner.

In relation to what I have learned about children's peer groups at school, I am able to observe how kids from my block constitute their friendships out of daily adjustments to the space they live in. Within this relatively circumscribed area children participate in various kinds of play: climbing trees, playing chase in the car park or football on the grass, inventing games and riding on their bikes, skates or scooters. In this way children actually come to live the space outside in a way that adults never have the time or inclination to do and that is why childhood matters so much in a place where people think of themselves as being born and bred. This is how people come, in time, to be thought of as being irrevocably attached to places: they belong to and are inseparable from the haunts of their youth.

True to my word, I go down into the car park and talk to the kids from my area. I explain to them that Baqir and Chetana are my friends and I emphasise to them that I want Baqir and Chetana to come into our area because they are coming to knock for my daughters. Surprised, but offering no resistance except to fill me in on their version of events, which also situates Baqir and Chetana as trouble-makers, Ian and Jenna agree. Ian is to our block what I imagine Gary is to his – a boy who makes his presence known – and he is often engaged in nefarious activities, finds himself frequently in trouble and is dominant among the boys of a similar age in the block because of the reputation of an older brother. The following week Baqir runs up to me in the playground at school, telling me that Ian is now his friend. I am surprised by Baqir's enthusiasm to be Ian's friend and also by the dramatic turn-around in neighbourhood relations which, I imagine, can't suddenly be quite as harmonious as Baqir portrays, but I am pleased for him.

I don't tell Baqir what Ian and Glen told me when I talked to them, which is that Baqir, Chetana and her brothers cause a lot of trouble around the estate and are always in trouble even inside their own area. That is the reason that Ian gives for why he and the other kids from my area chase them away: 'Even their own neighbours call the police on them,' Ian explains. Realising that the explanation they give about why they don't come to play in my area is obviously not as clear-cut as Baqir and Chetana make out, I'm eager to understand how children's neighbourhood relations vary from those relations formed at school, so I persevere.

Pokemon trading cards

Before long, and inquisitive now about the intervention that I have made on Baqir and Chetana's behalf, Jenna and her brothers begin to come up and knock for my daughters to come out to play. Relaxing my constraints on their play, I allow the girls to go out to play in the car park, where Ian and the other boys incorporate them into their game. When I call them up for dinner, my daughters report, excitedly, how Ian and his friend Glen were swapping Pokemon cards. Ian and Glen, having been told by my daughters about my Pokemon drawings, are too curious to stay away for long; within minutes they come up to our landing to knock tentatively on my door. Uneasily, because they don't know me very well, they ask to have a look at the drawings and I fetch my Pokemon folder to show them on the doorstep.[4]

The boys are impressed by my drawings, but not for long: they are more interested in showing off their Pokemon trading cards and they want to know if I have got any to trade. Ian, the more forceful of the two, is proud of his 'shinies' which are those Pokemon cards with holographic pictures of the characters on. I didn't even know you could get such a thing as shiny trading cards, so I am taken by surprise. The few cards that I have got aren't even worth showing so I decline to trade, and opt to show them my sticker collection instead. Ian gives them a disdainful glance. Unimpressed, he says disparagingly, 'Stickers are lame [rubbish, frowned upon]. At my school everyone collects cards.' Momentarily embarrassed about how worthless my sticker collection is in this new situation, I have no choice but to acquiesce to Ian's influence and I realise that if I want to get to know how the dynamic of children's relations works on the estate, I'd better quickly improve my trading card collection.

Learning to trade

My daughters, Ty and Fola, are keen to participate in this unexpected opportunity to trade Pokemon cards and to get to know Ian and Glen better. They accompany me on a trip to Toys R Us where we buy some packs of trading cards, a few of which I give to each of them as gifts. Whereas a pack of stickers only costs 30 pence, each pack of trading cards costs £2.50, so we can't afford to buy too many at once.[5] The cards come in shiny silver packets with Pokemon graphics on the front depicting which series the cards belong to; the first series are Jungle cards.[6] Each pack contains eleven cards. For our collection of cards to count we know we must get some shinies, but at this early stage we are just as excited to see which of the different Pokemon that we have become familiar with over the previous weeks are featured in the cards. We know, from watching Ian go through his cards, that the fighting Pokemon – those that have high hit points and do moves which inflict maximum damage – are valuable even if they are not shiny. Like the boys at Tenter Ground, Ian and Glen are most interested in the battling potential of various Pokemon, and it is on this basis, apart from their desire for shinies, that they are building their collections.

With much anticipation, feeling like Charlie looking for a golden ticket, my daughters and I open our packets and quickly flick through to see what we've got. Unlike in the stickers packs, there isn't a shiny in every pack of trading cards and much to her older sister's disappointment, only my younger daughter – Fola – gets a shiny, a beautiful one, featuring a Pokemon called Snorlax. Desperate to have a shiny of her own, Ty pleads to be allowed to buy 'just one more pack', so I give her money to run back in and buy one more. This time she is lucky: she finds a shiny Venosaur, which is an excellent battling Pokemon with 100 hit points and high damage potential. Ty knows instantly that this is a card that Ian will want to trade for. Filled with anticipation, she can hardly wait to get back to the flats. Hoping to find Ian and Glen, Ty is ready to attempt to make a trade.

After school the next day, my doorstep is cluttered with children who are crouching and sitting outside, looking at each other's cards and engaging in the difficult business of trade. Observing and listening carefully, I try to ascertain how the process of exchange between the children works. The older boys, Glen, and especially Ian, dominate proceedings because they have the best cards. Like me, quietly observant on the periphery of the group, younger children and children without cards to trade, sit and watch. Looking over the balcony, my youngest daughter, Fola, notices Baqir, Chetana and her brothers watching us from the car park outside; she alerts me to their presence. I lean over the balcony and call to them to come up, and when they do I try to make them feel welcome. Baqir and his cousins stand tentatively, just beyond the younger children, watching proceedings and no one attempts to chase them away.

Because Ian is interested in Ty and Fola's cards, each of them has to go through their cards, in turn, in front of him. This is how trading begins: each child holds his or her own cards and goes through the pile one by one, lifting the top card and placing it at the back of the pack to reveal the one underneath. When the younger children ask to look at the cards, they want to hold them themselves, but Ian quickly tells them off, saying, 'You don't touch other people's cards.' Holding someone else's cards is a matter of trust and when he gets to know us better Ian lets us, under his watchful gaze, hold and go through his cards, and we return the courtesy. Usually, however, this only happens if no other, and especially no younger, children are watching.

As Ty and Fola take it in turns to go through their cards, Ian and Glen make occasional remarks under their breath, which subtly indicate to us which cards they desire. Shinies evoke the most rapturous admiration. Good cards are described as being 'bare', 'rough' or 'buff'. A rubbish collection of cards is called lame. Once all the cards have been seen, Ian decides with whom he wants to trade first and he chooses Fola. He then goes through his cards for her to see; she sits quietly and looks carefully because she doesn't yet know what the terms of trade are or how value is established. Everything is new and exciting including the language which Ian uses to talk about the cards.

All the while assessing her trading skills, Ian begins negotiations, presenting a possible trade for Fola to consider: 'I'll give you my [non-shiny] Victreebel for your shiny Snorlax.' A strong trader, like Ian, tries to take advantage of the inexperience of the younger child, hoping to get rid of his worthless or less valuable cards in order to acquire her most valuable ones. If she senses what he is doing and has some knowledge about which cards are valuable she refuses the trade, suggests a more suitable one herself or waits for him to make another offer. In this case Fola declines the trade because she doesn't want to give up her new shiny Snorlax too easily. Ian makes another offer: 'I'll give you my Victreebel and my shiny Venomoth for your shiny Snorlax.' Looking quickly at her older sister for confirmation, Fola accepts the trade, cards are swapped and Ian declares, 'No refunds.' This means that if anyone should have a change of heart and regret the trade it is then impossible to go back to the person to try and get your cards back.

Turning to Ty now, Ian asks her to go through her cards again. She does so. When he and Glen see her shiny Venosaur, they draw their breath in and lean closer to have a better look. Feeling confident that she has something which they want, Ty waits for Ian to go through his cards again. He suggests a trade: 'I'll give you my shiny Snorlax for your shiny Venosaur.' Ty refuses straightaway. Looking frantically through his cards again Ian seeks another shiny to add to his offer. Speaking as if he is being hard done by now, he continues to trade: 'I'll give you my shiny Snorlax and my shiny Vileplume for your Venosaur.' Looking over her shoulder at me Ty seeks reassurance and advice but I don't know whether it is a good trade or not, so I shrug my shoulders as if to say, it's up to you. Ty decides to agree to the trade, cards are swapped and 'no refunds' declared. Glen immediately tells her, 'You got skanked [ripped off, robbed], it wasn't worth it on you, you could've got up to eight shinies for that Venosaur. Boys at Ian's school'd give you their '[wh]ole collections for that card.' Looking dejected and clearly caring a great deal, Ty replies, 'I don't care.'

Glen, eager to take his turn to trade with Ty and Fola, moves forward as Ian withdraws, but Ty, having had her fingers burnt, doesn't want to trade anymore. She retreats into the flat leaving her younger sister to handle Glen on her own. Glen asks to see Fola's cards again; he's got his eye on what was Ian's, but which is now Fola's, shiny Venomoth. He needs it to complete his collection of one of the grass Pokemon's evolution sequence – Parasect, Venonat and Venomoth. He shows her his cards again and suggests a trade: 'I'll give you my Bellsprout and Weepinbell to go with your Victreebel. Then you'll 'ave a set, 'cos Victreebel is the evolvshun [evolution][7] of Weepinbell.'

Glen talks up the desirability of the idea of having a complete set and when he thinks he's convinced Fola, he prompts her response, 'You give me your shiny Venomoth.' Thinking for a moment, and weighing up the prospect of having a whole evolution set against having a single shiny, Fola happily agrees to the trade. Pleased with himself, Glen swaps cards and quickly declares no refunds. Ian immediately tells Fola that 'it [the trade] wasn't worth it on her', and explains to her that she shouldn't have given him her shiny, but like her sister, trying to save face, Fola says she doesn't care.

The boys turn to me then, and ask me if I want to trade, but I'm not confident enough yet either about my trading abilities or about my cards because I don't have any shinies yet, so I decline their offer. I say goodbye to the boys and the other children and closing the door I go inside to see if Ty and Fola are in need of consolation. Fola is explaining to her sister the trade that she made with Glen and Ty tells her that it wasn't worth it, but Fola doesn't care, she's happy. Ty, on the other hand, is cross and disappointed that she got skanked by Ian. He has proved his position of influence among the children by trading aggressively and without mercy, but she is determined to make a comeback.

Not surprisingly she wants to know when we can go and get some more cards.

How is value established in practice?

Between us, over the course of the next six weeks, Ty, Fola and I increase our collection of Pokemon trading cards and improve our trading skills. We know that compared to the formality and complexity of categorisation on the card, the value of each Pokemon card is established by children relatively simply in the process of exchange. Shiny, rare and effective battling Pokemon have the highest value and evolution sets also have worth. Some children trade merely to accumulate a better set of shinies and others, like Ty, aim to achieve that at the same time as they want to complete the whole set of Pokemon cards. The transformational potential of this highly specialised form of exchange is demonstrated by the dramatic appreciation in the value of single shinies in a relatively short period of time. One pack of Pokemon cards costs £2.50 and one single shiny might appreciate to many times its own value over a period of about six weeks, becoming, for example, worth up to £35 or £40 in specialist shops, which start to sell rare cards singly.

In the same way that single cards can appreciate in value, a child can also increase his or her own influence and reputation among peers by becoming a skilled trader with a buff collection. Whoever has the most shinies has the most prestige and therefore the most influence. The way to get more shinies is, firstly, to have parents who can afford and are prepared to spend money on keeping up the regular supply of packs of cards as gifts, and secondly, to learn how to be a confident and canny trader. For some boys, becoming a skilful trader and acquiring more shinies involves a degree of intimidation, aggression and the wielding of influence. A clever Pokemon trader can, however, talk up the value of the cards she or he wants to offer and talk down the value of the shinies or rare cards she or he wants to acquire without resorting to aggression. Prestige is also constituted, therefore, by skilful trading.

Boys like Ian make much of the joy of trading with younger kids who don't know the value of what they are giving away and so are easily duped. Ty frequently lambasts Fola for not being a strong enough trader, for giving in to Ian too easily and, therefore, for not winning his respect. Meanwhile, the person who brings out an impressive collection of shinies, but who is not willing to trade, is frowned upon and put down aggressively. Completing the Pokemon card collection is not the point: trading is everything and it is through trading, as a means of establishing differential exchange relations, that relative influence between children on the estate is now constituted.

In the end the shinies circulate continuously, like valuables in a Kula ring,[8] and trading networks are formed on the basis of more or less stable trading partnerships between kids who are known to have a regular supply of new cards and know how to trade properly. These trading partnerships, like the peer groups I observed at Tenter Ground, are friendships based on a shared and continuously negotiated mastery over objects of specific significance. Excluded from these friendships are kids too young to know how to trade effectively, or kids from families too poor or unprepared to spend money on cards. Hard as it is, these children fail to develop a competitive mastery in this particular domain. The exchange of Pokemon cards, as a form of competitive economy between children, is exciting, fun and completely ruthless. It is the desire to gain access to this highly specialised sphere of exchange, in which my daughters and I are able to establish considerable competence, that makes Pokemon a craze like no other. Pokemon trading provides the opportunity for children to transform their social relations with each other simply by virtue of their capacity to compete for prestige. It is the immediacy of this social transformation that makes the exchange of Pokemon trading cards so thrilling an experience and so revealing a phenomenon from a theoretical point of view. What it helps us to understand is how social transformation is made possible precisely because the value of cards and kids is created, transformed and mutually established, in the moment, through the practice of exchange.[9]

Earning respect: space, age and gender

Just as I became a person of significance to boys at Tenter Ground by virtue of my specific competence in relation to particular objects, so by similar means my daughters, and especially Ty, become influential trading partners with the boys who dominate the area in which we live. Ty enjoys the way in which she has to work hard to earn respect, integrating herself thereby into a network formed on the basis of a highly specific form of participation. Ian, by virtue of his ruthless trading skills, retains the best collection of shinies and therefore the most prestige. Trading of Pokemon cards is predominantly the preoccupation of boys but girls are also involved and they can, like Ty, overcome the gendered expectation that girls won't know how to do it properly.

Younger children, in contrast, and those who are less confident and have fewer cards but who, nevertheless, want to trade, wait to bring their cards out until Ian and Glen are gone. They know they can rely on Ty and Fola not to be as ruthless with them as Ian and Glen frequently are. Meanwhile, boys as young as 2 years of age, who know nothing about the complex categorisation of value, are often seen on the stairways fervently swapping the common cards that older boys have given them as gifts because these kinds of cards are surplus to trading requirements.[10]

Baqir, Chetana and her brothers quickly accumulate a few shinies of their own. They seize the opportunity to begin trading with Ty, Fola and myself and in this way they are incorporated into the trading network in my area. Eventually we see them in the car park, striking their own deals with Ian and Glen and, for a while at least, it is clear that the territorial conflict which prevailed before can be battled out now with cards and cunning rather than with stones and blood. Back at school I hear endless stories from Baqir and Chetana about how they got skanked by Ian.

Ian is, then, the most influential boy in our area. He is tough, ruthless, has heaps of charisma and, unlike other children of his age, he has the freedom to exercise his influence in other areas of the estate beyond where his mother can see and supervise him. He brings these independent qualities to the way he makes Pokemon exchanges and they serve him well. His indomitable spirit continuously finds a way to win but he meets his match in Ty, who is also a canny trader. Ian quickly notices that Ty keeps her shinies in mint condition whilst his, often crumpled up in his pocket, become quickly scuffed and damaged. Often Ty refuses to trade with him for cards she would otherwise have wanted because Ian hasn't looked after them carefully enough. In time, because he is becoming infuriated with Ty's refusal to trade for badly cared for cards, Ian persuades his mum to buy him a folder for his cards just like the one Ty has. In this she proves her influence over him, but it soon becomes obvious that the main difference between Ian and Ty is that Ty's influence ends with the successful conclusion of trading at the doorstep.

She does not have the freedom, as Ian does, to extend and exert her influence among the children in relation to the wider spaces of the area in which we live. The constraints which I place on Ty's freedom of movement frustrate Ian too. Attempting to extend the competitive rivalry they enjoy into a friendship that extends beyond the doorstep, Ian invites Ty to accompany him on excursions into the wider territory of the estate, but I decline permission. I fear the trouble that I know freedom, his reputation, and the desire for influence can bring to boys like Ian. Like Jenna and the other girls in my area, my daughters must stay close to home, and the space of the neighbourhood becomes, therefore, gendered in relation to the limitations which are placed on girls' freedom to explore beyond where their mothers can keep a close eye on them.

Raising the stakes

During the school summer holidays in July, I take my daughters on holiday to Canada to visit my parents and there we discover, to our delight, that we can buy Pokemon cards from the next series, the Dark cards, which are not yet on sale in England.[11] Returning home triumphantly from their expedition into the wider world, with a new stash of trading cards that they know no one in England will yet have, Ty and Fola instantly demolish Ian and Glen's trading dominance. Ty skilfully talks up the value of the Dark Raichu which is her best shiny; it is the evolution of Pikachu and the rarest of the Dark cards. Overwhelmed, Ian offers Ty his whole collection of shinies for that single Dark Raichu. Ruthlessly, and without a second's thought, Ty agrees and declares, 'No refunds.' She is triumphant and Ian appears to be cleared out, but not for long.

Tables turned now, Ian, who no longer has cards to trade with, draws on his influence further afield in other areas of the estate. He brings an older boy, Steven, who is about 13 years old, from another block on the estate to trade with us on our doorstep. Ian is determined to get these new prestigious Dark cards out of Ty's hands and into the trading network, but he can no longer do it by himself. For several weeks the majority of our spare time is taken up with the heightened excitement of learning how to trade with this much more aggressive boy. He is a mixed-race boy from a family and block on the estate that we know nothing about[12] and Ian is careful to warn us that Steven is renowned for stealing cards from kids, but it is obvious that Ian gains influence amongst older boys, like Steven, because he is able to bring them to places where valuable trades can be made. Nevertheless, Ian still seems nervous and unsure of himself when he is around Steven who is that much older; here is a boy with a more menacing reputation for Ian to contend with and we all feel uneasy.

During that summer, the trading of Pokemon cards becomes a national and international phenomenon. The media buzzes with headlines and stories about the crazy things that children are doing just to acquire valuable rare cards. Parents despair and fail to understand: the story is cited of one young boy, who doesn't know how to trade, trying to swap the whole contents of his bedroom for a single rare card. Everywhere children, and especially boys, are seen – on their way to school, out on the street, on the bus, any chance they get anywhere – to be trading frantically. Before long the fact that some children will go so far as to steal Pokemon cards from other children, sometimes at knifepoint, hits the news. The thefts do not surprise me, however. What most adults fail to understand is that for children, the value of having the cards is not just for the sake of possessing them, but also for what they represent, which is the opportunity to trade and to gain, thereby, the chance to transform one's personal prestige relative to peers. The true value of Pokemon cards is both material and social: they contain transformational potential. This is because their value, as objects of desire, is constituted in the process of exchange and their worth is thus conferred upon their owners as the substantiation of the capacity to trade. It is a question of self-esteem. Without the process of exchange the trading cards are nothing, they are meaningless to children, and in relation to this process of exchange, the child without cards is, for that moment, as nothing, meaningless to his or her peers.

For any child, to be excluded from this phenomenon is, therefore, a desperate situation to be in. Some children accept it grudgingly; unwillingly, they look humbly on from the margins of frenzied trading groups at their peers' participation in the trading network. Other children, like Steven perhaps, who live in an area where being violent and ruthless are, in themselves, already the means for boys to gain prestige among peers, may think nothing of stealing to get what they want. Being able to steal well is, after all, a particular kind of competence: an intimidating and potentially violent one, but one that provides the means for certain kinds of tough boys to increase their prestige, especially if they are also prepared to carry an object which assumes a new and heightened significance for them – a blade (knife). Unlike Pokemon cards, which are expensive, being tough costs nothing at all; the incidence of thefts of Pokemon cards is, therefore, no surprise.

Prestige system

Reacting against the craze, schools everywhere begin to ban Pokemon cards because of the conflict which they apparently cause between children. This ban only serves, however, to make the trading of cards more exciting because it suddenly becomes a subversive activity that cannot be done in the open, in public spaces or in schools where adults and predatory children might be watching. This crisis in the state of the nation's childhood is supposedly the result of the explosion of child-on-child violence arising from the desire to get hold of these strange and highly valued objects – shinies – which adults cannot comprehend the significance of. From my point of view, however, it is clear to see that the trading of cards does not create conflict between children; it simply transposes the material means for conflict into a new medium of exchange.

At Tenter Ground and on the estate where I live and in my area, I observe that for particular kinds of boys, like Ian, being tough, being able to fight and do battle, to inflict damage and maintain prestige, are, as for Pokemon and other fighting characters, exactly those qualities necessary to gain respect and maintain one's reputation. On working class council estates this disposition towards violence, which, in time, all young boys must, somehow or other, learn to accommodate themselves to, precedes the Pokemon phenomenon. It is the basis of what makes boys' possession of prestige items, like mobile phones, significant and is the background against which teachers struggle to get boys to be nice to each other and to get on well together at school. In this light, it is not boys' ruthless struggle for prestige which is the source of the furore, but rather the fracturing of the adult idyll of childhood, which, I predict, is to be a dominant theme of the twenty-first century.

Mobile phones: ring-tones and face-offs

Interesting about the Pokemon phenomenon is the fact that in the face of adult ideas about children and childhood, here is a rare instance in which children are visibly creating for themselves and being noticed on a national scale for participating in their own value system. The effectiveness and the rapidity with which trading cards became a national and international medium of exchange between children shocks everyone because, by definition, children are supposed to be excluded and protected from the marketplaces that the monetary economy establishes. Little credit is given to children for participating in the creation of a system under their own control, in which the value of relatively cheap commodities is transformed, via the medium of exchange, into prestige items worth many times their original price. Anthropologists, on the other hand, are well aware that at the margins of capitalism, which is a space that children in the Western world are supposed, by definition, to occupy, gift exchange functions perfectly well.[13] It creates real opportunities for transformation both of social relations and the use value of objects.

By the middle of the summer holidays the Pokemon phenomenon is at its height. The block that I live in is alive with the frenzied exchanges of young trading partners, newly bound by the excitement of Pokemon competitiveness. Children continue to be preoccupied with trading cards throughout the holidays. By August, however, Ian, who has no cards left to trade with, has a new prestige item to show off to his friends and competitors – a brand new mobile phone. He is the first child in the block to get one and the whole point of having a mobile phone, like all prestige items, is to show it off and that's when the real trouble starts.

At the boundary of the space he is allowed to travel in, far beyond the other side of the estate, Ian and his friend Glen encounter a group of black boys who take a liking to Ian and Glen's bikes. These black boys also notice Ian's mobile phone and try to take it from him. Ian and Glen, none the worse for wear, but scared by their encounter with this group of older, teenage black boys, return quickly to the safety of home to report what has happened. Ian's older brother, John, is 16; he has just left school for good. A week before this incident I had been chatting with John's mum, Alice, about how John is doing and we had reminisced together about having watched him grow up on the estate. As a boy, John had spent every waking moment, when he was not in school, practising his football skills, in the garden square at the back of the flats. When we were chatting, I had told Alice about my research and asked her if she thought John would mind doing an interview with me, seeing as he seemed to have turned into such a bod lately. Alice had laughed, saying, 'It's true, he is a real Bermondsey bod now, since he's hooked up with a gang of white boys from down The Blue.'[14]

Alice had then explained that before, because John used to go to a school near the Walworth Road, whose pupils are mainly black boys, he was used to hanging out with black boys. Recently, however, there had been a few incidents in which John had been badly beaten up by black boys on the Walworth Road. As if to clarify something for me, Alice had then emphasised: 'I'm not racialist, I get on with everybody; anyone'll tell you that. I don't let my boys say racialist things in front of me, but I've [h]'eard 'em talkin' and I know what goes on.' She had then explained how worried she was because she felt that John always had to prove his reputation on the street. When she told him not to get involved, advising him to walk away from trouble, he would tell her that she would never be able to understand. He had tried to explain to her that if he walked away from confrontations he wouldn't have a reputation and he then wouldn't be safe on the street anyway. Cheering up somewhat, Alice had then changed the subject to tell me about how John has now got a lovely girlfriend and she was, she said, thanking God because now John would start spending a lot more time with this girl indoors instead of out on the streets with the boys where trouble starts. Alice had told me with pride that after the summer holidays, John was going to start looking for a job.

So, to return to the incident concerning Ian and Glen: John had heard Ian's story and then, probably against his mother's wishes, made his way straight round to these black boys' area to see if he could find them and teach them a lesson. Nobody in the block knows exactly what happened but at dusk the terrible sound of a woman, screaming in anguish, pierces the peace of the evening. I run to the front balcony to see what is going on and Alice is there, doubled over, holding her side and crying in pain. Pointing and screaming, she cries out, 'They're killin' '[h]im, they're killin' '[h]im, phone the police!' None of us who have come out onto our front balconies can see what or where Alice is pointing to, but witnessing the look of terror on her face, I run inside and phone the police straightaway. My partner, meanwhile, runs down to help Alice and to see if there is anything he can do, but by this time, John is long gone. Apparently he was being chased by a gang of twelve black youths. It is said that one of them came into our area after John's earlier incursion into their area and hailed John out from the street below his flat in our block. Thinking that he faced a one-on-one confrontation, John presumably went down without a second thought. At least ten more boys were hiding, however, waiting for him to come down, before they pounced.

Eventually the police arrive in numbers but they are not able to prevent the eventual assault, which happens several blocks away and down a quiet street. It emerges later that the boys managed to corner John and one of them used his mobile phone to call his dad for back-up. The father apparently arrived in a car with his baseball bat and assisted the boys in dragging John out from under a car where he had tried to hide. They then proceeded to beat him to within inches of his life. The next day, whilst his son lies in intensive care, John's father, who has a reputation of his own to defend, issues a warning to the man that he has heard is responsible for the attack on his son. It is a warning that everyone in Bermondsey can understand and it is not an idle threat. It is popular knowledge that Bermondsey has its own justice system that runs in parallel to and often against the efforts of local police. The foundation of this justice depends on the understanding that you do not 'grass' (tell the police anything) because the people who need to seek revenge will do so on their own terms.[15] If you grass you are implicating yourself in the cycle of revenge-seeking which is an extremely dangerous thing to do. It is against this background that the police struggle to bring people to conventional justice in Bermondsey and, not surprisingly, witnesses are a rare phenomenon.[16]

After some time the police accuse the man, who allegedly brandished the baseball bat, with attempted murder. Fearing for their lives the family is quickly moved to safe housing and the flat where this man used to live with his family, on the same housing association estate where Tom lives, is soon boarded up and empty. Meanwhile, Ian's mother and her family, fearing for their own lives too and disrupted beyond measure, struggle for the next eighteen months to try and secure a housing transfer from the council. That this incident should end up becoming an issue to do with the way that the council manages housing in Bermondsey is poignant. Time and again white people that I interview or speak to in Bermondsey accuse the council of mismanagement and incompetence because the pressing needs of local white people are overlooked for the sake of outsiders, who are perceived now to be black people and other kinds of immigrants, whose needs seem always to be given precedence. The question of who owns Bermondsey is thrashed out, then, in the tense dynamic between white people's sense of belonging to their manor and the council's legal responsibility to manage the land and housing rights according to national governmental legislation about housing those people considered to be in most need.

In an article describing the processes of gentrification in Bermondsey, a journalist asserts that the 'old Bermondsey' has finally been tamed. Presumably he hasn't spent time talking with local people and fails to realise that claiming a space is not just about buying up the land or its properties, which smacks of the arrogance of monetary control. Those people who are born and bred here, their allies and especially the young men at the warrior stage of their lives, still feel that Bermondsey belongs to them and some of them are ready to die defending it.

Space and race

To most people it seems outrageous that this level of violence could escalate all because of a mobile phone, but it is about much more than that. In part it is about the way in which male prestige, from the early years of childhood – from the age of 8 or 10 to about 18 or 20 years and sometimes beyond – is constituted through the capacity for violence and brutality. This is intimately related to the way in which control and influence are wielded over particular neighbourhood areas and which can sometimes lead to involvement in territorial gangs. This has always been the case in Bermondsey; there is nothing new in it. Young white working class men from Bermondsey battled against their enemies in adjacent manors in Peckham and Walworth long before immigrants from Africa, the Caribbean and Asia arrived. The long-standing dynamic of these territorial conflicts is the historical precedent that governs all present transformations.

When I speak to older men and women about this they say that all that has changed, nowadays, is that young men now carry knives and guns and they take drugs; they also have fewer amenities to distract them and so they get carried away more quickly. In addition, most Bermondsey people are quick to blame the presence of black people on the estates as a reason for what they see as the demise of Bermondsey in general and for the escalation of violent tension in particular. The story of what happened to John becomes the stuff of legend because it is the evidence for what white people perceive to be the truth about black people, which is that black people's violence is far more brutal and indiscriminate than their own. I am aware, however, that things are rarely as simple as racial explanations suggest.

Two days after John was ambushed, two gangs of white youths further into Bermondsey are involved in skirmishes, which result in a white youth of 15 years of age being stabbed to death. He was stabbed fifteen times. Obviously this was not reported as a racial assault because both gangs of youths were white, but I would argue that to differentiate between the assaults on the basis of race is to miss what the assaults share in common. The point is that what all young men in Bermondsey have to contend with is a prestige system based partly on their ability to be brutal and to withstand brutality in the defence of territorial areas. In this system the means for controlling the space, becoming a man and developing a particular kind of bodily competence via specific kinds of violent exchanges, become mutually specified. Being able to handle yourself on the street where territories are mapped out is what counts. Ian himself was beginning to learn this when he was chasing Baqir and Chetana out of our area.

The increased incidence of young black youths' involvement in violent skirmishes on the streets of Bermondsey simply means that as particular kinds of outsiders, they are now confident enough to begin to stick up for themselves and compete violently for prestige in this Bermondsey big-man system. Perhaps, as the children of immigrants from particular countries, like Jamaica, they, unlike Baqir and Chetana, are already learning from their fathers about a way of life in which the development of masculinity is inseparable from the capacity for territorial violence. In other words, perhaps some immigrant groups have big-man systems of their own. If so, this doesn't make their youths much different to Bermondsey bods. Significant about the focus on racial difference, then, is the way that it eclipses what black and white youths share in common in working class areas like Bermondsey: they all have to accommodate to how masculinity is defined, often violently, on the street.

The pertinent question, if we are at all interested in saving young men from their involvement in this big-man system is how to change a value system. Schools are obviously failing to show these boys how to create and transform their sense of self-value in a different way than the working class neighbourhood demands. In light of the theoretical hypotheses about participative learning that I have proposed in this part of the book, it would seem that part of the solution might involve increasing the numbers of opportunities available, outside school, for young men to transpose the territorial conflicts of the street into new and less dangerous, but, nevertheless, still meaningful forms of exchange. Currently, sport and music are the only alternative, but still legitimate, means that bods have at their disposal to make something of themselves without simultaneously damaging their reputations on the street.

It becomes clear then, that what it means to be working class is to do with a lot more than the attainment of adulthood in a world defined by differentiated kinds of low-status work. Becoming a working class person is a lot to do with learning how to become a particular kind of person by learning how to belong to a particular place. Involved in this learning is the development of a complex and embodied appreciation of how all the manifold conceptual distinctions like gender, race and culture intersect with familial reputation in such a way that kinds of common people become distinct in working class neighbourhoods. These categories of distinction are not out there in the ether, they have to be brought into being, embodied as a stance and made sense of anew in each generation.

Gender, space and developmental cycle

Ian, as a young contender in what I call this 'big-man system', and John, as a stronger and more confident youth, were both crushed by this incident with the gang of black youths. Just like in the fantasy world of Pokemon battles, rivals are destroyed and lose face unless they can demonstrate an equal capacity for damage and destruction. Ian, as a result of the assault on his brother, is not allowed to play out for a very long time, and mobile phones, as predicted, do go on to become the next big craze for children.[17] Not surprisingly, street crime rises commensurably. When I do see Ian outside again it is obvious now that he has to stay closer to home. One day I see him playing in the car park with Jenna and her brothers; he is encouraging Jenna to call the young African children, who are thrilled now to be old enough to come downstairs and outside to play, niggers. Refusing to allow them the freedom to play out, Ian intimidates the African children and forces them to go back inside.

Meanwhile, Ian has stopped talking to Ty and Fola and me altogether. I wonder whether this is because Ty and Fola are mixed-race and their father is black, but because I am trying to empathise with how he must be feeling, I don't say anything to Ian. I don't try to explain to him how complicated things are in Bermondsey or try to remind him that it was my partner who was the first to go down and help Alice when she was pushed aside by the black youths. I want to explain to him that racial difference is probably the least interesting aspect of what is at stake in Bermondsey and yet I know that it is what is on everyone's minds, so I keep my mouth shut and leave Ian to nurse his grievances.

Remembering what John's mother, Alice, had said to me about her expectations for John, I realise then how important it is to situate young men's involvement in street violence as just one period in the developmental cycle of the household in working class areas like Bermondsey.[18] As Alice had explained, at the point when bods with reputations on the street begin to date nice girls they start to spend more time indoors again. Ironically, the developing relationship between space and gender, which is what makes the difference between tough boys and nice girls, is what saves bods in the end. Starting to date a nice girl who wants and is expected to stay close to home is the best possible thing that can happen to a Bermondsey bod and it is what every Bermondsey mother hopes for in the end. This is because the nice girlfriend, in her domain, which is the domestic space, begins to take precedence over the boy's peer group which is usually a gang of troublesome youths preoccupied with their reputations on the street where violent skirmishes unfold.[19]

No wonder, then, that relations between daughters-in-law and mothers-in law can become very close in Bermondsey; the girlfriend is literally the mother's ally in the battle to secure her son's future and perhaps his life.[20] After or about the same time that he starts to go steady with a girl a Bermondsey bod might get a job, and that is what every mother hopes for because there is security in employment too; no matter that it is a routine occupation, being at work also keeps a young man out of trouble. The problem, however, is that having a reputation and becoming lord of his own manor, a Bermondsey boy is ill-prepared for the humility required for starting work at the bottom of the employment ladder. In the next and final chapter of this part of the book, I consider the reproduction of economic relations in the broader context of the question of how, in Bermondsey, young men learn at home, at school and on the street, what it means to be valued as a man.

10
Notes from an Armed Robber – Gone Straight

*'It all starts in the pub, when a man pulls out a wad of notes fatter than yer fist, "F*u*ckin' 'ell, 'ow d'ya ge' tha'?" ya say and 'e tells ya, "'s easy," as 'e lays a grand [£1000] on the bar and tells the barman to get everyone a drink.'*

Patrick, Bermondsey, 2000

Patrick is a middle-aged Bermondsey man, born and bred. Now in his late forties, he once served eleven years of a twenty-year sentence for armed robbery. Patrick is sure that going to prison was the best thing that ever happened to him because, he says, 'If it weren't for that I'd be dead by now.' The scar which runs from Patrick's temple to the middle of his left cheek gives testimony to a precarious past in which he was stabbed on three different occasions and shot at three times during one altercation with a rival East End firm. Explaining his past, Patrick says, 'When I was growin' up all the people who 'ad nice stuff, BMW car and all that, was armed robbers. Trouble is,' Patrick says, 'gangsters f[th]ink they can buy prestige.' The armed robber buys prestige with big money and spends it in the place where it matters who sees it and takes note – in the pub. The man with the wad of notes as fat as a fist makes it sound easy and has no qualms about explaining to younger men, like Patrick, how an armed robbery is done and who has to be seen to get what's needed for the job.

Having guns is what makes it seem simple; the step a petty criminal takes, when he buys a piece (gun), is to dare to purchase the power of an intimidation he knows no one can argue with. Patrick explains that guns are relatively cheap and easy to come by, but daring deeds require courage, in this case for crimes that carry steeper sentences and harsher penalties. A step up from thieving and scamming, moral qualms

160

overcome by the eager desire for the good things in life and respect of his peers, an armed robber graduates from other forms of physical intimidation learnt early in life. As long as he is ready to take the risks and goes on succeeding, the professional thief is 'Mr Big Potatoes' (a big man) in Bermondsey.

Patrick describes how, in no time, he was living large, dodging the Old Bill, bringing in five grand (£5000) for a week's work, and spending it in the same amount of time because dirty money (money from crime) can't be stashed. With flash suits and expensive shoes he soon became a proper chap (a well-dressed contender), driving a brand new BMW, confidently chatting up the best looking birds (women) in the pub and taking them to all the top West End clubs to show off. Meanwhile, Patrick explains, the allure of gangster life pulls a man into a dangerous high-stakes world, where he struggles to 'stay on top of his game' whilst drinking, taking drugs and making deals, all of which test loyalties and define turfs (territorial areas). It's not difficult to imagine how, in this fast and furious world, the necessary guile and ruthlessness sort the men from the boys. The odds were that Patrick would get wiped out quickly or learn all too soon of crime's proximity to punishment through carelessness born of self-destructive bravado, and bearing fruit at Her Majesty's pleasure.

In prison, Patrick emphasises, the economy of self-esteem changes and crushes prestige, making way for a humble new beginning or else it contributes to the reputation of the hard man made heroic by his ability to withstand the punishment of the state. He remembers all too well the tragic reverence of his son's friends, rising to shake the hand of a gangster, greeting him respectfully on the only day that he was allowed out of prison in eleven years, to visit his dying father. Categorised in relation to the degree of violence involved in their crimes, men in prison are classified according to the risk they pose to others and to themselves. With good behaviour, a man like Patrick can end his sentence in the company of category D prisoners who are inside (in prison) for relatively minor crimes such as petty fraud or corruption. There, in category D, Patrick met an ex-Oxford don, who was incarcerated primarily because he had lacked the criminal know-how to successfully sell-on the rare and precious books he had stolen from one of Oxford's famous libraries. Despite their widely differing backgrounds, what men in category D have in common is some appreciation and empathy for each other's pasts in which, aiming for self-respect, they have succumbed to greed and desperation. Men, like Patrick, from poor backgrounds learn there, in category D, that a background of poverty and deprivation is not the only motivation for crime.

New horizons

What distinguished Patrick in prison was his obvious flair for writing: he kept a prison diary and was soon dramatising his experiences for the sake of the other inmates' entertainment and his own personal transformation. The Oxford don, noticing Patrick's talents, was able to put his privileged education to good use: he assisted Patrick to develop his literary ambitions and gained, in return, an education of his own about a way of life quite different to what he was used to. Out of this unlikely encounter a friendship grew between the two men and when Patrick's parole came up again, after five previously failed applications, the Don, as Patrick called him, encouraged Patrick to apply for university. This was a possibility Patrick had never entertained before: Bermondsey men don't go to university, they get jobs and settle down to a working life or else, failing this, they sign on the social or end up dead or in prison. The Don persisted, however, encouraging Patrick to send off for the prospectuses and application forms and together they filled them in. Underestimating the value of his previous and only legitimate sources of employment – as a barrow boy in the market and as a dustman – Patrick wasn't filled with confidence. The Don insisted, however, that the sum total of Patrick's life experiences, combined with his determination to put it to a new and creative use would make him, compared to the run-of-the-mill, well-educated, straight-as-a-die applicants universities are used to, an outstanding university candidate. The Don was right: Patrick was accepted to read for a degree in media studies and this fact influenced the parole board positively: within six months Patrick was out of prison and in university with the prospect of a whole new horizon stretching out ahead of him.

Despite the difficulties of gaining well-paid employment with a criminal record under his belt, Patrick continues to struggle valiantly to redefine for himself the meaning of prestige. Honing his skills and, in the process, gaining rather than stealing self-respect, Patrick specialised in film-making at university and now takes pride in his own work and is supportive of the artistic endeavours of other aspiring creative talents in Bermondsey. Patrick explains how he still has to fight the battle against the desire to buy prestige, but it is a battle he is winning. Despite the dream of getting easy access to big money, Patrick continues to win the battle on a day-to-day basis out of his struggle to redefine the means for gaining respect. Avoiding the places where the ghosts of a more hazardous past might threaten the hard-won peace of mind he has found, Patrick is one amongst a few men who are struggling, by affirming the positive aspects of the Bermondsey way of life in their creative work, to set a different example for young men in Bermondsey.

Pilferin'

Against the historical background of dire poverty, the more recent closure of the docks in the 1970s and in the face of an increasing emphasis on the value of consumer consumption, theft has come to assume its own legitimacy in Bermondsey. An elderly woman explains to me how she used to smuggle chocolate out of the factory where she worked when she was a young woman. She had fashioned special undergarments in which she used to tuck away chocolates so that her children could taste what she knew she couldn't otherwise afford to buy for them. 'A bit of pilferin' didn't do no one no '[h]arm,' she says. 'It was expected.' Also reminiscing about old times, when his father still worked on the docks, an elderly man explains how, if his father wasn't picked to work in one week, there would be no food on the table by the end of that week. The man explains how his mother would then make sack bags for the children, sending them down to the river where cargoes lay on ships for weeks, waiting to be unloaded into wharves. The man tells how he and the other children would then either shimmy down the ropes to the ship decks or test their swimming skills against the notorious current of the River Thames in order to climb aboard ships and cut holes in whatever sacks of foodstuffs they could find. The same man also emphasises how his mother would dispense a rough justice on the children if they continued to steal when times were good. She would be quick to turn a blind eye, however, if their father miraculously came home with a whole side of beef. 'If you were lucky,' the man explains, 'work provided for the bread and butter, but everyone knew that cunnin' catered for the jam.'

Whilst Bermondsey men have a notorious criminal reputation and the status of gangsters is mythologised, the truth is that more often the majority of men are struggling to make an honest wage and perhaps a little something 'extra on the side'. It is impossible to understand what it means for a young man to become working class, without simultaneously appreciating the lure of the so-called underclass. Even a man who makes an honest wage will rarely turn his back on the ready supply of stolen goods. Patrick's half-brother, Paul, for example, has a perfectly legitimate job in television, but recalls having once had a lucrative sideline in pirate video production. He reminisces about teenage years spent raiding warehouses and trying to explain to his mother why his bedroom was suddenly packed floor to ceiling with designer jeans. Quashing any qualms she had with extra housekeeping cash, Paul soon persuaded his mother to turn a blind eye. When I ask Paul what his dad did for a living, he says matter of factly: 'Me dad? '[H]e was a thief.' Paul then goes on to describe how his father had capitalised on the closure of the factories and warehouses: pulling up in their vans in broad daylight, stripping the place of all the metal they could lay their hands on, piping and so on, they would then sell it on for scrap, making a tidy living in the process. For years, Paul explains, he thought his dad had a proper job, believed him when he said he was going out to work in the van and only found out much later that his dad was a professional thief.

Resisting social change: lamenting the death of the community

One of Patrick and Paul's best friends – Trevor – explains to me how he changed his mind about thieving the day that he had to suffer the humiliation of seeing his wife and young children come to visit him in prison. He resolved never to go back and he hasn't. He now manages the last wet-fish stall in Bermondsey in the market down the Blue. When I visit him there, and spend the afternoon with him on the stall, he points across the road to the frozen food shop, Iceland, and beyond to Tesco, unseen in the direction of Surrey Dock. Animated, he explains to me, 'You've come just in time you 'ave [to tell our story]. Remember those old films, where the wagons were turned over in a circle and people was defendin' 'emselves behind 'em, completely outnumbered by Indians but still ready to fight for their lives? That's what's happenin' in Bermondsey now: people are behind them wagons.' I ask Trevor who the Indians are and he says, 'Big business' and points across the road at Iceland again. 'They are the super-tankers on the ocean now.' 'And what are you?' I ask him, 'A fishing boat?' And he replies, 'Nah, I ain't even a fishin' boat: I'm just a cork makin' a point. Every time they push me down, I bob right back up again.'

Trevor explains that he doesn't have a market stall for the sake of the profit because there isn't any profit in it. He only manages to break even, but he keeps doing it because he wants to make a point about a way of life that is dying out. 'Everyone'll tell you that Bermondsey is dying 'cos of all the blacks comin' in,' he says. 'But it's not true, it's got nothin' to do with skin colour.' Trevor, then, is one of the very few people in Bermondsey who understand the changes in Bermondsey in economic and not cultural terms. Perhaps that is because he is struggling to run his own business in the time-honoured fashion, selling goods through a stall in the market-place, down the Blue. Lamenting the loss of the market which once represented everything that Bermondsey stood for, he explains what was distinctive about it: the market made possible a personal way to shop: 'You'd be bumpin' into everyone you knew; makin' time to chat; it could take you hours to get from one end of the market to another.' Trevor then laments, 'Nothin's personal no more. It's all about the individual now; no one cares about anyone else and the worst thing is that we're all tryin' to keep up with the Joneses. That's doin' more harm in Bermondsey than anything else.' I ask Trevor if keeping up with the Joneses is a new thing, didn't they have that before? 'Nah,' he replies, 'nobody 'ad anythin' so you didn't 'ave to worry about who 'ad what, you just got on with life and children made their own entertainment, but not anymore, now they're killin' each other over trainers that cost £100.'

Feeling desperate about Bermondsey, the place where he was born and bred, Trevor tells me that he now calls it 'Dodge City' because it is a lawless, ruthless place ruled by vendettas. Young men have now, he explains, become, ironically, the toughest but also the most vulnerable young people in the city. 'Now,' Trevor explains, 'if a bod has a score to settle, he's got to finish it off good and proper and only a carefully placed knife can do that. If he doesn't take that desperate measure he can be sure the knife will be in his belly before the year is out.' Trevor emphasises that he believes that the only way to reach these young bods now is through music. 'Music,' he explains, 'is a new thing for bods in Bermondsey and it is a lifeline.' Together, Trevor and Paul devote a large proportion of their spare time and energies to organising music events of all kinds for young people in Bermondsey and, in so doing, they dedicate themselves, without financial reward, to the provision of new and different opportunities for bods to transpose the conflict which rages on the street into a different and yet still meaningful medium of exchange.

Ways to get money

Patrick describes how the scale and scope of theft in Bermondsey has continuously changed over time as the forces of law and order have varied their strategies for catching and convicting criminals. This makes the Old Bill the enemy and the grass the scourge of the earth. Whereas Bermondsey was once labelled the 'Bermondsey (as opposed to Bermuda) Triangle' because there had been more armed robbers in that small area than anywhere else in the country, its reputation has now changed. Armed robbers are few and far between now and those who did make a success of it are 'living large' in Kent or Spain whilst the combined technologies of CCTV and coding and tracking systems have made armed robbery a virtually impossible scam to pull off. What is easy and, therefore, tempting now, is drugs crime.

Patrick's second cousins – David and Mark – are 19 and 16 years old respectively. They both work on a casual basis for a man who pays them £55 cash each per day for helping him to fit laminate floors. It's easy work, they say, because their boss doesn't give them any grief, but it is casual labour and some weeks they don't work at all. For now at least, David and Mark are forced to continue living at home because, without their mother's support, they couldn't make ends meet on their own. Their mother's only stipulation is that if they want to continue living at home after having left school, they have to give her housekeeping money every week. Support from the state in the form of unemployment benefit isn't an option until the age of 18, so younger school leavers, like Mark, would be particularly vulnerable in any case. Even for those youths who are old enough to claim it, there is no dignity in scraping by on the social which involves continuously having to prove to the job centre that you are job seeking.

Reaching school leaving age, young people must, of necessity, concern themselves with work and other ways to get money, but in Bermondsey this specifically economic dilemma emerges out of and in relation to a much deeper concern with getting respect. By school leaving age bods, like David and Mark, have developed a generalised disdain for conventional figures of power and authority that is mediated and constrained only by the intimacy of kin relations. They begin, therefore, to face a difficult paradox. On the street they have status and influence, which implies that they are becoming lords of their own manor. The problem, however, is that having a reputation on the street is not a position conducive to the humility required for initial success at the bottom of the employment ladder, which is the place where bods who have failed at school and left with no qualifications find themselves.

The problem for bods is that their preoccupation with a subversive and dominant male peer group sabotages the chances of legitimate success at school, and by implication in conventional working life, unless humility can be learned or enforced. Older Bermondsey men, who had, as youths, served their apprenticeships in various crafts and trades, were not unfamiliar with this dilemma. One man, Charlie, explains to me what it was like for him when he started work. When he left school at a young age, he got an apprenticeship as a fine mould plasterer. On his first day he was ritually humiliated: stripped naked and dunked in the liquid plaster, he then has his bollocks painted with lacquer by the older men. These kinds of ritual humiliation were, Charlie explains, standard practice for apprentices in all kinds of trades. After that, he says, 'I knew where I stood: I knew that at work I was nobody 'til I could work my way up.'

Unless he can accept the humiliation of starting at the bottom and working his way up the employment ladder, little by little the door opens wider to the world of illegitimate gains that bods are accustomed to through their fathers', uncles', cousins' or older siblings' lives of crime. As a boy becomes a man the all-important respect gained through the capacity for street violence must be matched with conspicuous consumption, and so cash matters, but it is hard to come by with no chance of a well-paid job. The point is that in Bermondsey the development and reproduction of economic and political relations are inseparable from the specific means of getting prestige. This transforms from one generation to the next and evolves as a developmental cycle over time: people who were involved in crime in their twenties are much less likely to be so in their thirties and forties when they are more likely to have been tamed by the necessities of trying to provide the necessary financial and moral support for family life.

So, for a young man at least, crime comes to seem like the easy way to get money and work becomes the harder option and harder still to come by if you have left school at 14 or 15 with nothing but a reputation on the street to trade by. Low wages and little opportunity put a bod at the bottom of an employment pecking order that undermines his reputation and leaves him with little choice but to continue living at home, dependent on a devoted mother whose patience is sorely tested but who won't see him go without. Thinking of a way out of economic stagnation, desperate for the respect given to a self-made man, thieving, and now especially drug dealing, becomes the last resort of the daring dispossessed in Bermondsey. Once notorious for its armed robbers in particular, the profession of crime in general remains a last-chance choice for Bermondsey bods who dream of a bigger and better life than manual, menial or semi-skilled labour can provide.

Puff

David has just recently been to court; he was charged and acquitted of possessing cannabis with intent to supply. Police raided the house after a tip-off, probably from an envious or revengeful acquaintance, but luckily there was insufficient evidence to prove that the cannabis found was not for personal use. David was fortunate to escape a custodial sentence; it was a first offence and his mother, Carolyn, was able to call upon the local priest to give a character testimony to the effect that leniency would be constructive. Carolyn emphasises how David now has a steady girl-friend who has got a good job in an office. She is relieved that he now spends a lot of his spare time with this girl at home. Evenings are usually spent indoors with 'a pizza, a puff [a marijuana cigarette] and a video' and David is, therefore, much less likely now to be out on the street looking for trouble with his friends.

On the day that the priest calls at Carolyn's to talk about the details of the testimony, I am there with Carolyn and her sister Claire. Carolyn is already distraught because David and Mark had been involved in a fight the night before with Roaders: these white boys had come looking for trouble in the pub opposite where the boys live. At the time, Carolyn had been out at the opera with her new boyfriend and was dressed accordingly. Arriving home late in the evening she had found her boys involved in a brawl outside the pub. Tough as nails herself and having no qualms about being able to handle herself in a fight, Carolyn had kicked off her elegant high heels and got stuck straight in whilst her companion hesitated on the sidelines. Breaking up the fight and taking the risk of getting hurt herself, Carolyn had been determined, as always, to protect her boys from harm. When I arrive at Carolyn's door the morning after the night before, one shoe remains where it was thrown off on the lawn outside the house. Like Cinderella's slipper, the elegant shoe bears testimony to a glamorous night out away from the troubles of Bermondsey life.

When the priest enters I am shocked to hear him swearing and blinding about the 'cunts' that had made it impossible for him to park properly outside. Later, after he has gone, Carolyn tells me about the time when she was still living with the boys' father and the same priest had called round. Everywhere cocaine had lain in piles, waiting to be weighed up and sold, and while Carolyn had got flustered about the priest's presence she noticed him calmly lick his finger and take a dip, saying nothing about it to her, but muttering appreciatively. Carolyn laughs in dismay about a priest without whom they would be lost but who has, nevertheless, been completely corrupted by his parishioners' ways. He is, she says, used to giving character testimonies and is called upon regularly.

The priest asks to see a recent photo of David so that he will know who he is talking about in court the next day, and when Carolyn hands him some family photos he recalls the notorious reputation for violent crime of David and Mark's father, from whom Carolyn is now estranged. All the credit for getting two sons close to manhood relatively unscathed, which is no mean feat in Bermondsey, goes to Carolyn. She is completely determined to get them safely through these last few years of their youth and she is tenacious in the face of the seductive danger of the precedent set by the boys' father and the lure of what it means for them to make their reputations on the street.

Following the court case, I ask David and Mark how they will walk the fine line between the choice of whether to make money out of work or crime. David does most of the talking because he is the older and respected brother and, in his presence, Mark defers to him:

David: 'I dunno really, ya just get on with both; like I work and think, I dunno, everyone wants money, it's just whether ya choose to make money legally or illegally really in'it? Most of our friends that do things illegally a lot of them are in prison, aren't they so . . .? A lot of my friends that are like a little bit older than John anyway, like a lot of your friends are still about [not in prison] ain't they? But I've still got a lot of friends that are about but a lot of friends that chose to like try and make big money at a young age a lot of them are in prison.'
Gillian: 'Does that stop you?'
David: 'It does make you think: is it worth it? But then again you could go and work and work for like ten years for what? On the other hand there ain't no point in workin' either, you can't really win.'
Gillian: 'So where does school fit in?'
David: 'At school you don't wanna lose face; everyone's the same really but that's in school, it ain't too serious when you're in school: you're just all tryin' to prove a point to each other, like you ain't really got money or nothin' at that point anyway so that don't matter.'
Gillian: 'Is that more about having a laugh [at school]?'
David: 'It's just makin' a name for yourself really ain't it when you're at school? And then, when you leave, it's more people then wanna earn money and that's when people make it in different ways?'
Gillian: 'So, it starts out like just a bit of a rep[reputation] at school?'
David: 'You leave school and then it really does hit ya. You think: shit what am I gonna do now and you do see people earn money that are doing things illegal and then see some people that are earning money doing things legal but then again there's people like our friend: he's like really brainy he stayed at sixth form and all that and now he's livin' with his girlfriend; he can't get a flat, can't a job can't get nothin', and like he's always been our friend but he was really clever at school and he stayed on and it ain't got him nowhere. You're takin' a chance really, like people say: it's a lot easier to go it legal but I think going legal . . .'
Gillian: 'It's harder [going legal]?'
David: 'It's 'ard to explain. You see people earning money like what you'd be working like six months for.'

Gillian: 'So, why is it then that at school, you know the stuff you were saying about having a name for yourself, why is it that school work can't be part of that?'

Mark: 'It's a culture in'it?'

Gillian: 'Tell me about that, when you say it's a culture.'

David: 'We wouldn't talk about it like that: our friends wouldn't look at it like that; it's a different sort of thing.'

Gillian: 'Is it just what you're used to?'

David: 'It's just when you do start secondary school and like you see the older boys and your older cousins or whoever you know that's older, if they're from round 'ere that's how they're actin' and really you're just followin' in their footsteps, I s'pose. And it's easier I s'pose in'it, when you're at school to like, not do your work and 'ave a laugh than to do your work and study. I mean if everyone's havin' a laugh it's a lot easier to just turn around and say look: I can't be bothered to do that – let's be naughty – than sit down and do it. That's basically it. It starts from school don't it? In'it? But it's when people leave school that it really hits ya, like what are they gonna do?'

Mark: 'See your mates drivin' buff cars now and you think. . . . (laughter)'

Gillian: '[Do you think:] How am I gonna get one?'

Mark: 'I'll just wait 'til I can drive me Bentley (laughter)'.

David and Mark realise, then, that the desire to make a name for themselves, which they have succeeded in, has at the same time thwarted their chances of getting or working towards a well-paid job or profession. At the same time, they struggle with the humiliation that taking a low-paid job entails. They are not convinced of the rationale of education, which suggests that if he works hard at school a boy will be guaranteed a better future; they reassure themselves that a million sacrifices made over thousands of days in school classrooms in order to work hard and do well may yield no greater rewards for a boy than the pleasure of as many pranks. I ask David and Mark if they imagine staying in Bermondsey and Mark instantly replies in the negative, explaining how much he wants to 'get out', but David, in contrast, describes how much he wishes Bermondsey were the kind of place that he could imagine his kids growing up in one day. I ask him why that is impossible and he says: 'It's not like it used to be. It's not a close community anymore, not like it used to be when everyone looked out for everyone else. There's 'ardly any Bermondsey people left here now, look at it.' David then points out of the window at the cranes which reach out of the construction sites close by and over the house where he now lives. 'These are not Bermondsey people movin' in 'ere. The new Bermondsey is for yuppies.'

Pub culture

Talking about how much and how quickly things have changed for young men in Bermondsey, Patrick describes for me the transformation in what he calls the pub culture. Whereas contemporary Bermondsey bods' fathers would, at a young age, have been in the pub making manhood out of beer, their sons are more likely now to be indoors with friends enjoying a pizza, a puff and a video. Patrick remembers smoking weed in his pre- and early-teens but, in those days, he explains, you couldn't buy puff in Bermondsey; you had to go all the way to Deptford to buy it from the West Indian café. If you wanted something more exotic you had to go as far as Leicester Square to get speed (amphetamines), for example, or LSD. When Patrick was young, smoking weed was something associated with black and specifically Jamaican men; bods had to be extremely streetwise to get hold of it. He recalls being 14 years old, doing 'penny for the guy' with his mates, desperately trying to get 10 shillings together so that they could send someone running down to Deptford to buy some puff. In those days it cost 10 shillings an ounce whereas now it is more likely to be £60–£80 and, like harder drugs, it is freely available and consumed all over Bermondsey, London and the rest of the country more generally.

Because puff is illegal, takes time to consume and has a pungent smell, consumption of it usually takes place behind closed doors. As a result, the economy of Bermondsey leisure time is now rapidly changing. Where once there was a thriving pub culture with beer at its heart, a pub on every corner and people drinking to the sound of live music and ready to get up and sing a good song themselves, all that is changing. The traditional practices associated with going to the pub, like getting dressed up for a Sunday lunchtime drink and dinner, are in decline. Pubs in Bermondsey are closing down by the month. Like vultures, eager developers stand ready to snap up those pubs which have failed to survive the decline in custom. Only the middle-aged and elderly remain staunch regulars in pubs where space is allocated according to who's who and which regular has sat where for the past thirty years.

One of the lads: on the gear: cocaine

Terry, aged 31, another middle-aged Bermondsey man, born and bred, who lives in the neighbourhood of Tenter Ground School, explains to me how, for men of his age, taking drugs goes hand in hand with, rather than displaces, the pub culture. This is possible, he says, because the drug he is talking about – cocaine – is more easily consumed in the pub. Revealing what the pressures of this pub/drug culture can be like for young men in Bermondsey, Terry blames the death of Bermondsey on the influx of drugs. He explains why he wants a different future for his young son and accounts for his own near-demise, from the perspective of the hard-won changes he is now struggling for in his own life:

> *Terry*: '[In the pubs] you got the piss 'eads, who you take no notice of; they get a bit lairy, you just give 'em a slap. Then you got, you got them categories: you got lairy ones, rowdy ones and the quiet ones; they're all Bermondsey people, but 'alf of 'em, well 99 per cent of 'em, are all taking cocaine anyway. They're all, if you walk in, ideally the King's Head, down the Blue, that's a Millwall/Bermondsey pub, everyone's "smart" [well dressed] sorted – cocaine. You walk in there everyone's on it and I'm talking from 15 up until 60 – everyone. If you ever go to a pub in Bermondsey you just watch how many men go to the toilet together (laughter). I'm being serious, you go to, well anywhere, it's not just Bermondsey, its any white male-dominated pub, everyone's on coke: you watch how many men go to the toilet together and it's all little packets, and that's it. You've got yer alcoholics who are low-life shit, you know who let their self go or you got alcoholics who are smart, on the gear, faces [men who are respected for something or men with a tough, criminal reputation] because everyone drinks, everyone, but in Bermondsey, it's the culture: you're brought up on the drink, cocaine. And you got two ways of doing it, you're either going to end up dead, heart-attack, alcoholic, lose everything or you could say, "No, I don't want that."
>
> 'Now, I'm lucky, I said no. I was an alcoholic. I was there, I was suicidal mate. I was gonna commit it, 'cos I was doin' it, but I'm 31, a lot of people couldn't 'andle it; they can't 'andle it because everyone's on it, that's why you got so many people fuckin' losin' it in Bermondsey now. But you can either say no, I was lucky, I got a second chance in life; half the people I talk to or see now, they're gonna go one way . . . either way you look at it, even though they've got a good life now 'cos they're drug dealers, as I say they ain't doin' nothin' but they're on the gear [drugs]. It only takes so long and you're dead, but the drink, once you 'ave cocaine you can drink as much as you want. So where . . . Everyday you're an alcoholic but when you're on cocaine you don't think you're an alcoholic 'cos that 'ang over's gone, you're there.'

Gillian: 'So, you don't feel like an alcoholic, you feel like a million dollars?'

Terry: 'Yeah all the time, oh yeah, but then that's only paranoia; you get paranoid about it and then you need more and more until the end of it – bang! You're gonna lose it, you're gonna die. Not so much die, yeah, well, that's the way I perceive it, 'cos that's where I was headin', that's where I would 'ave been. If I'd been, if I'd still 'ave been drinkin' I think I'd 'ave been dead now. Christmas I think I would 'ave lost it, but that's through abusin' myself you know? But I was lucky; I stopped, 13 months. First six was hard, but where I broke up with all that shit, when I was 21, got out of all the gang shit, but see I got married young, 24.'

Gillian: 'So, you broke up with your gang before you got married?'

Terry: 'Oh yeah, she was the barmaid in the pub we used to drink in. But even though I broke up with them I still [used to] see her every now and then but I was in my own world by then. I still [used to] see me close mates but I used to be taking cocaine, drink, drink, drink. I got made redundant in 1985, that's when it really hit me 'cos I got ten grand (£10 000) and then another eight [grand], so I had 18 grand in my pocket, done that within six months – horses, coke, booze, phew – gone, Jack the Lad then.

'You know, for that six months period, I can't really remember a lot, then I 'ad a fit. It got me. I was indoors, like, with me wife, but I just woke up, phew, I'm gonna die, that's how I felt, couldn't feel myself. Went to 'ave a bath, next thing I knew I woke up in 'ospital, but pissed myself, shit myself, broke my nose, bit my tongue, ambulance, bang! I went, no, that's it, I'll stop. Stopped for six months, no drinks, no drugs, nothin', got back in work . . . But by this time I'd done 18 grand, it was playin' on me mind . . . But no, I blame it on me childhood, no, not me childhood I can't blame that, but where I thought I was one of the boys, I thought I could 'andle that.

'You got two people [in Bermondsey], no, three people: doughnuts [people who don't get any respect], people who think they're gangsters or not gangsters, a face, or think they're something. And you've got people who are something, but really everyone's just wankers. I look at them now and I'll be honest with you, they don't bother me. You know? A lot of people go: "Oh, but . . . Frankie Frazer", 'cos he was a nutter, but anyone can be a nutter, anyone can take an axe to someone. So that doesn't . . . (pause)'

Gillian: 'Doesn't impress you?'

Terry: 'Nah.'

Gillian: 'So what does impress you now?'

Terry: 'What impresses me now? When I wake up in the mornin' and look at me kids. Me, I impress meself, 'cos I'm alive, stopped the drugs. I'm brave enough and I've admitted that I'm an alcoholic, 'cos it's not embarrassing to me, I took the wrong road and I'm not afraid to admit it . . . No, but I explain that on me thinking I want this life, I want to be one of the lads.'

Gillian: 'What I've seen is that the schools blame the parents, the parents blame the school, but on the street it seems like boys are constantly vying to see . . .'

Terry: 'You're seeing if, whose the guv'nor? Where you want to be in. You know?'

Gillian: 'Whether you can compete or not? It's about being a boy really isn't it?'

Terry: 'It's about being a boy in Bermondsey, Peckham, Brixton; you know; you've got it. It's impossible for you university people to understand. You've got it everywhere; it's just that Bermondsey is Bermondsey. Everyone knows Bermondsey is a racist area; everyone looks after each other, but that's a load of shit now, that's gone, that's finished, that finished ten years ago. That don't work like it anymore. Bermondsey's basically finished.'

Gillian: 'So what's finished it then?'

Terry: 'Drugs. A lot of friendships have split up 'cos of drugs.'

Gillian: 'So, it's almost like it's caving in from the inside?'

Terry: 'Yeah, it started, you 'ad the villains in the 60s, 70s . . . do the armed robberies, that's where they got their names from, your family [name] brings up [your family gets a reputation] 'cos his dad or his uncle is an armed robber, he's got a name. So that's where it starts from. In them days I s'pose I would have done armed robberies in the 70s; I would 'ave done that. But why go and do that with a gun when you can sell drugs? This is where it's gone over, you see? So from the early 80s up until today, it's drugs, drugs, drugs, drugs. So that's, and that's where it's fucked up 'cos people on drugs turn to crackers, you lose yer self respect and you lose yer respect for other people and people are competing . . .'

Gillian: 'So, it's like this closeness between people is being worn away?'

Terry: 'Oh, it's gone, it's finished.'

Gillian: 'But it's almost as if it's collapsing on the inside and people are blaming what's coming in from the outside.'

Terry: 'Nah, nah, nah . . . Everyone blames black people, brown, whatever. It's nothin' to do with that. They [Southwark Council] moved other people [in], and they fucked the housing estates up, they fucked it up. That's the way people will, are perceiving it now, everything's gone, that's why you get all this race hate shit goin' on.'

Terry, like Patrick, is proud to have survived what Bermondsey culture means for young men: dicing with danger and death through involvement in the self-destructive bravado that being 'one of the boys' in the pub demands. They have, at a young age, experienced it all – crime, booze, drugs and violence – and still come out the other side, glad to have got away with their lives. Terry now works two jobs: he has a regular day job and also a night job 'in the print' because he is saving up to put his baby son through private school. He knows that he has got a fight on his hands to save his son from what becoming a Bermondsey bod implies, which is a contender – a big-man in a short-life culture. Patrick, meanwhile, has struggled for the last ten years to help his only son, who is now in his early twenties, to kick a heroin habit. It is not getting his son off the gear that is a problem; every time his son does time (goes to prison) for another petty theft committed in the attempt to service his habit, he easily gets through the 'cold turkey' (withdrawal symptoms). The much harder challenge, Patrick explains, is keeping his son away from the peers who have influence over him and with whom he soon starts taking drugs again as soon as he's out of prison. Terry's strategy is to get away from Bermondsey, to move to Cornwall, which he has discovered through his passion for fishing. Whatever it takes, Terry is prepared to do it. He is desperate to secure his children's future because, he laments, Bermondsey has become a 'shit-'ole.'

Notes

1. Introduction: Social Class and Education

1. Wherever I quote actual speech I try to give a sense of the sound of the language, indicating, for example, where syllables are merged and consonants dropped, but there is nothing systematic (in a linguistic sense) about the way that I do this.

2. The classic British sociological antecedents, in the 1960s and 1970s, of this kind of study include Corrigan's *Schooling the Smash Street Kids*, Douglas's *The Home and the School* and Willis's *Learning to Labour*. At least three decades of research have followed but, despite much debate and untold numbers of policy initiatives, the issue of the relationship between social class and education remains as relevant now as it has ever been. I make no pretence, however, to have mastered the relevant literature in the sociology of education and neither do I come to the subject as a teacher, sociologist or educator. I am not, therefore, an expert in the field and my approach to it is, therefore, somewhat presumptuous.

   As a social anthropologist I am interested in the diversity of ways that humans come to be the particular kinds of persons that they are. I am fascinated by the social processes through which people come to be differentially valued and, purposefully naive about the literature on social class and education, I set out to see what kinds of new insights, if any, might arise from a contemporary ethnographic study of educational failure. Rather than focusing on social class *per se*, my theoretical and substantive attention is directed towards what it means, in any specific locality, to become a particular kind of, in this case, British person. My theoretical aim, following Toren's (1990, 1999) broadly phenomenological and anthropological theory of the learning person, is to work towards a theory which allows for ethnographically grounded, historically specific studies of people in situ and which is, at the same time, equal to the task of hypothesising about generalities in the processes concerning human development. Rather than imposing existing analytical categories on to those people that I encountered during my fieldwork research, my intention, rather, was to make analytical the ethnographic categories through which people make sense of their everyday lives. In a sense, then, I have ordered my research practice in a reverse direction: I approach the literature only after having first produced my ethnography, which is a highly unusual, but hopefully productive way to have gone about things.

3. In Britain, compulsory education (for 5 to 16-year-olds), which is free at the point of access, is the outcome of Butler's Education Act of 1944. This Act set out the structure for the post-war British education system, raising the school-leaving age to 15 and providing three types of schools: grammar, secondary modern and technical. Butler's hope was that schools like this would cater for different academic levels as well as other than academic aptitudes. Entry to the various schools was based on the 11+ examination. Over time, however,

criticism grew about the idea of selection at 11 because those children going to secondary moderns were not getting as good an education as those children in grammar schools. A few Local Education Authorities (LEAs) started to experiment with the idea of comprehensive schools which were designed to provide a better education for children of all abilities. Initially there was a lot of resistance to the idea of comprehensive schooling but by the 1960s the government, which was at that time Labour controlled, began to prepare for a gradual transition away from grammar schools. This policy was supported by subsequent Labour and Conservative governments and by 1990 most grammar schools had gone independent or become comprehensive. Because, in contemporary times, the standard of education in many comprehensives is now relatively poor, scepticism is expressed about the wisdom of having phased out the grammar schools. Those children from working class families who would have passed the 11+ examination and benefited from a grammar school education can now no longer do so and they are much less likely, therefore, to fulfil their academic potential.

4. Speech by David Bell HMCI – Annual Report 2003/4 press conference, Ofsted (Office for Standards in Education), UK. A copy of the full report is also available: Annual Report of Her Majesty's Chief Inspector of Schools 2003/4, Ofsted, UK, 2005.

5. Feinstein (1998). Feinstein uses data from the 1970 British Cohort Study (BCS70), which is an ongoing and multi-disciplinary longitudinal study conducted by the Centre for Longitudinal Studies at the Institute of Education in London. The subjects of study are people living in Britain who were born between 5 and 11 April 1970. The first survey of about 17 000 subjects, which took place in 1970, was a medical survey conducted at birth because there were concerns that foetal malnutrition, as a result of the mother living in poverty, might be the cause of congenital brain abnormalities which could, through impaired brain functioning, affect children's later development. Since then several other information-gathering exercises have been undertaken with the same cohort of subjects. Each new survey has broadened its scope to include first physical and educational development, for example at age 5, and then physical, educational and social development at the ages of 10 and 16. The assessments, which were carried out by health visitors, included tests of intellectual, emotional and personal development. At the point at which the subjects were 26 years of age another survey was taken of the cohort's physical, educational, social and economic development. In 1999/2000 BCS70 collaborated with the National Child Development Study (NCDS) to interview subjects who were then aged 29, about an even broader range of subject matters.

6. Because factors in children's outside-school background are so significant for educational achievement, Feinstein's research undermines the Labour government's strategy of aiming to reduce overall inequality via targeted investment in Britain's schools. Hence the most recent debates about the best means of supporting children to learn successfully prior to compulsory schooling and policy initiatives for increased investment in pre-school education, e.g. Sure Start. It has been suggested, however, that the low adult-to-child ratios in these kinds of pre-school learning environments makes it highly unlikely that the overwhelming significance of factors outside school will be outweighed through pre-school education.

7. See, for example, Eysenck (1971), Jensen (1969) and, more recently, Herrnstein and Murray (1994). The genetic argument is based on the following ideas about intelligence: it is fixed and can be measured using scientific IQ (Intelligence Quota) tests; such tests have shown that working class students are less intelligent that middle class ones; that within each class black students are less intelligent than white ones; that these differences in IQ scores explain educational inequalities; and that class differences correlate with educational attainment because intelligence is inherited. The arguments against this kind of explanation suggest, on the contrary, that IQ tests only measure the way that innate intelligence interacts with the social environment and particular aspects of the social environment are weighted in the IQ tests. The point is that it is not possible to separate out the part of the test that measures the influence of social environment and that which measures innate intelligence. There is, therefore, no agreed definition of intelligence. IQ tests cannot, therefore, tell us about any particular child's potential nor can they account for the conditions under which the tests are taken which may be familiar to some but highly unfamiliar to others.

8. For a fascinating history of working class self-education see Rose's (2001 [1952]), *The Intellectual Life of the British Working Classes*. It is notable that literature searches about working class children's educational successes produce very few easily accessible results; the focus on failure is overwhelming.

9. Influenced by Bourdieu's phenomenological theory of practice (1977) and interested in investigating the differences between formal and informal learning with a particular focus on apprenticeship, Lave and Wenger (1991) argue that informal learning is characterised by its distinctive, socially situated and participatory character. The novice's position is best described, they suggest, as one of legitimate peripheral participation. Simply stated this means that novices, as relative outsiders – those on the periphery of any particular 'community of practice' – must accommodate to the structurally specific form that participation takes. In so far as they acquiesce, novices' learning is legitimate. By implication, resistance to the form that participation takes becomes illegitimate learning and exclusion of participants is also a denial of their legitimacy. The potential for conflict is, therefore, inherent in the participative form that learning how to belong takes. The point to emphasise is that it is in and through learning, in practice, how to participate appropriately that a novice comes to understand (a) how relations between people in the community are structured and (b) what that means for his or her own social position vis-à-vis others.

10. Professor Stephen J. Ball, author of *Class Strategies and the Education Market*, argued in his inaugural lecture at the Institute of Education that, 'The effort that goes into the assembly and maintenance of an able middle class child is largely the result of work by the mother.' Professor Ball calls this effort 'intensive parenting'. Diane Reay (2005), adapting Bourdieu's notion of 'cultural capital', calls the kind of work that is done by middle class mothers to increase their children's educational life chances 'emotional labour', and classifies the advantage that accrues to middle class children as a result of it as 'emotional capital'. Other authors of research about middle class parents and children have stressed how much pressure this kind of parenting can put on young people. Professor Sally Power, author of *Education and the Middle Class* (2003)

explains how, despite relatively high levels of attainment, high expectations of academic success can lead to feelings of low esteem. Middle class young people in high-achieving schools can often feel that if they're not the very best in their class or didn't get a place at the very best universities then they're not good enough.

11. This kind of early social segregation through schooling also tends to be perpetuated in later life: middle and working class people encounter each other at work where the basis of the unequal relation between them is substantiated and maintained, but outside work, because of the different kinds of homes and neighbourhoods they live in and differences in the kinds of leisure activities they pursue, middle and working class people tend not to mix in an environment where they can encounter each other on a more equal basis.

2. Sharon: Common-as-Shit

1. According to Sharon's way of classifying people, a posh person is someone who thinks they are 'upper' (upper class), i.e. better than common (lower class) people like her.
2. Names of estates have been changed.
3. A 'manor' is a working class term for the local territory a person belongs to in London; it is a borrowing from the aristocratic equivalent and has its origins in the aristocratic history of the area. During the period of my research, for example, the official title of Lord of the Manor of Bermondsey was auctioned with bids starting at £50 000. Bermondsey, which was once classified as being outside London's boundaries in the borough of Surrey, was originally called Beormund's Eye; in the Domesday Book it was listed as belonging to the King. In the eleventh century an abbey was built which, for centuries, dominated as a site of religious and royal significance in what was otherwise an essentially rural, village-based location. The abbey was home to Queen Catherine who was consort of Henry V and Elizabeth Woodville who was Queen of Edward IV. Henry VIII confiscated the abbey in 1539 and later sold it to a private owner who had it torn down during the Reformation.
4. Bermondsey people make the same kind of jokes about people from Deptford, who live less than half a mile away to the southeast. Deptford people are also teased about having their own Irish-based language, which Bermondsey people call 'pikey', 'gypsy' or 'diddikoi' slang.
5. Astonishing about this discovery is the way that it mirrors, almost fifty years on, what Willmott and Young (1957) found to be true of working class communities in London in the 1950s. Other examples of anthropological studies of English communities formed on the basis of born-and-bred kinship relations include those by Edwards (2000) and Strathern (1981), in which the authors show how the question of what it means to be a so-called 'real' member of these communities, is continuously worked out in relation to people's preoccupation with kinship and residence criteria.
6. To bowl is to walk in a way that embodies confidence and pride in having and maintaining a tough reputation. A person might accuse a man of arrogance, saying, 'Look at him: he's got a bowl on him, ain't he?' A man who

bowls is often seen with a tough-looking fighting dog, such as an English or Staffordshire bull terrier, which becomes an accessory to his intimidating stance.

7. A bod is a Bermondsey youth or young man with a tough street reputation.

8. In Bermondsey, because there is the perception that everyone knows everyone else, there is the necessity for a degree of caution about gossip. There is every likelihood that the person one is talking about might be known or related to the person one is talking to. I quickly realise that loyalty to friends and family requires discretion. Anita explains to me that whilst she is aware that for some people 'keepin' to your own' means not mixing with black people, for her it means that 'you don't shit on your own doorstep': the loyalty of friends and family means more to her than following social taboos, so that a black person who is her friend is worth more to her than a stranger who is white.

9. The Blue is an area most likely named after the Blue Anchor pub on Blue Anchor Lane. It is at the heart of Bermondsey life because the street market that was there was once the principal shopping location. The shops on either side of Southwark Park Road are still frequented, but only a handful of market stalls remain.

10. When I refer to manners my intention is to bring the reader's attention to the whole range of bodily dispositions by which different class positions are held to be identifiable. For example, a common woman hails me as I walk past a pub where she is having a drink and she remarks, laughing, 'I'd recognise that walk anywhere, Gillian: head held high, chin up. You're so posh, you don't walk – you glide. Even when I saw you pissed in the Alscot [a pub], I still recognised you by the way you walk.'

11. At a young age, instead of translating my education into a well-paid career, I fell in love and had children with a talented, dedicated, but at that stage, penniless musician; when our eldest daughter was a baby we were, therefore, both living on benefits and claiming housing benefit for our council flat.

12. The increasing kudos in Britain associated with being working class is evinced in the increasing numbers of public figures who 'talk common', especially on television. Jamie Oliver, an Essex boy who became a celebrity chef, is a good example. 'Talking proper' or what might once have been called 'BBC English' is becoming a thing of the past and people who talk like this find themselves discriminated against in the media and confined to serious news-type programmes. Anita maintains that the increasing visibility of common people in positions of importance is a sign of the changing times because, in the old days, she says, working class people only ever knew power collectively, as a group.

3. Common Women: Working Class Values

1. For a sociological analysis of class-related processes of distinction see Bourdieu's classic book entitled *Distinction: a Social Critique of the Judgement of Taste* (1984).

2. It is interesting that the embodiment of social class position even means learning what constitutes an acceptable decibel level in private speaking tone and also in comportment pertaining to the voice in public situations.

3. Anita explains to me that because 'talking proper' is associated with being gentle and polite, common women often worry about being perceived, by posh people, as aggressive.
4. Sharon's partner keeps himself scarce when I spend time in the house. Waiting until 'that posh cow' has gone, he usually hides himself away in the bedroom, playing on his Sony Playstation.
5. Long before fish and chips or kebabs, pie n' mash was the traditional fast food of working class London. It occupies a place in many people's hearts because it is the kind of food that they were treated to as children: their mums or nans would take them for pie n' mash on a Saturday for a special treat. Not all people like it, but those who do are often fiercely loyal about which pie n' mash shop they frequent. One man that I interview proudly describes how he travels all the way back from Bromley to have pie n' mash at Manze's on Tower Bridge Road and he won't eat pie n' mash anywhere else. He values the place and its food as an inseparable part of Bermondsey's tradition; he loves the old-fashioned benches for sitting at and the preserved features of the old décor.
6. Tulips (a pseudonym) is an after-school, church-related group similar to Brownies.
7. Catalogue debt is especially prevalent because the catalogue is the means by which the often close neighbourhood relations of working class women are turned into a discount for the woman running the scheme as a concession from her home.
8. An elderly woman explains to me that she wasn't allowed to go to grammar school because her older sisters hadn't got places. Her mother was too worried that going to grammar school would make her daughter feel that she was better than her sisters. The elderly woman uses this example to illustrate the point she is trying to make, which is that, 'Workin' class people can be their own worst enemies.'
9. See Part II, Chapters 5–7.

4. Trouble on the Estates

1. See Parts II and III.
2. Stephen Lawrence, a young black teenager, was stabbed to death in a racially motivated murder on 22 April 1993. There were five main suspects, three of whom were brought to trial in a private prosecution in 1996, but all were acquitted due to lack of evidence. Committal proceedings against the two other suspects were also dropped for the same reasons. These five men are still suspects but having once been tried for murder they cannot, under current British law, ever be retried. Stephen's parents were never satisfied with the first murder investigation conducted by the Metropolitan Police Service (MPS) and the Home Secretary, Jack Straw, later ordered an official inquiry into the death which was led by Sir William Macpherson. The inquiry found that the first investigation by the MPS was indeed flawed in various ways and concluded that the underlying cause of police failure was institutional racism. This accusation was rejected by Sir Paul Condon, the then Police Commissioner, who acknowledged that individual officers can be racist and that racist attitudes can, therefore, pervade an institution, but, he suggested, the label of institutional

racism would cause more problems for the police and the community than it was going to solve.

3. It is important to emphasise that the prejudice, which working class people in Britain may feel towards black and Asian people, is not so very different to the prejudice that middle and upper class people have historically felt towards the working classes. What matters is that whilst the middle and upper classes took for granted the inferiority of the working classes, the working classes also took for granted the inferiority of the 'coloured' peoples subjugated by British rule. During the era of industrialisation in Britain, when liberal-minded philanthropists and politicians became interested in, and/or horrified by, the living conditions of the labouring classes in the slums of the cities, the squalor they discovered was sometimes likened to the living conditions of the 'Negroes in Africa':

> For as the British contemplated the unprecedented numbers massed together in their new industrial cities, they tended to compare these great towns at home with the dark continents overseas and thus equate the workers in factories with coloured peoples abroad. The 'shock cities' of the 1830s were seen as resembling 'darkest Africa' in their distant, unknown and unfathomable menaces; and during the third quarter of the nineteenth century London's newly discovered 'residuum' and 'dangerous classes' were likened in their character and their conduct to the 'Negroes of Empire'.
>
> (Cannadine 2002: 5–6)

The end of Empire has, however, transformed that hierarchical relationship between the white working classes and the black and Asian subjects of British colonial rule. As the Empire has retracted it has, like a centripetal force, bought with it – onto the doorsteps of the council estates – the face-to-face reality of a relationship between different kinds of British subjects that was only previously maintained at a distance, across the miles and largely in the imagination. With this change has come the challenge of equality for all British subjects regardless of their racial, ethnic, cultural or class background. This relatively recent ideal of equality strains, however, against the historical precedent of an overwhelmingly hierarchical history in Britain. Most interesting about this is the way that anger about inequality is more often directed down, and not up the social ladder.

4. One elderly woman explains to me, for example, that when she had brought the man she loved home, to meet her father, she was nervous because it was a young man from Peckham – a white man – but an outsider nevertheless. The woman explains that she will never forget her father's response. He had said to her scathingly, 'What d'ya wanna bring a bloody foreigner in the family for?'

5. Although the right-wing BNP (British National Party) has gained a foothold in several traditionally white working class communities in England, it has failed to do so in Bermondsey because the organisers (the same is also true for the NF (National Front)) are always classified, by Bermondsey people, as outsiders and are, therefore, rejected. Racial politics in Bermondsey are most often worked out on the ground, among youths, on the street, on the estates and, on the periphery, in territorial battles with youths from beyond Bermondsey's boundaries with other manors.

6. During campaigning for the general election in the year 2000 the Conservative Party attempted to fight for a cohesive cultural vision of England and Britain which they portrayed as being under threat from the twin evils of liberalism at home and uncontrolled immigration from abroad. The Labour Party broadcasts, meanwhile, side-stepped the delicate ground of racial and cultural politics in an endeavour to stick to rationally calculated economic agendas. Liberal Democrat Home Affairs Spokesman and Member of Parliament for North Southwark and Bermondsey, Simon Hughes, accused William Hague, then leader of the Conservatives, of inflaming racial tension with ill-chosen words about asylum seekers, and Simon Hughes was, in turn, accused of playing the race card himself. Most people are unaware, however, of the extent to which rhetoric that incites racial hatred poses a very real danger in Simon Hughes's constituency.

7. The cultivation of a specific ethical disposition may or may not include religious instruction. For Emma's Bangladeshi Muslim friends, their understanding of what it means to become a viable person is undoubtedly influenced by religious instruction, but for Emma this is far from true. As for myself, I become aware of how far the idea of what it means to be middle class is, in Britain, closely related to a particular religious history. Even though I have had no religious instruction myself, because my parents were atheists, and I have given my daughters no religious influence whatsoever, I am conscious of the fact that I am only three generations removed from a working class background, and, on my mother's side, only two generations removed from a strict Methodist upbringing. The case for a relationship between the rise of particular forms of Protestantism and the development of capitalist economies has been argued by Weber (1930) and applied, by E. P. Thompson (1963), to the English case in his classic historical study of the relationship between the rise of Methodism and the formation of the working classes.

5. Tom at Tenter Ground

1. *South Park* is an American cartoon featuring a group of young children who are constantly engaged in nefarious activities; they never do as they are told and they swear a lot. In every episode one among them dies during their escapades. I often hear Tom brilliantly mimicking the voices of the *South Park* characters; he can also draw them from memory. Cartoons like *South Park* and *The Simpsons* cleverly satirise conventional ideas about childhood and family life.

2. For the sake of confidentiality the name of the school and all children and adults mentioned in the book have been changed.

3. Part of the reason for improved living standards amongst London's poor and for the formation of a Victorian middle class was the popularisation of birth control methods, which gave women a degree of control over family planning. Note that whilst Tom's mother Anne objects strongly to Tom having to share a small bedroom with his sister, she takes for granted the family's sole use of a living room, kitchen, dedicated bedroom for the parents and a bathroom/toilet. Mrs Waldman, in contrast, had to share a bedroom with eleven other family members – adults and children – and baths were taken in a tub in the kitchen. Nowadays, parents would ideally like each of their children to have a bedroom

of their own, especially when siblings are not of the same gender. Pressure for council accommodation is, however, extremely high because there is no longer a state commitment to new building and it is virtually impossible for a family to get rehoused just because of overcrowding. Often the flats that are available are hard-to-let properties in a state of disrepair which have frequently been turned down many times by other prospective tenants. Those families who are currently on the council housing list are classed as emergency cases; they are usually housed through referral to independent housing associations, which have higher rents than council properties.

4. The Ragged School Movement was established by the charitable efforts of churches and individual members of the gentry during the era of industrialisation. The aim was to provide education for destitute children.

5. The regeneration of Bermondsey began when Terence Conran purchased a huge area of derelict riverside dock and warehousing during the 1980s for conversion into a residential and continental restaurant complex. In the early 1990s some of the wharves and warehouses were still being used to store imported spices and on breezy days the whole development was filled with the smell of cinnamon, cloves and other delicious odours. Capitalising on this romantic association, the new luxury apartment blocks have been named after the various spices. This property development, which has transformed the redundant riverside industrial sites into premium value residential areas, has spread slowly into the interior of the borough and along the length of the South Bank. The irony is that these expensive property developments are interspersed in an area that has one of the highest densities of council estates in the country. This means that apartments worth a minimum of half a million pounds often overlook run-down council estates where tenants pay on average £60–£80 a week for their flats.

When Butlers Wharf was still derelict it was squatted by a group of artists who did it up and lived there for a long period of time. When the development of the wharf began they were told they could stay but would have to move temporarily so that the roof could be repaired. Alas, once they moved out they weren't allowed back, but the council rehoused them around the area and the group went on to form the BAG (Bermondsey Artists Group) which now runs the Café Gallery in Southwark Park. They are founders of a housing co-operative in Rotherhithe Street and, like Bermondsey people, they are opposed to the 'posh yuppies', which is what they call the wealthy people who have moved into the converted wharfs apartments. Yuppies are just one kind of outsider in Bermondsey; they are resented because they bring nothing to the established working class community, they don't frequent the pubs, don't send their children to local schools or spend money in local shops and businesses. In contrast, local people embrace BAG because the group do a lot of creative work in the community.

6. There is a long history of Irish immigration to Bermondsey beginning when Irish men were brought over to build the docks. Their strength and tenacity has become the stuff of legend; they laboured by day, drank all evening and slept in the warehouses by night because no residential accommodation was provided for them. The strong Irish contingency on the docks supported the Catholic Church in Bermondsey, which remains influential today. At the dockers' social club an elderly man tells me that his father was out of work for long periods

of time because the Irish Catholics controlled the distribution of work on the dock and his father, who was a Protestant, was often overlooked. An Irish nun in Bermondsey also explains to me how strong is the level of prejudice among Irish immigrants in Bermondsey against black and Asian immigrants. She never ceases to be surprised at how longstanding immigrants, like the Irish, are often the ones to express the most vehement levels of discrimination and prejudice against more recently arrived and more visually identifiable groups of immigrants.

7. Kent has a romantic place in many Bermondsey people's hearts because they remember going there as children to help their parents with the summer work picking hops. This was as close to a summer holiday as most poor families in Bermondsey ever got. Nowadays, rather than moving out of Bermondsey, the few couples with young children who have become homeowners here mark the changing fortunes of the place and its people; they are the first generation of Bermondsey people for whom owning their own property was ever conceivable. Increasingly, however, because of the hyper-inflated market for central warehouse conversion apartments, private property in Bermondsey is out of reach for first- or even second-time local buyers. Decent quality housing at affordable prices is extremely scarce in Bermondsey as it is elsewhere in London. Many people who can afford to buy their own property and would prefer to stay close to the community they grew up in, near family and friends, are forced to move out of the area unless they choose the right to buy their council flat. For young families, however, this is not usually an option and they usually end up staying in overcrowded conditions in their parents' or grandparents' homes while they wait to find suitable accommodation of their own.

8. Anne has had no contact at all with Tom's father for over a year, and that's how she prefers it because he is unreliable and causes too much trouble. Middle-aged women in Bermondsey, many of whom are no longer with the fathers of their children, recall their parents' generation for whom marriage was still a sacred institution which, whether it was a happy marriage or not, meant that couples stayed together until death. Many women tell me that it is a rare thing now to find, in Bermondsey, a middle-aged couple that are still married with children living at home. This historical shift in the structure of kinship relations and household organisation is of course not unique to Bermondsey and many sociological trends here mirror those in England and Britain more generally.

9. 'Likes a drink' is a phrase used to describe people who drink a lot; it can be a polite way of describing someone who verges on becoming, or has actually been, an alcoholic.

10. Cocaine is widely available in Bermondsey but you have to know which pubs to get it from without any recriminations. The joke amongst women is that men used to think that women went to the toilet together because they liked the female company but of course now it might literally be because they want to 'powder their noses'.

11. Whilst boys and young men bowl when they walk, Bermondsey women, like Anne, who have had to be tough in the past, also have a distinctive body posture. Anne stands upright and proud, shoulders back and chest forward; it is something like a fighting stance. This is a posture which says as much about

Anne's pride and resilience as it does about the necessity for her to constantly demonstrate her capacity for self-defence.

12. Children from one block of flats tend to hang together and may pit themselves against other groups of children from other blocks on one estate. Otherwise, children from one estate might gang together against those from other estates, but more established teenage gangs or 'firms' (groups of teenage boys) who are antagonistic towards rivals gangs within Bermondsey's boundaries, will, nevertheless, come together if a group of enemy boys from outside Bermondsey threatens them.

13. 'Digging out' means to have a go at, moan at or threaten someone or something. So for example a person might say, '[H]'e was diggin' me out [he was having a go at me]', 'I dug [h]'im right out when I see [h]'im [I had a go at him]', or 'She was diggin' out me new shirt [she took the piss out of or said she didn't like my new shirt].'

14. See Part I for a description of the differences between kinds of common girls. Girls, like Emma's older sister Sophie, and indeed women like Anne, who have a reputation for being able to fight, exist in contrast to 'nice girls', like Tom's sister, Mary, and 'decent' women like Pete's sisters in Kent.

15. Compare her case with that of Sharon's daughter Tracey (see Part I).

16. This is an example of just one among the many kinds of exchanges through which the development of fieldwork relationships are made possible.

17. Although I have less time to observe Tom's relationship to Pete because Pete is most often at work when I am visiting, the parental relationship seems to be one of respect, which means, for example, that I don't observe the same degree of joking between Tom and Pete as Tom enjoys with his mother.

18. In conversation with a Special Educational Needs Co-ordinator (SENCO) who has worked for twenty years in the same Bermondsey secondary school, I learn about her impression of an emerging trend: she suggests that the children of first- and second-generation immigrant families, such as those of West African backgrounds, are now surpassing their peers' achievements at school. She stresses that it is often the Caribbean and white working class children who are being left behind. Another head teacher of a local primary school explains how she often gets white working class parents coming in to school because they are worried about the negative influence which they fear black boys might be having on their children's education. In response, she says, she has to explain to those parents that, in fact, her greatest concern is for the often chronic low achievement of white working class boys. Her apprehension stems, she says, from her awareness that in some local families, boys come from a background in which there have been generations of disregard for education.

A middle-aged Bermondsey man suggests to me, in contrast, that in 'the old days' working class people had always been in awe of teachers. Treating them as if they were somehow 'superhuman', parents would have been loath to approach them for any reason. At the same time he emphasises that, in those days, there had been no expectation that children should be prepared, by their parents, for school work. Nowadays, the man remarks, Bermondsey parents would probably be accused of 'bad parenting' because parents are expected to do more for their children, but, he points out, this idea was unheard of years ago. He tells me that when he was a boy he regularly heard fathers say to their children, 'I can't read or write and it ain't bothered me', but despite this lack of parental involvement he has no recollection of boys misbehaving so badly in class the way that they do now; this, he says, is because when he was young teachers were highly respected and still had authority.

19. In the 1990s a plethora of books and articles were published about the changing relationship between gender and education. This research took a number of different directions and it followed on from earlier feminist studies of education that sought to redress a gender imbalance, which has historically meant that women and girls in Britain have not enjoyed equal opportunities with men and boys in employment and education. The research brought the rising levels of girls' achievements to academics', the public's and policy-makers' attentions. Statistical analyses were beginning to show, for example, that girls were closing the gender gap and indeed, in time, reversing the trend in which boys had always been expected to outperform girls. See, for example, Epstein et al. (1998) and Arnot et al. (1999). This educational trend, which is now widely discussed and much-researched, is labelled as the problem of boys' underachievement.

In 1996, Chris Woodhead who was then HMCI, reported on boys' increasing failure to match girls' educational achievement and particularly problematic, he suggested, was white working class boys' failure to learn. He suggested that it was one of the most disturbing problems we face within the education system. Diane Abbott later suggested in an article written for the *Sunday Observer* in 2002, that the most difficult crisis facing the British educational system was the chronic underachievement of black boys. The problem with separating the problem of white working class boys' underachievement from that of black boys, however, is that with respect to white boys, what is emphasised is their social class position and what we learn about black boys is always to do with their racial, ethnic and cultural difference. My suggestion, if we are to make sense of this crisis of boys' underachievement, is for studies which enable us to appreciate (a) how similar black and white working class boys are and (b) how relevant the racial, ethnic and cultural distinctiveness of white working class boys in Britain is. Thereafter we need to understand, for both black and white boys, how their understanding of what makes them different is constituted in social practice.

In order to approach this task, I propose here a theory of the person, which can account for gender, race, ethnicity, class and culture as inseparable and embodied aspects of what it means to become British. For this kind of study we need a theory of becoming (Toren 1999): a theory of what it means, over time, to become a particular kind of person and develop a specific 'way of being' in relation to others. It is this 'way of being' that Bermondsey people are trying to account for when they talk of their cultural distinctiveness and so, to understand those 'ways', we need to advance our theories about and conduct studies of how, through the processes of learning in childhood, people come to take their way of being in the world for granted.

20. The achievement of a conscious awareness of being a Bermondsey bod doesn't usually occur until the teenage years anyway. This is because it arises out of the territorial conflicts that Bermondsey youths have with outsiders from Peckham, the Walworth Road and Tower Hamlets to the north of the

river. It is in the course of these conflicts, either at secondary schools or on the streets, that Bermondsey children find out who they are because others give them the ascription that they are 'Bermondsey'. This means that young children whose parents are resident in, but new to the area, and know nothing about its industrial history or the genealogical precedence of key families, can still become more 'like Bermondsey'. These marginal youths often try harder to prove themselves in the peer group because of the self-conscious desire for acceptance from a group of young people that meet the criteria of belonging without having to try so hard.

21. Tom was permanently excluded from his last primary school because of persistent altercations with the classroom assistant.

6. The Classroom and School

1. For a fascinating historical and ethnographic record of children's playground games see the classic work on the subject by Peter and Iona Opie entitled *Children's Games in Street and Playground* (1969).

2. Piaget's theories of child development (see, for example, 1926, 1929, 1953, 1958, 1971), although widely criticised in contemporary times in part because of the underestimation of infants' abilities and neglect of the social underpinnings of consciousness, were revolutionary because Piaget established that the foundation of mind as the condition for human knowing is sensory-motor action. Before children ever acquire language they must first embody the physical, temporal and spatial properties of the material world. They do this via sensory-motor engagement with objects in the world, which led Piaget to go so far as to argue that all thinking is repressed movement.

3. The difference between the way the middle class teachers deal with children and the way that common mothers deal with them was brought home to me when I accompanied the class on a school trip. Some of the mothers joined us to help out with supervising the children and when Mara, the softly spoken head teacher, was failing miserably in her attempts to get Tom to behave while we were waiting for the coach to arrive, Sharon, Emma's mother, stepped in. From right at the back of the line in which we were trying to get the children to queue up, she screamed, 'Tom, you get back 'ere by me you little bastard. I'll keep an eye on you.' Mara then came to talk to Sharon, saying, 'We don't talk to children like that at school.' Laughing, Sharon then said to Mara, 'Oh yeah, well you wanna start 'cos he won't give me no problems when I'm dealin with 'im the way 'e knows.' Happily Tom then ran to stand next to Sharon and was good as gold whilst she teased him kind-heartedly, swearing fit to burst about what a troublesome boy he is.

Whilst corporal punishment in schools ended many years ago, there is also, in recent times, a move towards ending parents' rights to physically punish their children. This is commensurate with recent developments in the area of children's rights, which, in turn, is reflective of modern political change in the last century during which time rights of all kinds have been extended to previously marginalised groups. As a consequence of these developments our ideas about what it means to be a child are changing in contemporary times. For scholarship about how the idea of what it means to be a child is socially constituted see the groundbreaking sociological and anthropological contributions of James et al. (1998), James and Prout (1997) and Jenks (1996). For an understanding of how ideas of the child have changed in different historical periods see, for example, the work of Ariès (1973).

For teachers, the question of what to do about disruptive boys in general, and violent behaviour in particular, is a pressing one, but it is a fallacy to suppose that success in formal learning is guaranteed when children's tranquil comportment is hard won by teachers through strict discipline. When corporal punishment was at its highest level in Bermondsey secondary schools, academic results were no better, but life must have certainly been a lot easier for the teacher in the classroom. From a historical perspective the problem posed by disruptive boys at school is to do not only with the way that these boys disrupt their own chances of fulfilling their potential at school, or how they sabotage the prospects of other children who want to learn and have the potential to do well, it is also about how these boys disrupt our assumptions concerning adults' unquestioned power and authority over children.

4. Permanent exclusion means that a boy, if he cannot gain access to an alternative school, then has to attend a certain number of hours a week at what is called a PDU (Pupil Deferment Unit). Here, of course, he will meet and have to accommodate to another peer group that is likely to be even more hardened than the one he has left behind at school. The drop-out rate at these units is extremely high, which means, ultimately, that the street has then claimed the child.

5. Towards the end of my research, by the time Gary has finished primary school, he, like some of the more academically able boys in the class, is offered one of a few places for able children at a summer school held during the holidays in one of the local secondary schools. Gary accepts the place but is unable to toe the line and he finds himself expelled after only a week's attendance. In September 2000 Gary begins secondary school, but before the end of the first term, he is, as Christine predicted, permanently excluded from school.

6. The school year in Britain runs from September to the middle of July with a long summer holiday throughout August; there are also extended breaks at Christmas and Easter.

7. Each primary school varies in the degree to which the relation of respect between children and teachers is constituted in formal terms, such as in the use of titles for teachers, like Mrs, Miss or Mr so and so, rather than children being on first-name terms with teachers and other staff members. Tenter Ground also has a relaxed attitude to school uniform policy: there are school colours and a school sweatshirt but no formal uniform, which is frowned upon by some parents who see it as a relaxation of formality and, therefore, of discipline. There is nothing to say, however, that schools with high degrees of formality don't have problems with discipline because they often do; neither can we assume that schools which encourage informal relations between teachers and children will inevitably have problems with discipline.

8. The fixed and angry stare is one among many behaviour management techniques that Christine utilises to quell inappropriate behaviour.

9. During a normal school day the majority of the time is taken up with lessons in literacy, numeracy, and to a lesser degree, science. Relatively little time is devoted to other pursuits such as humanities, art, music, drama or sport.

10. Whilst disruptive boys demand the most attention in class, David is more likely to be worried, he explains, about those children, and girls in particular, who might be abnormally quiet and withdrawn. These children can easily go unnoticed but they often pose the greatest risk to themselves and present the hardest kinds of problems for the psychotherapist to solve.

11. The management, within the school, of children's behavioural problems is seen to be the joint responsibility of the Special Educational Needs Co-ordinator (SENCO) and the head teacher who between them are supposed to follow the national code of practice for children with educational, emotional and behavioural difficulties. In practice, however, there is very little funding for this kind of work and when the SENCO at Tenter Ground retires there is no money to replace him so the burden of the job falls squarely on the head teacher in whom the teachers have no faith.

12. Good enough parenting is a concept taken from the work of D. W. Winnicott, who came up with the idea of the 'good enough mother'.

13. Fearing for her health and finally admitting defeat, Christine resigns in December of the year 2000 at the same time as my fieldwork also finishes.

7. Who Rules the School?

1. Fatema is a woman of Bengali Muslim descent who lives locally. She runs extra English classes for the Bengali children at school. During those groups she focuses on developing the children's confidence to speak out and answer the teacher's questions in class without being shy about mistakes in front of their peers. The children for whom English is a second language are often reticent about classroom participation because they lack confidence in English language skills.

2. Because of the disproportionate number of boys in this class there is a marked increase in solidarity amongst the girls and very little of the bitchy peer group exclusiveness and verbal character assassination that is typical of girls in other classes lower down the school.

3. Many of the supply teachers in London come from Commonwealth countries such as New Zealand, Australia and South Africa. Increasingly they are called upon to supplement the severe shortage of teachers in inner city schools.

4. Ade is the son of first-generation Nigerian immigrants of specifically Yoruba descent. The family have only recently arrived in England and, even though his English is quickly improving, Ade still struggles with language difficulties; when he speaks he has a strong Nigerian/Yoruba accent and sometimes this is a source of embarrassment to him when other boys, including those of second- or third-generation African immigrant descent who have no accent, make Ade the butt of their teasing jokes. Mark, Ade's friend, is also the child of Nigerian immigrants but because his mother is a second-generation immigrant Mark has no accent and gets teased less.

5. Because I don't want the children to think of me as a teacher or classroom assistant and because I have Christine's full support in trying to discover what school is like from the children's point of view, my participation in the classroom environment varies from what children are used to. Sometimes I sit at the tables with the children and just observe their interaction and

behaviour, noting the details down in my notebook without making any direct interventions, and at other times I engage in the kind of more conventional participation that is expected of adults in a classroom situation. Vygotsky (1978, 1986) describes the relationship between adults and children in a learning environment as a 'zone of proximal development' in which the adult provides the conceptual tools for the child to reach from its existing understanding up to the next level of knowledge. Because caring and learning are synonymous for me, I have to force myself not to engage in a conventional zone of proximal development with the children and, in time, I become more like a friend to them rather than a teacher or classroom assistant. For example, even though I observe distracting and disruptive behaviour directly, I never tell on children to the teacher unless there is a direct risk of harm.

6. Fat Boy Slim is a popular music DJ (disc jockey).

7. Nathaniel is the son of first-generation immigrant Ghanaian parents. He is probably the most academically able boy in the class but he is also friends with Gary and is often, therefore, distracted by him.

8. Some of the children, like Tom, are persistently late for registration and this is just one of the ways in which the rigid parameters of the school timetable are disrupted. This issue is usually referred to Kofi, the home–school liaison officer, who then chases up the parents of individual children. Teachers tend to perceive this lateness as being to do either with parents' disrespect for school rules or to do with familial difficulties, such as when the mother is struggling with complicated morning childcare routines. With this in mind Mara begins a breakfast club in a nearby hall so that children can be dropped off as early as 8 o'clock in the morning and once there they can also enjoy a healthy breakfast.

9. The Kray twins – Ronnie and Reggie – were infamous gangsters who built up a criminal empire from the East End of London. They were probably London's most notorious gangsters during the 1960s.

10. One among the most disruptive of the boys, Winston, is the son of a single-parent, first-generation immigrant Jamaican mother.

11. At times the form of competitive equality amongst the boys can seem like one in which they are competing to see how best to destroy each other. For example, there is, in Bermondsey, a game played by boys as young as 8 years old which is called 'Roast Chicken'. This game involves getting in a car, setting it on fire and seeing who the last boy is to get out. The first one out is chicken (coward) and the last one out risks getting roasted alive.

8. Pokemon and Peers

1. The boys who play football take it extremely seriously. A novice must prove his or her skills quickly or he or she is immediately intimidated off the pitch.

2. Pilgrim's is the secondary school that Gary and many of the boys in the class end up going to in September 2000, but, like Tenter Ground, it has a bad reputation locally and officially it gets poor results.

3. At the beginning of their last year at primary school children have to decide which secondary schools they are going to apply to, so that by December in

any academic year these decisions will already have been made. Most children will already have visited those schools with their parents. However, even if a child has all the requisite personal and objective qualifications, the most desirable schools with the best reputations and results are extremely difficult to get into. Those boys like Gary and Tom, who have poor behavioural records, actually have very little choice about which secondary they will go to; usually they move straight from sink primary to sink secondary school.

4. Pokemon was first an electronic computer game on the Nintendo Game Boy hand-held computer games console developed in Japan, but most of the boys at Tenter Ground heard of it through watching television. Part of the extraordinary success of Pokemon is due to the exploitation of multi-media international marketing opportunities; most of the children's parents subscribe either to satellite or cable as well as terrestrial television systems.

5. Laughing to myself, I don't mention the fact that my Mercedes is twenty years old and can't go faster than twenty miles per hour up hills.

6. Darth Maul is a (Jedi) knight; he fights on behalf of the dark side (evil) in the *Star Wars* movie called *Phantom Menace*.

7. Action Man is an action figure designed for boys' play; it is the equivalent in boys' affections to what Barbie is for girls.

8. The children use a street slang when they talk to each other which, although they are not aware of it, is one derived from Jamaican patois and black American language use. It is what was once thought of as 'black talk' but which has now become the common slang of young people – black, white and Asian – growing up in the city. Even the quietest immigrant children whose first language is not English quickly pick up and learn this peer group language which they may never use in any other context. Whereas white working class people in London could once have been distinguished on the basis of the differences in their dialect, nowadays their children are more likely to be influenced by this so-called black street slang and it is difficult, therefore, to tell them apart.

   White working class language traditionally includes rhyming slang and this is mixed and matched with outside influences in an ongoing creative synthesis that extends beyond language use to other cultural borrowings. In the dialogue quoted here when the boys are saying things like, 'That's bad', where bad obviously means good, I am interested in the linguistic inversion of adjectives referring to value so that things that are bad become good and things that are good become bad. There is a considerable degree of innovation amongst the boys in this specific slang use, such that a boy gains prestige among peers by introducing a new term that becomes accepted and widely used in the peer group. During my fieldwork, for example, new words are introduced about once every three to six weeks. These are usually introduced by boys, like Gary, who have access to an older teenage peer group through older siblings and street experience. One of these words, for example, is 'buff' which supplants the use of 'wicked' to mean the best or excellent.

9. The same is true for adults too of course, but the process is often more difficult to observe among adults because they are more likely to be engaged in linguistic exchanges in which the mediation of objects appears to have been transcended.

10. Not until I visit Tom at home do I discover that Tom is also an expert at colouring in his pictures. He keeps his Pokemon folder at home and colours

in the drawings using pens his mother has bought for him especially. His care and attention to the drawings is amazing; it proves that he is capable of careful concentration and shows that he can take pride in his work.

11. Football takes the highest priority in the disruptive boys' choice of what to do with their time. There are two football captains who are accepted as being the best two players in the class and each of them chooses their team anew each day. Their play is tough and unprincipled, without any referee. The home–school liaison officer who organises the school team attempts to organise and coach the boys but is frustrated by the lack of school management support and by the boys' inability to work as a team which would involve them in having to overcome aggressive individual competitiveness. When he attempts, for example, to prepare the boys for the inter-school football league and to enter them for some matches the boys' efforts are continuously thwarted by the antagonism between them.

12. Thinking of any game theoretically, in terms of how social relations between people come to be structured for the duration of the game, it becomes interesting to compare and contrast one game with another: think about the difference, for example, between what is going on in a game of Premiership football with what is happening in a game of world-class chess.

13. Football has traditionally been a working class men's game whilst cricket, tennis and rugby are considered to be middle class and public school boys' sports.

14. Dreamcast is a games console designed and produced by the American games company, Sega.

15. Although I have not investigated them here, it seems likely that object and exchange centred therapies ought to be highly successful with children (and indeed adults). I am reminded that objects are the bridges over and through which children encounter each other. Therefore, when there has been a disruption or breakdown in a child's social relations, either at school or at home, it makes sense that, in an effort to repair them, the mediation of significant objects would be vital to the re-establishment of trust. I imagine that talking therapies alone are probably insufficient.

9. Place and Prestige

1. The garden-square-type design for public housing was one of the housing improvement initiatives of Dr and Ada Salter.

2. Children from the block of flats where I live play on the concrete area at the front of the block, in the communal garden behind and in the adjacent car park.

3. All the children call their homes houses, not flats. They might say, for example, 'Do you want to come to my house?' A house is another word for a home.

4. I am conscious of the unspoken rule amongst the children and parents in the block which prevents children from going into other families' homes unless the parents themselves are already friendly. The doorstep becomes, therefore, a significant boundary between what happens 'indoors' and what goes on outside and it is the boundary across which intimacy between various families in the block is established.

5. Part of the reason for the prolonged duration of the Pokemon phenomenon is the fact that the cards are expensive, and so it takes a long time for all the

rare cards to enter into circulation. Also, as soon as children began to master one set of cards, another series of cards is released, which introduces more rare cards into and revitalises the trading networks.

6. New series of cards are released every few months; this is marked by an increased frenzy in trading as rare and desirable cards enter the sphere of exchange.

7. Both Ian and Glen say 'evolvshun', because they can't pronounce evolution; this kind of mispronunciation of 'big words' is typical in common families where, like in Sharon's family, for example, the introduction of new words into everyday vocabulary is actively restricted.

   Pokemon is the original creation of a Japanese man, Satoshi Tajiri, who, as a child, was obsessed with insects and their evolution. He was also a video game freak who spent most of his time in Tokyo's arcades. Eventually he was employed as a game designer by Nintendo and there he devised Pokemon for Game Boy.

8. Kula is a ceremonial exchange system in Papua New Guinea. It was first described by the anthropologist, Malinowski (1922). The system includes eighteen island communities and participants travel hundreds of miles by canoe to exchange valuables consisting of shell-disc necklaces which move in a northwards direction and shell armbands that move in a southern direction. The terms of participation vary from region to region and in the Trobriand Islands exchange is monopolised by chiefs.

   The anthropological literature is replete with ethnographic descriptions of various kinds of exchange economies. I refer to this literature only nominally here because the insights I have reached about children's exchange relations arise not from that source but mainly from ethnographic observation and an interest in the application of a broadly phenomenological theory of learning (Toren 1990, 1999), which predisposes me to attend closely to subject/object relations.

9. As a form of exchange Pokemon trading effects transformations in social relations so quickly because, unlike football or drawing which require dedication and practice over long periods of time, Pokemon trading doesn't really require mastery of specific forms of bodily competence.

10. A year after the summer of 2000, and even as late as 2002, young children and especially younger boys in my area, who were completely precluded from gaining influence amongst the older kids before, are still trading cards. They are safe now in the knowledge that older kids have moved on to other preoccupations and they can, therefore, impress each other with their cards and trading skills without attracting unwanted attention from older children.

11. The restriction of children to the estate and its environs and the close relationship that develops between children and the place where they grow up is heightened, of course, if they don't have the opportunity to travel further afield, either in London to other areas or abroad. Where we live, for example, is very close to the South Bank and all its amenities, but families with children in my block, either because of poverty or because of preoccupations closer to home, are rarely seen along the river. This kind of restricted geographical mobility and inward-looking community life continues to be a typical feature of working class life for some families in Bermondsey. Others, in contrast, live what would conventionally be thought of as a more middle class lifestyle, taking foreign holidays, owning houses abroad and managing up to two cars.

12. These boys are about 12 or 13 years old which is about the limit of the age that boys continue to be interested in Pokemon cards.

13. The classic scholarly work on gift exchange is that by Mauss (2002) entitled *The Gift*.

14. Ian and John have both grown up close to Bermondsey's northern border but their parents are not Bermondsey people. This means that although they are growing up here, they do not have the genealogical credentials of born-and-bred Bermondsey people. These kinds of children, and youths like John, who start to hang out with 'real' Bermondsey bods like those from 'down the Blue', are marginal both genealogically and geographically to what being a real Bermondsey bod requires. They can, however, as John has, become accepted into bods' peer groups where, because of their desire to belong, they try twice as hard to prove their credentials. For example, when I speak to one of the youth workers at a local youth club about Bermondsey bods, he happens to mention John and explains how proud John was of his forays over Tower Bridge where he set out to cause trouble with the 'Pakis' who dominate the territory north of the river. The youth worker explains that he had asked John why he and his friends were doing that and John had apparently replied, ''Cos we're Bermondsey ain't we, that's what bods are, they're racist.'

15. To 'grass someone up' is to give evidence about them to the police.

16. A Bermondsey man tells me about a murder case a long time ago in which the victim was stabbed to death in a crowded pub. The policeman investigating the case had apparently said that if there were no witnesses to this murder there must have been 200 people in the pub's toilet that night.

17. Mobile phones become and continue to be a craze among young people for several reasons. What preoccupies children about them are the various differentiating features of various phones. The following kinds of questions about the phones are important to them: What brand of phone is it? Which make of phone is it? What face-off or fascia does it have? (Fascias can be removed and changed as fashions change.) What logo does it have as a graphic on the screen? Can you download multiple choices of graphics from internet sites? What ring-tones have you got? What games can you play on it? Does it have a camera and/or a video? Does it have an MP3 player? These differentiating features are the secret of a successful craze. Because peer group formation works on the basis of a shared, but finely differentiated mastery over objects of specific significance, the more levels of difference there are to explore, the longer the object will enthral and continue to mediate relations among friends. Unlike Pokemon cards, the phones cannot physically be exchanged because their initial worth is too high. The function they serve doesn't lend itself to exchange between one person and another. There is, however, still a form of exchange in operation. What is important to young people is the comparison of prestige that possession of the object engenders, but to me, the most interesting thing about mobile phones is the way that the inter-subjective relation, which the object mediates, is made absolutely explicit because the object is itself a medium for verbal communication. The mobile phone substantiates the social relations that the child is engaged in. Who phones? How often? The answers to these questions directly address the important issues of peer group formation, which are those to do with how to be popular and have friends.

18. The concept of the developmental cycle of the household was developed by Goody (1958) in his book entitled *The Developmental Cycle in Domestic Groups.*
19. The difference, between the kinds of things that men like to do together and which are the basis of their relationships with each other, and what men do with their girlfriends or wives at home, is the source of tension between the woman and her husband or boyfriend's friends. This tension finds ritual expression in pre-martial occasions such as the 'stag' and 'hen' nights. Where should a man's allegiances lie – with his mates or with his wife who saves him from them? This specific social tension is also the source of much English comedy as well as advertising for domestic products and services, such as in adverts where the furious wife attends upon her husband and his mates who have taken over the living room to watch a game of football on a Sunday afternoon.
20. I do not want to overemphasise the occurrence of violent or racist incidents on council estates. The majority of families do live a decent, trouble-free life, just trying to get by on the estates. Trouble tends to come to those who look for it and in so far as it is within parents' means to keep their children, and especially sons, preoccupied with other pursuits, they may escape having to watch in vain as their sons develop a reputation for being able to hold their own on the street. Like an undercurrent, the social dynamic of violent conflict in Bermondsey is always there, but it never becomes the predominant feature of the overall flow of life until, every now and again, trapped in its eddy, a young man screams aloud as he tries to escape from its irresistible pull. We are then reminded of what risks these boys take with their lives in the desperate effort to gain respect: 'big-man system', 'short-life culture'.

References

Abbott, D. (2002) 'Teachers are Failing Black Boys', *The Observer*, 6 January 2002.

Ariès, P. (1973) *Centuries of Childhood* (Harmondsworth: Penguin).

Arnot, M., David, M. and Weiner G. (1999) *Closing the Gender Gap: Postwar Education and Social Change* (Cambridge: Polity Press).

Ball, S. J. (2002) *Class Strategies and the Education Market: the Middle Classes and Social Advantage* (London: Routledge/Falmer).

Bell, D. (HMCI) Annual Report 2003/4 press conference (UK: Ofsted, 2005). A copy of the full report is also available: Annual Report of Her Majesty's Chief Inspector of Schools 2003/4, Ofsted, UK, 2005.

Bourdieu, P. (1977) *Outline of a Theory of Practice* (Cambridge: Cambridge University Press).

Bourdieu, P. (1984) *Distinction: a Social Critique of the Judgement of Taste* (London: Routledge & Kegan Paul).

Cannadine, D. (2002) *Ornamentalism: How the British Saw their Empire* (London: Penguin).

Corrigan, P. (1979) *Schooling the Smash Street Kids* (London: Macmillan).

Douglas, J. W. B. (1967) *The Home and the School: a Study of Ability and Attainment in the Primary School* (St Albans: Panther [orig. London: Macgibbon & Kee, 1964]).

Edwards, J. (2000) *Born and Bred: Idioms of Kinship and New Reproductive Technologies in England* (Oxford and New York: Oxford University Press).

Epstein, D., Elwood, J., Hey, V. and Maw, J. (1998) *Failing Boys? Issues in Gender and Achievement* (Buckingham: Open University Press).

Eysenck, H. J. (1971) *Race, Intelligence and Education* (London: Temple Smith Ltd for 'New Society').

Feinstein, L. (1998) 'Pre-school Educational Inequality? British Children in the 1970 Cohort', *Centre for Economic Performance Discussion Papers*, 0404, Centre for Economic Performance, LSE.

Goody, J. (1958) *The Developmental Cycle in Domestic Groups* (Cambridge: Cambridge University Press for the Department of Archaeology and Anthropology).

Herrnstein, R. J. and Murray, C. (1994) *The Bell Curve: Intelligence and Class Structure in American Life* (New York and London: Simon & Schuster).

James, A., Jenks, C. and Prout, A. (1998) *Theorising Childhood* (Cambridge: Polity Press in association with Blackwell Publishers Ltd).

James, A. and Prout A. (1997) *Constructing and Reconstructing Childhood: Contemporary Issues in the Sociology of Childhood* (London: Falmer Press).

Jenks, C. *Childhood* (London: Routledge).

Jensen, A. R. (1969) *Environment, Heredity and Intelligence* (Cambridge, MA: Harvard Educational Review).

Lave, J. and Wenger, E. (1991) *Situated Learning: Legitimate Peripheral Participation* (Cambridge: Cambridge University Press).

Macpherson, Sir William, of Cluny (1999) *The Stephen Lawrence Inquiry: Report of an Inquiry* (London: HMSO).

Malinowski, B. (1922) *Argonauts of the Western Pacific: an Account of Native Enterprise and Adventure in the Archipelagoes of Melanesian New Guinea* (London: Routledge & Kegan Paul).

Mauss, M. (2002) *The Gift: the Form and Reason for Exchange in Archaic Societies* (London: Routledge [orig. 1925; Eng. trans., London, 1954]).

Opie, I. and Opie, P. (1969) *Children's Games in Street and Playground: Chasing, Catching, Seeking, Hunting, Racing, Duelling, Exerting, Daring, Guessing, Acting, Pretending* (Oxford: Clarendon, Press).

Piaget, J. (1926) *The Language and Thought of the Child* (London: Kegan Paul).

Piaget, J. (1929) *The Child's Conception of the World* (London: Routledge & Kegan Paul).

Piaget, J. (1953) *The Origin of Intelligence in the Child* (London: Routledge & Kegan Paul).

Piaget, J. (1958) *The Growth of Logical Thinking from Childhood to Adolescence: an Essay on the Construction of Formal Operational Structures* (London: Routledge & Kegan Paul).

Piaget, J. (1971) *Structuralism* (London: Routledge & Kegan Paul).

Power, S. (2003) *Education and the Middle Class* (Buckingham and Philadelphia: Open University Press).

Reay, D. (2005) 'Gendering Bourdieu's Concepts of Capitals: Emotional Capital, Women and Social Class', *Sociological Review*, 52, 2: 57–74.

Rose, J. (2001) [1952] *The Intellectual Life of the British Working Classes* (New Haven, CT; London: Yale University Press).

Strathern, M. (1981) *Kinship at the Core: an Anthropology of Elmdon, a Village in North-west Essex in the Nineteen-sixties* (Cambridge: Cambridge University Press).

Thompson, E. P. (1963) *The Making of the English Working Class* (London: Gollancz).

Toren, C. (1990) *Making Sense of Hierarchy: Cognition as Social Process in Fiji* (London: Athlone).

Toren, C. (1999) *Mind, Materiality and History: Essays in Fijian Ethnography* (New York: Routledge).

Vygotsky, L. (1978) [1936] *Mind in Society: the Development of Higher Psychological Process* (Cambridge, MA: Harvard University Press).

Vygostky, L. (1986) [1934] *Thought and Language* (Cambridge, MA: MIT Press).

Weber, M. (2001) [1930] *The Protestant Ethic and the Spirit of Capitalism* (London: Routledge).

Willis, P. (1981) [1977] *Learning to Labour: Why Working Class Kids get Working Class Jobs* (USA: Columbia University Press).

Willmott, P. and Young, M. (1957) *Family and Kinship in East London* (London: Routledge & Kegan Paul).

Winnicott, W. D. (1971) *Playing and Reality* (London: Tavistock Publications).

Woodhead, C. (HMCI) (1997) *Annual Report of Her Majesty's Chief Inspector of Schools: Standards and Quality in Education 1995/1996* (UK: Ofsted).

Index